Liberalism:
Find a Cure

Mark Dice

Table of Contents

Introduction

The differences between liberals and conservatives used to be pretty clear-cut and well known to those who paid even the least bit of attention to politics. People generally knew where someone with opposing political views stood on important issues involving immigration, gun control, abortion, war, gay marriage, social welfare programs, etc. While not everyone has always been clearly defined by the general attributes of what the "usual" core beliefs are of someone who is a Republican or a Democrat, the primary differences and objectives of each ideology have been deeply rooted and widely understood.

Historically there have been compelling arguments put forth by both sides of a debate, but recently the seemingly endless tug of war between the Left and the Right took a dramatic turn. The Left's well-established counter positions, some of which had been at least reasonable on the surface, have been replaced by a variety of new and bizarre ideas that are hard to even take seriously, let alone understand.

It's as if we're living in an episode of *The Twilight Zone* where we are witnessing an outbreak of some strange mass psychosis that's sweeping across the country. We're seeing the mainstream media, Hollywood celebrities, and professors on college campuses promoting such preposterous agendas about race, sexuality and life in general, that it's impossible in many cases to distinguish their ideas from satire poking fun at them.

Liberalism has ballooned into a mental health crisis, and it's not just an epidemic of odd behaviors and proposed new laws from a small number of disturbed individuals, who in past generations would be featured as circus freaks or guests on the *Jerry Springer Show*. These positions are being embraced, endorsed, and promoted by the liberal mainstream media establishment and entertainment industrial complex.

Not only are these once-fringe individuals and beliefs being glorified and celebrated by the media, but there are also a growing number of laws and corporate policies being put in place that demand everyone else accept these lunatics and their behavior as if they're totally normal.

Facebook now recognizes literally countless "genders" after first expanding the options from the "old fashioned" male and female to 58 different gender options in 2014, but that wasn't "inclusive" enough, so now the gender listing isn't a checkbox with either "male" or "female" — it's a fill-in-the-blank where you can list anything from peanut butter to an attack helicopter as your gender.[1]   The state of New York now legally recognizes 31 genders and made it a crime if you don't refer to someone by their "preferred pronoun."[2]   That means if someone "identifies" as "gender non-binary"

---

[1] BBC "Facebook to Offer Users Custom Gender Options" by Victoria Sill (February 14th 2014)

[2] The Daily Caller "New York City Lets You Choose From 31 Different Gender Identities" by Peter Hasson (May 24th 2016)

you cannot refer to them as he or she. Some people are now "identifying" as dragons,[3] elves,[4] and even aliens.[5] Equally insane views on race and sexuality are spreading. You've probably heard some of this lunacy but unless you've been monitoring the trend closely for the last several years, what you've seen and heard is only the tip of the iceberg. Beneath the surface is an epidemic of utter madness that's trying to rise up and take control of our culture. Criticizing much of this new liberal agenda has recently been deemed "hate speech" and the Leftists are increasing their levels of violence in order to intimidate those who speak out against them.

We've seen a growing trend of violence on college campuses by students determined to stop conservative speakers from giving talks. The perpetrators justify their terrorist behavior by labeling speech and ideas "violent" and claim that they must then use violence to stop what they say is a "fascist" ideology being adopted by conservatives who are simply arguing against this modern day liberalism. It's now commonplace for those on the Left to defame average conservatives and Trump supporters as "white supremacists" and "Nazis," which

---

[3] Daily Mail "Transgender former banker, 55, has her ears and nose REMOVED to transform into a 'dragon lady' with scales, a forked tongue and a horned skull" by Unity Blott (April 5th 2016)

[4] Daily Mail "EAR he goes again! Human 'elf' who has splashed $60,000 to turn himself into a creature from a fantasy novel reveals extreme results of his latest surgeries" by Martha Cliff (December 19th 2017)

[5] The Sun "Man who wants his GENITALS removed to become a 'sexless alien' is warned it could be impossible... as he'll have no way to urinate" by Becky Pemberton (May 26th 2017)

has created a dangerous political climate not seen in America in recent history. Leftists encouraging and celebrating violence against average Trump supporters is a regular occurrence on social media.[6] Many have equated red Make America Great Again hats with a Nazi swastika.[7] And a wave of anti-Trump mass hysteria has swept across the country.

Throughout history, cultures around the world have thought that strange behaviors like inserting large plates into their lips or stretching the necks of members of their tribe was completely normal.[8] Performing other dangerous body modifications like head or foot binding were a standard practice in some societies, but today we look back and marvel at these primitive cultures and have a hard time understanding how such unhealthy and unnatural acts were conceived, let alone seen as normal.

Hopefully the same will be true in our future, and we can look back at how liberals almost unraveled the basic fabric of society because of their poisonous ideas, but thankfully we were able to reign in their craziness and restore normalcy, but only time will tell. If we can't put an end to their madness soon, the human race will be psychologically scattered in a million different directions and crawling all over each other trying to survive like a bunch of ants after someone steps on their colony.

---

[6] Town Hall "20 Liberal Calls For Violence Against Conservatives in Quotes" by John Hawkins (June 15th 2017)

[7] Fox News "Teacher compares Trump's 'Make America Great Again' slogan to swastikas" by Todd Starnes (September 47th 2017)

[8] The Guardian "The Ethiopian Tribe Where A Lip Plate Makes You More Attractive" by Njideka Agbo (January 11th 2018)

Maybe crazy people just have too much time on their hands these days, since idle hands are the Devil's workshop, as the saying goes. Or maybe what would have been a fleeting curiosity by a few isolated mentally unstable individuals has been given a breeding ground since different people with the same bizarre fetishes and delusions can now connect with each other through the Internet, and instead of having friends who would discourage these kinds of abnormalities, they find strangers half way across the country who share in their madness and foment it.

Logic and science are no longer accepted by a growing number of Leftists. In fact, different points of view from what they hold aren't even allowed anymore. They feel like real life interactions should be identical to their social media feeds, where they can customize who they follow and exactly what they see and hear, as well as who they can block out with a tap of their finger.

Their life has become a bubble they feel should be their own personalized safe space Utopia, filled with only things they like, without any opposition, disagreements, or challenges. But that's not how the real world works. And they're very upset by that. And when they get upset, they get even more unstable.

The only rational explanation for why this is happening is that the Liberal Establishment is strategically trying to unravel the social fabric of society as part of a hostile takeover. The basic unit of this fabric is the nuclear family, and as liberal activist Linda Gordon said, "the nuclear family must be destroyed...Whatever its ultimate meaning, the break-up of families now is an objectively revolutionary process."[9]

Destroy the family, and the long-established traditions of the human race will vanish, and people will be left without any support structure instilling morality, loyalty, responsibility, or spirituality. The government will decide what is right and wrong, and provide the basic needs such as food, shelter, and financial assistance. Or, as George Orwell wrote in *Nineteen Eighty-Four*, one of the primary aims of the tyrannical government in his book (called the "Party") was, "to prevent men and women from forming loyalties which it might not be able to control."[10]

We are under attack by those who want to grow the government so large and powerful that it will be an all-encompassing entity that is involved with every facet of our lives. They want the government to be "God."

A lot of this insanity started on college campuses in the early 2010s. College is the first time kids are completely free from parental supervision and is the beginning of a new life. Often it's in a new city, with new people, new places to explore, new ideas to think about, and an opportunity to shed the labels and restrictions they've had following them around since middle school or high school. They're also still very impressionable and can easily be convinced to believe radical ideas, no matter how irrational or impractical.

Recent studies show that adolescence lasts until the age of 24, which means that a person isn't really an adult until two years after they graduate college, assuming they

---

[9] AZ Quotes "Linda Gordon Quotes"

[10] Orwell, George - *Nineteen Eighty-Four* page 58

went to college (which you don't need to do to have a good career). But instead of preparing kids for the "real world," many college professors seek to indoctrinate them with their own radical liberal agendas, and in this "safe space" culture they've created, instead of growing up, many of the students are actually regressing. Their minds are filled with useless and unrealistic ideas about how the world works and many get so fixated on past injustices they can't navigate through our modern society without seeing everything through a distorted lens that's stuck looking in the past.

With elementary school kids having their own cellphones and tablets, they now have access to a dangerous online world filled with YouTubers and social media stars who introduce them to ideas and activities no child should be subjected to. Parents are at a loss and feel that if they don't let their child have a smartphone or tablet, their classmates will ostracize them since "everyone" else has one, and preventing them from consuming inappropriate content once one is in their hands is impossible. So children are being raised by viral videos, trending topics, and social media stars — instead of parents; and it's setting up society for a disaster of unimaginable proportions.

Today's children are growing up in a sea of attention-seeking tweets and Instagram posts, and each have a million different things screaming for their attention and trying to take as much of it as possible, ruining their capacity to concentrate, their long-term memory, and even their ability to think. As media analyst Neil Postman noted, they're amusing themselves to death.[11]

The Millennials have been called the Lost Generation because most of them can't fix anything on their cars or around the house.[12] One survey claimed that twelve percent of people under the age of 35 don't know how to change a light bulb.[13] Another famous study even suggested that many people now have the attention span of a goldfish, and can only focus on a subject for eight seconds before their mind starts to wander.[14] It's probably not a coincidence that's about as much time as it takes to read a tweet or look over an Instagram post.

The younger generations are now so desensitized and have been so dehumanized that when they see someone get injured in an accident or assaulted on the street, their first thought is to pull out their cell phone and take a picture or record a video of the situation so they can post it on social media, instead of calling for help or actually helping the victim themselves.[15]

---

[11] The title of his historic book is *Amusing Ourselves To Death*.

[12] The Telegraph "Young people are 'lost generation' who can no longer fix gadgets, warns professor" by Sarah Knapton (December 28th 2014)

[13] Daily Mail "Millennials might be good on their phones but many STILL don't know how to change a light bulb or boil an egg" by Phoebe Weston (March 22nd 2017)

[14] Time "You Now Have a Shorter Attention Span Than a Goldfish" by Kevin McSpadden (May 14th 2015)

[15] The Independent "Passers-by film women trapped in crushed car instead of helping" by Matthew Moore (January 29th 2016)

Despite this cruelty, they think they're helping make the world a better place. They go out of their way to "virtue signal" to others that they are the "good" people by supporting the latest trendy social justice warrior causes. As the Urban Dictionary explains, virtue signaling is, "To take a conspicuous but essentially useless action ostensibly to support a good cause but actually to show off how much more moral you are than everybody else."[16]

Every day more people seem to get further detached from reality, and sink deeper into a synthetic world of contradictions and confusion. When Conservatives make a joke now, many Liberals think we're being serious. When Liberals are being serious, sometimes we think they must be joking. The story about a 34-year-old man who "identifies" as a 6-year-old and "dominates a cross-fit kids class" is a parody.[17] But the one about a man in his 50s identifying as a 6-year-old-girl, is not.[18]

In the 1990s men dressing up as women was a common occurrence in sketch comedies and sitcoms, but now men who dress up as women are participating in weightlifting competitions and MMA fights against (actual) women, and dominating them.[19]

---

[16] Urban Dictionary - Definition of Virtue Signaling

[17] The Overheard Press "Man who identifies as 6-year-old dominates cross-fit kids class" (July 7th 2017)

[18] The Independent "Transgender father Stefonknee Wolscht leaves family in Toronto to start new life as six-year-old girl" by Kate Ng (December 12th 2015)

[19] ABC News "Transgender teens outrun track and field competitors but critics close behind" by Karma Allen (June 13th 2018)

Many people are wondering what happened to free speech in America, since anyone who questions this growing madness is denounced as a "fascist" or a "hateful bigot." Everything is racist to liberals, but blacks can't be racist because they're always the "victim" of racism, they say. And racism "always" comes from white people who are seen as the cause of all of society's problems. The snowflakes now complain about Thanksgiving because it reminds them of what the early settlers did to the Native Americans.[20] Remember when we used to call them Indians? Well, that's too offensive today as well, so now they're "Native Americans." Liberals hate Columbus Day for the same reason.

They even hate the Fourth of July because they claim it's a celebration of "white men" who "stole the land" from the natives. Many black people complain about the Fourth of July because they don't want to celebrate the founding of the United States because some of the Founding Fathers owned slaves.

They get upset about Valentine's Day because it makes people who are single feel ostracized and "perpetuates cisgender heteronormative" couples.[21] They hate Christmas because Santa Claus is white and it's a Christian Holiday.[22] They hate Easter for the same

---

[20] Washington Times "'Big Bang Theory' star: Thanksgiving 'one of the grossest examples of genocide'" by Douglas Ernst (November 21st 2017)

[21] The Cougar Chronicle "Heteronormative Valentine's depictions marginalize LGBTQIA+ community" by Samantha Carrillo (February 7th 2018)

[22] Slate.com "Santa Should Not Be a White Man Anymore" by Aisha Harris (December 14th 2015)

reason. Many can't even celebrate Martin Luther King Day because instead of remembering the legacy of the man and the impact he had on Civil Rights, they use the day as an excuse to blame white people again for all of the problems in the black community.

Liberals even complain about Mother's Day and Father's Day now because they make "non traditional families" feel bad, and the holidays celebrate the traditional family, traditional gender roles, and heterosexual couples.[23] All of this insanity will be examined in detail throughout this book, and it's really going to blow your mind; so I hope you are ready, because things are about to get even more weird.

Regarding "climate change," liberals went from promoting reasonable ecological solutions aimed at reducing further environmental damage to paranoid fear-mongering about how global warming is supposedly going to wipe out the world's chocolate supply, make maple syrup "extinct," and cause the Internet to shutdown.[24] Bill Nye "the Science Guy" wants to throw global warming "skeptics" in jail,[25] and Arnold Schwarzenegger has threatened to sue Big Oil companies for "first-degree murder" because fossil fuels are "causing

[23] Huffington Post "Three Reasons Why Father's Day Should be Abolished" Huffington Post." by Jeremy Davies (June 14th 2017)

[24] Axios "Global warming poses 'devastating' threat to the internet, study says" by Andrew Freedman (July 17th 2018)

[25] Washington Times "Bill Nye, the science guy, is open to criminal charges and jail time for climate change dissenters" by Valerie Richardson (April 14th 2016)

climate change."[26] That's how insane they are now. One NASA scientist even warned that aliens may exterminate the human race in order to save our planet from more man-made global warming.[27]

As crazy as this all sounds, it doesn't come close to the level of madness I'll be detailing in this book regarding liberals' latest views on race, gender, and sexuality. If a television commercial shows a white family enjoying a barbecue in the back yard, they say it contains "micro aggressions" against blacks, Asians, and Latinos because it's not "inclusive" of other races.

If it's a normal family with a husband, wife, and a few kids, that's not "inclusive" enough either because it doesn't have enough "diversity" and is said to be "divisive" because it "ostracizes" gays and lesbians. That's why many commercials in the last few years now feature interracial couples, and many Fortune 500 companies like Coca-Cola, Tylenol, Honey Maid, Chevrolet, and others are airing commercials featuring gay and lesbian couples or transgender people.[28]

"Diversity" is basically a codeword meaning less straight white people. Or, in other words, more black and brown people, and plenty of freaks and weirdos. Everything is now under scrutiny by the "diversity" police

---

[26] USA Today "Schwarzenegger says he wants to sue global oil companies for first-degree murder" by David Carrig (March 13th 2018)

[27] The Guardian "Aliens may destroy humanity to protect other civilizations, say scientists" by Ian Sample (August 18th 2011)

[28] Huffington Post "Gay-Themed Ads Are Becoming More Mainstream" by Leanne Italie (March 6th 2013)

to make sure that blacks, gays and transgenders star in tons of television commercials, sitcoms, and movies. But adding "people of color" to popular film franchises isn't enough. Liberals are demanding lead characters from Luke Skywalker to Captain America be depicted as gay in future versions of the films.[29] I'll cover this in more detail later.

These "social justice warriors" as they're called, are even ruining comedy. When the television series *Friends* was added to Netflix in 2018 it reached a whole new audience who were too young to follow the show when it first aired in the 1990s, but many Millennials found it too offensive and took to Twitter to complain about the "sexist," "homophobic," and "transphobic" elements in some of the plots.[30]

Jerry Seinfeld spoke up about the new PC police and said he won't perform at college campuses anymore because the kids always complain about jokes being too "racist," "sexist," and "prejudice," adding, "They don't know what the hell they're talking about."[31] Chris Rock won't perform at college campuses anymore either, saying they are "way too conservative," clarifying, "Not in their political views—not like they're voting Republican—but in their social views and their willingness not to offend

[29] Daily Beast "Give Captain America a Boyfriend: The Campaigns to Make Disney's Big Franchises More Gay-Friendly" by Jen Yamato (June 25th 2016)

[30] The Independent "Millennials watching 'Friends' on Netflix shocked by storylines" by Ilana Kaplan (January 11th 2018)

[31] Entertainment Weekly "Jerry Seinfeld: College students don't know what the hell they're talking about" by Dana Rose Falcone (June 8th 2015)

anybody."[32]   Other comedians like Joe Rogan and Tim Allen feel the same way about the younger generations being hypersensitive about simple jokes that everyone used to enjoy.[33]

It's not much of an exaggeration to compare what's happening today with a zombie apocalypse, even though such comparisons have become cliché. And while it is amusing (on one level) to see the bizarre activities and beliefs of liberals today, it is also becoming increasingly scary as their ideas and behaviors are being encouraged and endorsed by mainstream media outlets, pop culture celebrities, and even becoming protected by law.

Many people are wondering "why is this happening?" How could such insane ideas be accepted as normal and promoted as cool?   The answer lies in what's called Cultural Marxism. The Left is aiming to tear apart the basic fabric of society, starting with the traditional nuclear family, gender roles, social norms, and acceptable behaviors.   They want to smash the moral compass in people's consciences to erase all boundaries between what's right and wrong.

This enables the construction of a larger bureaucracy to control society, and with people no longer adhering to the values which used to be instilled in them by their parents, grandparents, and peer groups—the government or "the State" is looked at as the ultimate authority in all

---

[32] Washington Post "Chris Rock, campus conservatism, 'The Interview' and the outrage economy" by Alexandra Petri (December 18th 2014)

[33] New York Post "Tim Allen joins docudrama taking down PC culture" by Marisa Schultz (January 29th 2018)

things. Mainstream news, and particularly pop culture and celebrity influencers are an extension of this authority, and their puppets serve as the role models and arbiters of what people should think and how they should behave.

One of the primary goals of Communist parties after their revolutions were successful was to eradicate religions and the basic family unit in the countries they control. The government replaces God. The government determines what its citizens should do with their lives. Without tight-knit family structures and local communities, it's much easier to prevent people from uniting together for a common cause such as resisting the increasing tyranny of a dictatorship and the restrictions on civil liberties they impose.

Authoritarian regimes want everyone to obey the power structure and their false prophets, or be destroyed. The more powerful a fascist regime gets, the more difficult it is for people to oppose it. And we're seeing the same mechanisms of control being put in place by the Liberal Establishment in America today, and their useful idiots being dispatched as foot soldiers on the ground trying to enforce them.

We must take a closer look at the various facets of today's liberal agenda if we hope to stop it. From the demonization of white people, to the explosion of gender identity insanity, to the promotion of perverted sexual practices and their double standards for free speech. We are, to paraphrase JFK's warning about Communism, opposed by a ruthless and monolithic conspiracy, but these perpetrators aren't half way around the world—they are inhabiting our own country, and they are completely out of their minds.

Imaginary Racism

Some manifestations of mental illness cause those who suffer from them to have visual or auditory hallucinations, or radically misinterpret benign events or actions of others as hostile. One form of hallucinations that many liberals suffer from today is seeing racism around every corner, where none exists. Much of this imaginary racism is being "discovered" in one of the least racist places on the planet—college campuses.

Racism exists because human beings are tribal creatures, like most mammals, and have historically lived in communities consisting of the same race and struggled and fought against outsiders who have different priorities, values, and customs. In our modern society we have largely been able to peacefully work and live alongside each other despite our different ancestry and history, but unfortunately some of these differences still cause racial tensions in certain communities and interactions.

But generally, most people in the United States treat each other as Americans, not as a member of a particular race. That's not to say racism doesn't exist, or that we don't have a stain on our history because of slavery, but today many liberals seem to be haunted by the ghosts of our racist past and think they see racism being perpetuated by white people everywhere.

17

Police investigated a "noose" hung up on a door handle at Michigan State University after a black student saw it and panicked, but their investigation revealed it was just someone's lost shoelace that another student had found on the floor and put on a stairwell door handle hoping whoever lost it may spot it.[34]

Similarly, a student at Bowling Green State University in Ohio reported she saw a KKK meeting going on in a classroom when walking by outside and happened to notice "Klan members" through the window dressed up in their white robes and hoods. Campus police investigated and discovered that the student had mistaken some lab equipment that was covered up with white plastic dust covers as the KKK hoods.[35]

The student senate at Santa Clara University in California refused to allow a Turning Point USA chapter to form on campus, a nationwide conservative student activist club, because they thought it would make other students feel "unsafe."[36] A Power Point presentation given at the student senate meeting before the vote painted Turning Point USA as a white supremacist group despite Candace Owens (who is black) being one of their most well-known members.

But it's not just college students who keep imagining racism everywhere these days. Many professors are

---

[34] Lansing State Journal "Police: 'Noose' found in Michigan State dorm was a shoelace" by RJ Wolcott (October 4th 2017)

[35] Washington Free Beacon "College Student Confuses Covered Lab Equipment With KKK Rally" by Emily Ferguson (January 24th 2017)

[36] The Mercury News "Turning Point USA student group denied chapter at Santa Clara University" by EricKurhi (February 9th 2017)

experiencing the hallucinations too. One at Michigan State University warned students that white people who do yoga are perpetuating racism.[37] Several San Diego State University professors alerted students that they thought farmers' markets were racist. "Farmers' markets are often white spaces where the food consumption habits of white people are normalized," they said.[38]

A similar delusion broke out at the University of Illinois where a professor began claiming that math, algebra, and geometry promote "white privilege."[39] A professor at Clemson University in South Carolina proclaimed that simply expecting people to show up to work or school on time is racist.[40] One at the University of Washington created a poster and hung it up in the school's writing center claiming that American grammar is racist and an "unjust language structure."[41]

She was upset that black people who use broken English and bad grammar are seen as uneducated and less intelligent than people who speak proper English. The

[37] Fox News "Americans who practice yoga contribute to white supremacy, Michigan State University professor claims" by Caleb Parke (January 29th 2018)

[38] Campus Reform "Profs: Farmers' markets cause 'environmental gentrification'" by Toni Airaksinen (December 27th 2017)

[39] Fox News "White privilege bolstered by teaching math, university professor says" by Robert Geary (October 24th 2017)

[40] National Review "Clemson Diversity Training: Expecting People to Arrive on Time Is Culturally Insensitive" by Katherine Timpf (April 10th 2017)

[41] Washington Times "College writing center: Proper grammar perpetuates 'racist,' 'unjust language structure'" by Douglas Ernst (February 21st 2017)

professor claimed that there was no "inherent 'standard' of English," and that language is constantly changing, so, "These two facts make it very difficult to justify placing people in hierarchies or restricting opportunities and privileges because of the way people communicate in particular versions of English."[42] It appears she is trying to justify Ebonics, and is upset that the "ghetto accent" we're all familiar with is looked down upon.

The University of Southern California's mascot is a white horse named Traveler that is trotted out during Trojans football games with a jockey dressed as an ancient Trojan warrior riding him, but since Confederate General Robert E. Lee also had a horse named Traveler, the USC Trojans mascot came under fire by the Black Student Assembly whose co-director considered it a symbol of white supremacy.[43]

White marble statues, like the ones commonly associated with ancient Greece, are "white supremacist" too, according to a University of Iowa professor. "The equation of white marble with beauty is not an inherent truth of the universe; it's a dangerous construct that continues to influence white supremacist ideas today," she said.[44] One Stanford University professor even thinks that Dungeons and Dragons perpetuates racism and white

---

[42] Ibid.

[43] Los Angeles Times "Traveler, USC's mascot, comes under scrutiny for having a name similar to Robert E. Lee's horse" by Nathan Fenno (August 18th 2017)

[44] National Review "Professor: White-Marble Sculpture Contributes to 'White Supremacy'" by Katherine Timpf (June 9th 2017)

privilege because characters are divided by their species, such as elves and dwarves.[45]

Even every kid's favorite lunch, peanut butter and jelly sandwiches, have been labeled racist by a school principal in Portland. "What about Somali or Hispanic students, who might not eat sandwiches?" she asked, expressing concern that peanut butter and jelly is considered a quintessential American food.[46] Peanut butter and jelly isn't the only food that's been labeled "divisive" or racist.

Milk is now a symbol of white privilege and white supremacy to liberals. As you know, milk is promoted as a primary staple of a healthy diet, but apparently a large number of black people are lactose intolerant, and so milk being promoted as a "standard" food is considered a symbol of the "white normativity" perpetuated in America.[47]

PETA, the People for the Ethical Treatment of Animals, calls milk, "a thinly-veiled allegory for racial purity" and "the perfect drink for supremacists everywhere."[48] Trolls on 4Chan, an online forum known for its creative pranks and hoaxes, decided to run with this

---

[45] Breitbart "Stanford professor: Dungeons and Dragons perpetuates systems of white, male privilege" by Tom Cicocotta (April 17th 2018)

[46] The Daily Caller "Now peanut butter and jelly sandwiches are racist" by Eric Owens (November 22nd 2013)

[47] Mother Jones "Are the US Dietary Guidelines on Milk Racist?" by Josh Harkinson (August 3rd 2016)

[48] Boston Globe "Arguable: Milk is for Nazis, says PETA" by Jeff Jacoby (April 3rd 2017)

idea and began spreading the "news" that white supremacists had indeed adopted milk as their new symbol, prompting some outlets to publish stories with headlines like "Milk, a symbol of neo-Nazi hate,"[49] and "Milk is the new, creamy symbol of white racial purity in Donald Trump's America."[50]

Since one of President Trump's nonverbal quirks is his frequent use of the "okay" hand sign, many Trump supporters have adopted the gesture to show support for the president and his agenda. But some jokers on 4Chan thought it would be funny to troll anti-Trump fanatics by spreading a hoax that the hand sign represented "white power." They created diagrams claiming the middle finger, ring finger and pinky symbolized the "W" while the wrist along with the circle that the index finger and the thumb formed was the "P."

Sadly, not only did liberals on social media fall for the hoax, but some journalists did as well. After a blogger named Cassandra Fairbanks got a temporary press pass to the White House briefing room, she posted a photo online of herself standing at the podium while giving the "okay" hand sign. Several liberal outlets including Fusion TV, a social justice warrior cable channel aimed at Millennials,

---

[49] TheConversation.com "Milk, a symbol of neo-Nazi hate" (April 30th 2017)

[50] Mic.com "Milk is the new, creamy symbol of white racial purity in Donald Trump's America" by Jack Smith IV (February 10th 2017)

published articles claiming she flashed a "white power" hand sign in the press room! She sued for defamation.[51]

A few months later when a photo of the current White House interns was published, one of the interns could be seen making the same hand sign, so *The Washington Examiner* and other outlets published stories identifying him by name, claiming that he too flashed a white power hand sign.[52]

Instagram removed a selfie of a young woman showing her wearing a MAGA hat while giving the "okay" hand sign, claiming it violated their terms of service after people flagged it for including the "white supremacist" hand sign.[53] Apparently none of the morons noticed the woman in the picture was Asian!

After Kanye West posted a selfie of himself wearing a Make America Great Again hat alongside a couple of his friends, one of them (Lyor Cohen who is the head of YouTube Music) was making the "okay" hand sign and got smeared in the press as well, so YouTube had to issue a statement that the gesture was meant to represent a company he founded called 300 Entertainment.[54]

---

[51] New York Daily News "Right-wing reporter sues Fusion writer over 'white power hand gesture' tweet" by Christopher Brennan (June 2nd 2017)

[52] Washington Examiner "Former White House intern poses with 'white power' hand gesture in photo with Trump: Report" by Naomi Lim (December 28th 2017)

[53] https://twitter.com/PoliticalKathy/status/974490928244125697

[54] TMZ "Kanye West's MAGA Pic No Alt-Right Gesture ... That's a Company Sign!!!" (April 25th 2018)

When Donald Trump revealed his "Make America Great Again" slogan, that too was labeled racist. The strange rationale for this accusation was that his supporters supposedly thought America was great during the 1800s when there was slavery, and want to return to that era. On the campaign trail for Hillary in 2016, Bill Clinton actually said it was a racist dog whistle,[55] forgetting that he himself had used the same exact "Make America Great Again" line in one of his speeches during his campaign in the 1990s, but of course that didn't matter.[56]

And during the entire eight years of the Obama administration, all of his critics were "racists" who didn't disagree with his policies or oppose his political agendas because they're members of the Republican political party. No. They were just "racists." That's the only reason Republicans opposed Obama, liberals say. MSNBC's Chris Matthews thinks that people who are against raising the minimum wage are "racists."[57] Other cable news hosts have said the same thing.[58]

---

[55] Huffington Post "Bill Clinton Says 'Make America Great Again' is Just a Racist Dog Whistle" (September 7th 2016)

[56] Washington Times "Bill Clinton vowed to 'make America great again' in 1992, now says slogan is racist" by Jessica Chasmar (September 9th 2016)

[57] Mediaite "MSNBC's Chris Matthews rails against these racists who oppose raising minimum wage" by Noah Rothman (December 201th 2013)

[58] News Busters "Ed Schultz: GOP Not Raising the Minimum Wage Is 'Every Bit as Racist' as Donald Sterling" by Scott Whitlock (April 30th 2014)

The viral video content farm "NowThis" produced a segment titled, "The word 'marijuana' is rooted in racism — here's why you should say 'cannabis' instead," which consisted of some Mexican guy begging people to stop using the word marijuana, "because it's racist as fuck."[59] It seemed like a parody, but he was serious, and even admitted "the word isn't inherently racist, but it was used by American prohibitionists to exploit racism and xenophobia, so by using the 'M word,' you're ignoring a long history of oppression against Mexican immigrants and African Americans."[60]

The *Guardian* covered this made-up controversy and reported that because the word "marijuana" comes from Mexico, it evokes thoughts of Mexicans, and those who supported making it illegal painted pot as a drug for "Negros and Hispanics." The writer said, "Today 'cannabis' and 'marijuana' are terms used more or less interchangeably in the industry, but a vocal contingent prefers the less historically fraught 'cannabis.' At a time of intense interest in past injustices, some say 'marijuana' is a racist word that should fall out of use."[61]

Even social justice warrior Laci Greene commented that, "a big part of why some social justice stuff online has gone off the rails is the click economy. There's a demand to be constantly producing content. Once they've

---

[59] https://twitter.com/nowthisnews/status/959158919095398400

[60] Ibid.

[61] The Guardian "Marijuana: is it time to stop using a word with racist roots?" by Alex Halpern (January 29th 2018)

covered real problems, some outlets pivot to trivial stuff, like whether saying 'marijuana' makes you racist."[62]

The Huffington Post published a story titled "Becoming A Racist: The Unfortunate Side Effect Of Serving Your Country?" and blamed serving overseas in the U.S. military for causing white veterans to become racist because after fighting in the Iraq/Afghan war many soldiers, "return with a new-found hatred for those different from them, especially after their mission is one of liberation from those who kill and persecute anyone of different faiths/beliefs."[63]

After Charlie Rose was fired from PBS for sexual harassment allegations, one black "journalist" accused him of being racist because he only allegedly harassed white women.[64] When President Trump helped get three UCLA basketball players released from jail in China after they were arrested for shoplifting while on a trip there, one of the boys' fathers' refused to thank President Trump. And when the president later said he thought the man was "ungrateful" for his help in releasing his son, Black Lives Matter activist and *New York Daily News* columnist Shaun King responded saying, "Ungrateful is the new nigger."[65]

---

[62] https://twitter.com/gogreen18/status/959618027783204866

[63] Huffington Post "Becoming A Racist: The Unfortunate Side Effect Of Serving Your Country?" by David Fagin (August 17th 2017)

[64] Information Liberation "Black Journalist Suggests Charlie Rose Is Racist For Not Sexually Harassing Her" by Chris Menahan (December 20th 2017)

[65] https://twitter.com/ShaunKing/status/932404094219771907

The term "law and order" is also said to be a white supremacist code meaning "control and contain" black people, and "thug" is also said to be a code word for the n-word, according to CNN's Don Lemon and *Tonight Show* band leader Questlove.[66]

After Google fired James Damore over an internal memo he wrote refuting the company's militant stance on "diversity," conservative activists organized the "March on Google" to protest the tech giant's increasing intolerance of conservatives, and so the mainstream media labeled the protest a "white supremacist" event.[67]

After online outrage over the Confederate flag being "racist" boiled over, reruns of *The Dukes of Hazard* were pulled from TV because their iconic orange Dodge Charger (named The General Lee) has one painted on the roof.[68] Amazon.com pulled all Confederate flags from their website, and Apple even removed Civil War video games that included the flag in their icons.[69] (Apple later reversed this decision after people ridiculed them for over-reaching.)

Then a best-selling author of true-crime books, Rebecca Morris, sent a "news tip" to her local paper (the *Seattle Times*) alerting them of a "Confederate flag" that was flying on a flagpole in front of one of her neighbor's

---

[66] https://twitter.com/questlove/status/592869780757082112

[67] Vibe "White Supremacists To 'March On Google' In 9 Major U.S. Cities This Saturday" by Marjua Estevez (August 16th 2017)

[68] ABC News "TV Land Pulls 'Dukes of Hazzard' Reruns" by Luchina Fischer (June 1st 2015)

[69] Reuters "Apple removes games featuring confederate flags from App Store" by Reuters Staff (June 25th 2015)

homes.[70]   She didn't want to confront the neighbor herself, so she emailed the paper suggesting they look into it. So they did. What they found was a pole flying an American flag at the top, and below it was another flag, and sure enough it was a red flag with a blue cross on it — It was the Norwegian flag! The homeowner had put it up when the 2018 Winter Olympics started because his parents emigrated to the U.S. from Norway in the 1950s.

Hallucinations of "racism" are only getting worse, and it might be easier to make a list of things that aren't racist instead of keeping track of the things liberals now believe are. But to further illustrate my point about the imaginary racism epidemic, in the next few pages I'll break down a few more of the countless examples in case you have any remaining doubts.

Walmart's Hair Care Products

A black woman in California sued Walmart, claiming they were "racist" because her local store put certain hair care products that were frequently stolen behind a locked glass case and required a store clerk to get them out for customers.   "I noticed all of the African American products was locked up under lock and key," she said at a

---

[70] The Seattle Times "'Suddenly there is a Confederate flag flying' in Seattle's Greenwood area – well, not quite" by Erik Lactis (February 22nd 2018)

press conference, claiming she feels black people are being treated like criminals.[71]

What unscrupulous lawyer would file such a ridiculous lawsuit? Gloria Allred, the infamous feminist activist (or as some call her, "extortionist"). At the press conference Allred said the goal of the suit was, "To stop Walmart's business practice which we contend perpetuates discrimination, and which we contend Esse [the plaintiff] and the general public, to suffer irreparable injury, shame, humiliation, and mental suffering."[72]

Other black people have posted pictures on social media of the glass case, saying it's racist. "If Walmart is gonna lock up hair products they need to do it for all of them not only the ethnic hair products," said one woman.[73] Another guy tweeted a brief video showing the case, saying, "When did Walmart start locking up black hair care products? Talk about racist."[74] The reason they're locked up is because they are some of the most stolen items by black people, which is why when Black Lives Matter supporters riot after police shootings oftentimes weave stores get looted.[75]

---

[71] Newsweek "Woman Sues Walmart for 'Segregating' Beauty Products, Alleges Racial Discrimination" by Summer Meza (January 27th 2018)

[72] Ibid.

[73] https://twitter.com/Kadia2_/status/955284663064342528

[74] https://twitter.com/ronniesidneyii/status/957028177540468736

[75] CBS 58 "Looting, tensions dash tenuous peace in Ferguson's streets" (August 16th 2014)

Hotel Shampoo

A bisexual bimbo singer named "Halsey" went on a Twitter rant to her almost 10 million followers about how the little bottles of shampoo in hotels don't work very well for black women's hair. She tweeted, "I've been traveling for years now and it's been so frustrating that the hotel toiletry industry entirely alienates people of color. I can't use this perfumed watered down white people shampoo. Neither can 50% of your customers. Annoying."[76]

Even though her dad is black and technically she's half black, she looks white. So white that Rachel Dolezal is more of a black woman than her. When reading through Halsey's tweets about this you may think she should check herself into a psychiatric hospital instead of a hotel, and the jokes just write themselves because in one of the tweets ranting about hotel shampoo she said, "It's not just hotels. I stayed in a psychiatric hospital as a teenager and they didn't have hair products for any patients who were POC. It's hard enough being in there as it is, but then your gonna too feel ugly and dry n frizzy too? Nah. Anyways. Y'all still missing the point."[77]

She continued, saying, "Your 'normal' does not = everyone else's. When you make white products the standard, it makes white the 'normal.' I was only trying to provoke some thought about the way these things

---

[76] https://twitter.com/halsey/status/989680930926166016

[77] https://twitter.com/halsey/status/990130531420418048

impact our perception."[78]   She's referring to "white normative" where "whiteness" or "white culture" is seen as problematic when it is the "standard" or the majority, and other races and cultures are deemed "other."

Reaction GIFs

The BBC published a report claiming that white people sharing reaction GIFs of black people making funny faces is "digital black face," and racist. Reaction GIFs are the funny or cringy animated pictures that are a second or two long which are taken from scenes in TV shows or movies, often of celebrities reacting to something.

They're popular on social media as a way for people to express their feelings about a post by using an animated GIF instead of typing words.   (Think of the Michael Jackson eating popcorn GIF or Mike Tyson slapping his leg in hysterical laughter.)

"But you've probably noticed, the most popular ones are of black people being dramatic," the BBC presenter says. "This, is digital blackface."[79] She goes on to say that "blackface" is when a non-black person uses make-up to "blacken-up" and that old theater shows depicted black people in negative ways by whites performing in blackface.

"They exaggerated black people's facial features and their expressions, and 'digital blackface' is the 21st

---

[78] https://twitter.com/halsey/status/990129124940238848

[79] BBC "Is it OK to use black emojis and gifs?" by Victoria Princewill (August 14th 2017)

century version of that. White people using GIFs to perform some kind of exaggerated blackness."[80]

She went on to complain about white people using dark skinned emojis too. "This is a form of cultural appropriation," she says. "So what's wrong with white people posting these GIFs and using these emojis? Black people are not here for other people's entertainment. We're not symbols of excessive emotion. And we aren't here to make you look more sassy, more sexy or more street," she says.[81]

Teen Vogue magazine echoed these concerns, saying, "These GIFs often enact fantasies of black women as 'sassy' and extravagant, allowing nonblack users to harness and inhabit these images as an extension of themselves. GIFs with transcripts become an opportunity for those not fluent in black vernacular to safely use the language, such as in the many 'hell to the no,' 'girl, bye,' and 'bitch, please' memes passed around."[82]

It goes on to say, "Ultimately, black people and black images are thus relied upon to perform a huge amount of emotional labor online on behalf of nonblack users. We are your sass, your nonchalance, your fury, your delight, your annoyance, your happy dance, your diva, your shade, your 'yaas' moments. The weight of reaction GIFing, period, rests on our shoulders. Intertwine this proliferation of our images with the other ones we're as

---

[80] Ibid.

[81] Ibid.

[82] Teen Vogue "We Need to Talk About Digital Blackface in Reaction GIFs" by Lauren Michele Jackson (August 2nd 2017)

likely to see — death, looped over and over — and the Internet becomes an exhausting experience."[83]

Most Movies are Racist

When the *War for Planet of The Apes* (2017) trailer was released, one of the apes could be seen wearing a blue vest, and so Black Lives Matter activist Deray McKesson (whose trademark look is wearing a blue vest) cried "racism," believing the producers were mocking him.[84] Even many of his own supporters thought it was a ridiculous claim and he was delusional.

After comedian Jordan Peele's *Get Out* was nominated for a Golden Globe for best comedy, black people on social media freaked out thinking it was racist to call the film a comedy, and said it should have been in the horror category. This was more evidence, they thought, of "oppression" of black films. It turns out that the writer and producer actually submitted the film for the comedy category himself because he saw it as a dark comedy.[85]

The movie is a "social thriller" about a group of old rich white people who kidnap black people and have their brains transplanted into their bodies so they can continue

---

[83] Ibid.

[84] The Daily Caller "Deray McKesson Mocked After Being Offended Planet of the Apes Character Wears a Vest Like His" by Derek Hunter (July 11th 2017)

[85] SyFy "Jordan Peele responds to Get Out being considered in Golden Globe comedy category" by Brian Silliman (November 17th 2017)

to live in the young "strong" black bodies. It was said to be a metaphor for how white people allegedly "live off the labor" of black people.

Producer Tim Burton, who made films like *Edward Scissorhands* (1990), *Beetlejuice* (1988), and *The Nightmare Before Christmas* (1993), caught the eye of the Diversity Police who caused him to trend on Twitter due to their complaints that he cast too many white people in his films.[86]

Apu, the Indian convenience store owner in *The Simpsons,* was then targeted because he is "a problematic stereotype."[87] One social justice warrior even produced an entire documentary on his quest to have Apu removed from the show! Hank Azaria, who voices the character, then publicly said his "eyes have been opened" and he's willing to "step aside" from playing him.[88]

When the remake of Stephen King's *It* was released in 2017, that too was problematic because it was full of "white, straight, able-bodied males."[89] The classic *Gone With the Wind* (1939) which takes place down south during the Civil War and resulted in the very first Academy Award given to a black actor (for best

[86] USA Today "Tim Burton's diversity comments blew up Twitter" by Carley Mallenbaum (September 29th 2016)

[87] NPR "A New Documentary Calls Into Question The Simpson's 'Apu'" by Eric Deggans (November 19th 2017)

[88] The New York Times "Hank Azaria Offers to Stop Voicing Apu on 'The Simpsons' After Criticism" by Matthew Haag (April 25th 2018)

[89] Science Fiction Film and Television "Stephen King's Science Fiction" by Simone Brown and Regina Hansen (Volume 10, Issue, 2, Summer 2017)

supporting actor) was scheduled to be shown at a Tennessee theater as part of their annual Summer Movie Series in 2017, but the screening was canceled after concerns and complaints that the film was "insensitive" to slavery. "The social media storm this year really brought it home," said the president of the theater company.[90]

When *Star Wars: The Force Awakens* came out in 2015, MSNBC host Melissa Harris-Perry (who is black) went off on a bizarre tangent painting *Star Wars* as racist because Darth Vader's costume is black. "I know why I have feelings — good, bad, and otherwise — about *Star Wars*. And I have a lot. I could spend the whole day talking about the whole Darth Vader situation," she said, which got her a strange look from a panelist at the table, who replied, "Really? You could?"[91]

"Yeah, like the part where he was totally a black guy, whose name was basically James Earl Jones. While he was black he was terrible and bad, awful and used to cut off white men's hands, and didn't actually claim his son. But as soon as he claims his son, goes over to the good, takes off his mask and he is white — yes, I have many feelings about that."[92]

When *Star Wars: The Phantom Menace* came out in 1999 many critics called one character (Jar Jar Binks)

---

[90] Los Angeles Times "'Gone With the Wind,' deemed 'insensitive,' has been pulled from a Memphis theater" by Christie D'Zurilla (April 28th 2017)

[91] NewsBusters "MSNBC's Harris-Perry Gripes Over 'Totally Black Guy' Darth Vader As Evil Character" by Brand Wilmouth (December 13th 2015)

[92] Ibid.

racist because he sounded like a Rastafarian from the Caribbean. Other characters in *Star Wars* (like Nute Gunray) are also accused of being racist because they sound like they have an Asian-American accent.[93]

After *Star Wars: The Last Jedi* came out, *Variety* thought they would investigate the racial makeup of the writers and directors for various films in the franchise and lamented that, "96% of its film universe writers and directors are white men."[94]   Shortly after their "investigation" was published, other articles followed suit.

Mashable declared, "*Star Wars'* obsession with white guy filmmakers is hurting the franchise" and said that by "continuing to hire only white men, Lucasfilm is not helplessly reflecting some unfortunate but unchangeable norm.   It's making an active choice to reinforce a status quo that rewards white men while systematically shutting out anyone else."[95]

"Baby Got Back"

When actress Blake Lively attended the Cannes film festival in 2016 she posted a photo on her Instagram showing off her curves and her gown with the caption, "LA waist with an Oakland booty" referring to the

---

[93] Los Angeles Times "A Galaxy Far, Far Off Racial Mark?" by Eric Harrison (May 26th 1999)

[94] Variety "'Star Wars': 96% of Its Film Universe Writers and Directors Are White Men" by Maureen Ryan (February 6th 2018)

[95] Mashable "Star Wars' obsession with white guy filmmakers is hurting the franchise" by Angie Han (February 9th 2018)

popular 1990s Sir Mix-a-Lot lyrics from his song "Baby Got Back."[96]

Millennials who are too young (or weren't even born yet) when the song was popular thought she was insulting black women, and they tweeted so much hate about her that she started trending on Twitter. She was simply making fun of how big her butt had gotten since she was gaining weight from her pregnancy. Sir Mix-a-Lot said he was surprised by the backlash she received and defended her.[97]

When Rapper Kendrick Lamar brought a fan on stage to rap along with him to one of his songs during a concert in Alabama, he stopped the show in the middle of the performance to berate the girl in front of the whole audience after she used the word "nigga" (which is in the lyrics) because, as you know, there's a huge double standard about white people not being "allowed" to say the "n-word" even when singing along to their favorite rap songs.

Of course, the n-word has an "er" on the end, not an "a" so it looks like there are two "n-words" not one, despite "nigga" supposedly being a "term of endearment" among blacks, but white people are still denounced as "racists" when they say it out loud or even type it. And most black people fail to see that it is actually racist to demand that white people should not be allowed to use a

---

[96] US Weekly "Blake Lively Defends Her Controversial 'Oakland Booty' Comment: 'I Was Celebrating My Body'" by Evan Real (June 21st 2016)

[97] Hollywood Reporter "Sir Mix-a-Lot 'Surprised' by Outrage Over Blake Lively's Instagram Post" by Sam Reed (May 19th 2016)

word that black people throw around all day like it's nothing. Even using the word in *any* context is seen as the equivalent of stringing up a black person from a tree or burning a cross.

Comedian Louis CK (who's white) has a hilarious bit about this hypocrisy where he talks about words that people are offended by and says he's offended by the n-word. "Not nigger, by the way," he continues. "I mean 'the n-word.' Literally, whenever a white lady on CNN with nice hair says 'the n-word'...you say 'the n-word' and I go 'Oh, she means nigger.' You're making me say it in my head! Why don't you fucking say it instead, and take responsibility...just say it, don't hide behind the first letter like a faggot. Just say nigger."[98]

Calling Rioters "Animals" is Racist

In 2016 Charlotte, North Carolina experienced one of the many Black Lives Matter riots that year after police shot and killed another armed and dangerous thug. Of course, morons thought the "racist" police "murdered" the man (who was armed with an illegal handgun and had previously been in prison for shooting at someone), and so they rioted again.

It was trending on Twitter and so the Seattle Mariners' catcher Steve Clevenger tweeted that the rioters should be "locked behind bars like animals" and pointed out that the dead thug was armed and got shot by a *black* police

---

[98] Louis C.K.'s bit on being offended by the n-word.

officer.[99]   A few days later the Seattle Mariners reprimanded him for his tweets and suspended him for the rest of the season without pay.[100]

The mainstream media and Democrat members of Congress pretended that President Trump's comments about MS-13 gang members being "animals" were racist, claiming he was referring to *all* immigrants from Mexico.[101] A video clip of Trump's "animal" comments went viral but had the first few seconds edited out, which clearly showed he was referring to the vicious MS-13 gang members who were being protected by Democrats in "sanctuary cities" refusing to cooperate with Immigration and Customs Enforcement (ICE) officers to detain and deport them.[102]

Speaking of animals, a life-size statue of a gorilla was removed from a child's circus-themed playground in Texas after complaints that it was "racially insensitive."[103] As you know, most playgrounds have "monkey bars" for kids to climb on, and most white parents call their

---

[99] New York Times "Charlotte Officer 'Justified' in Fatal Shooting of Keith Scott" by Richard Faussett and Alan Blinder (November 30th 2016)

[100] USA Today "Mariners suspend Steve Clevenger without pay for remainder of the season" (September 23rd 2016)

[101] NBC News "Trump: 'Animals' was about the violent MS-13 gang" by Jonathan Allen (May 17th 2018)

[102] Washington Free Beacon "Media Fuels 'Fake News' Criticism With Misleading Reports on Trump's 'Animals' Comments" by David Ruiz (May 17th 2018)

[103] CBS DFW "Gorilla Statue Removed After Complaints It Was 'Racially Insensitive'" (February 28, 2018)

children "little monkeys" because they don't sit still. Many parks and playgrounds also have statues of animals and animal-themed equipment and drinking fountains, but after some liberal lunatic got triggered and posted a picture of the gorilla statue on their Facebook page, the city received a few phone calls complaining about it.

Sadly, instead of telling the people they're insane, the mayor released a statement saying, "We can understand this, because we have an obligation to listen to all our citizens, to determine what is offensive and not, especially in public places," and took the statue down![104]

Some sane parents who couldn't believe the city did such a crazy thing, brought flowers, balloons, and stuffed animals to the playground and made a "memorial" for the gorilla as a way to protest the city's idiotic decision to remove it.

After an ESPN announcer referred to Venus Williams' aggressive style during a tennis match as "guerrilla tactics," idiots on the Internet thought he was comparing her to a gorilla so he was fired. He then sued for wrongful termination because it should have been obvious that he was referring to her unconventional gameplay (as in guerrilla warfare, which is spelled differently than gorilla the animal).[105] Nike had even produced a

---

[104] Ibid.

[105] New York Daily News "Doug Adler, broadcaster suing ESPN after he was fired for Venus Williams 'guerrilla' comment, says network 'killed me'" by Jake Becker (August 25th 2017)

commercial featuring Andre Agassi titled "Guerrilla Tennis."[106]

ESPN's imaginary racism problem is so bad that they pulled an Asian-American announcer from narrating a college football game in Virginia because his name is Robert Lee, and the network was concerned it sounded too similar to Confederate Army general, Robert E. Lee, and didn't want anyone to get offended.[107]

After Florida gubernatorial (running for governor) candidate Ron DeSantis said voters don't want to "monkey up" the state's economy by voting for a progressive Democrat who's funded by George Soros, the liberal media pounced on him, claiming he was calling his opponent (who is black) a monkey.

Obviously "monkey this up" means "screw this up" just like when your mom or grandma told you to stop monkeying around when you were a kid, she meant stop screwing around, but the talking heads said with a straight face that Ron DeSantis used the term as a "racial slur" against his black opponent. Democrats obviously got their talking points and sounded like a broken record, all saying this wasn't just a "racist dog whistle," it was a "bullhorn."[108]

---

[106] Vanity Fair "Pete Sampras and Andre Agassi Held a Total 90s Retro Match in the Streets of New York" by Bill Bradley (August 25th 2015)

[107] New York Times "ESPN Pulls Announcer Robert Lee From Virginia Game Because of His Name" by Matthew Haag (August 23rd 2017)

[108] Sun Sentinel "Ron DeSantis uses 'monkey' to describe Andrew Gillum's agenda; Democrats brand it racist" by Anthony Man (August 29th 2018)

The National Anthem

The black activist organization, the NAACP (National Association for the Advancement of Colored People) wants our national anthem banned, claiming the "Star-Spangled Banner" is too "racist." They sent letters to members of Congress saying the song is "one of the most racist, pro-slavery, anti-black songs in the American lexicon," and cited their allegiance to former NFL player Colin Kaepernick.[109]

They point to a third stanza in the song, which is never included in its modern rendition where it says, "Their blood has washed out their foul footstep's pollution. No refuge could save the hireling and slave. From the terror of flight or the gloom of the grave." Some say the lyrics refer to slaves hired by the British to fight against the colonists, so they of course would have been seen as enemies as well. Others believe the reference to hirelings and slaves refer to the British soldiers themselves who were seen as "slaves" of the king[110]

Salon.com jumped on the anti-American bandwagon and said, "It's time to examine the words and the origins of our national anthem" and called it, "another neo-

---

[109] Sacramento Bee "Remove 'The Star-Spangled Banner' as national anthem, California NAACP urges" by Alexei Koseff (November 7th 2017)

[110] PRI.org "Historians disagree on whether 'The Star-Spangled Banner' is racist" by Christopher Woolf (August 30th 2016)

Confederate symbol."[111]   CNN pundit Angela Rye agreed, saying that the national anthem "itself" is "problematic."[112]

After the CEO of Papa John's Pizza spoke out about the dwindling NFL ratings resulting from many fans refusing to watch during the 2017 season because players were disrespecting the national anthem by refusing to stand, the liberal media claimed the company was the favorite pizza of "racists."

"Why the Alt-Right Now Loves Papa John's" read the *Huffington Post's* headline.[113]   He later apologized for being "divisive" and stepped down as CEO. *Newsweek* framed his resignation in a false light with the headline, "Papa John's CEO Steps Down After Gaining Neo-Nazi Support."[114]

A high school near San Francisco has banned the national anthem from being played during pep rallies, which had previously kicked off the events.   The president of the Associated Student Body claimed it was "outdated and racially insensitive," adding, "As our

---

[111] Salon.com "It's time to examine the words and the origins of our national anthem, another neo-Confederate symbol" by Jefferson Morley (August 27th 2017)

[112] Washington Examiner "CNN pundit: The national anthem 'itself' is 'problematic'" by Naomi Lim (June 5th 2018)

[113] Huffington Post "Why the Alt-Right Now Loves Papa John's" by Luke O'Brien (November 2nd 2017)

[114] Newsweek "Papa John's CEO Steps Down After Gaining Neo-Nazi Support" by Cristina Maza (December 22nd 2017)

culture shifts to one that is more diverse and accepting of all types of people, so must our traditions."[115]

Students at a California high school near Sacramento were reprimanded for chanting "USA" during athletic events.[116] The principal sent out an email to parents saying that while the school wasn't outright banning the kids from chanting "USA," she warned that the chant could send an "unintended message," meaning that students of Mexican heritage might be offended.

Snowflake students at another California high school demanded that other students remove their American flag t-shirts they wore on Cinco de Mayo, a popular Mexican holiday in Southern California, because they were considered to be "offensive."[117] The American flag is now offensive, in America! The students sued, claiming the school violated their First Amendment rights by banning their shirts, but the 9th Circuit court ruled in favor of the school![118]

[115] The Sacramento Bee "National anthem banned from high school's rallies for being 'racially insensitive.'" by Don Sweeney (February 14th 2018)

[116] Washington Times "Calif. high school warns students against chanting 'USA' at sporting events" by Jessica Chasmar (September 14th 2017)

[117] Fox News "California Students Sent Home for Wearing U.S. Flags on Cinco de Mayo" by Joshua Rhett Miller (May 6th 2010)

[118] CNN "Court: School was within its rights to ban U.S. flag T-shirts on Cinco de Mayo" by Catherine E. Schoichet (March 3rd 2014)

Fourth of July

Since many liberals are uncomfortable with the American flag and our national anthem, you can imagine how they feel about the Fourth of July. A *Huffington Post* writer claimed, "Given the racial dynamic that still exists in this country today how can African-Americans celebrate a holiday that accentuates your perceived inferiority by your oppressor?"[119]

The writer noted that many Americans will be firing up their grills, and that, "I will fire up my grill as well, but it won't be in celebration of Independence Day. It will be in recognition of the centuries of lies perpetrated upon me masked as the truth by the so-called Founding Fathers."[120]

The holiday doesn't remind him of the freedoms we all enjoy in the United States today, but instead, "This holiday reminds me *not* of American independence; it reminds me of the hypocrisy this country has seduced us to blindly follow without questioning its authenticity."[121]

An Op-Ed in the *Philadelphia Tribune* titled "Should Blacks Celebrate July 4th?" answers that question, saying, "Simply stated, the answer is "No!"[122] One year comedian Chris Rock tweeted, "Happy white people's Independence Day," adding more fuel to the Leftists' anti-

---

[119] Huffington Post "Independence Day Is A Celebration Of American Hypocrisy" by Dexter Rogers (July 4th 2017)

[120] Ibid.

[121] Ibid.

[122] The Philadelphia Tribune "Should Blacks Celebrate July 4th?" by Michael Coard) July 1st 2017)

American fire.[123] Every Fourth of July floods of anti-American and anti-white tweets fill Twitter from angry black people who are so upset with what they've read about slavery in school, that they can't take a moment to enjoy the blessings we all have by being Americans today.

Food is Racist

New York University recently posted a special menu in the school's cafeteria to honor Black History Month, which included traditionally "black" foods like barbecue ribs, corn bread, and collard greens. It also included a watermelon-flavored drink and Kool-Aid, which are very popular in the black community. But, as you can imagine, some students thought the menu was racist and complained. (Probably white students).

The university's president then called the menu "inexcusably insensitive" and said that the employees who came up with it were fired. The dining hall's head cook revealed that those employees were themselves black, and thought it was a great way to honor Black History Month.[124]

A firefighter in Detroit brought a watermelon for his fellow firefighters to enjoy after he was transferred to a new station, but since he is white and 90% of the

---

[123] https://twitter.com/chrisrock/status/220512157937315842

[124] New York Times "Black History Month Menu at N.Y.U.: Kool-Aid, Watermelon and Controversy" by Maggie Astor (February 21st 2018)

firefighters at that station are black, some of them thought it was "racially insensitive," so he was fired.[125] Are watermelons racist, or is it only racist when a white person offers a slice to a black person? I just can't keep up anymore. Maybe grocery stores and farmers' markets should suspend watermelon sales so nobody gets triggered. What's the problem? Different cultures enjoy different kinds of food. Italians like pizza. Chinese people enjoy noodles. Mexicans like burritos—it's an obvious fact, but facts hurt liberals' feelings. Saying black people like watermelon is no different than saying people in Wisconsin like cheese, or people in Texas like barbecue.

This is just another one of countless examples of hypersensitivity, and in our backwards world today nobody seems to know what's right or wrong, or what's appropriate or inappropriate. And it's all because a few bad apples keep spoiling the bunch.

When a CNN contributor named Hilary Rosen saw a student at Georgetown University wearing a bacon costume to a basketball game against Syracuse University, she declared that the student was anti-Semitic and taunting Jews (who don't eat pork), apparently because there is a Jewish community in Syracuse. "This is a Georgetown #Hoyas fans anti-Semitic smear to the Syracuse team," she tweeted.[126] After Georgetown lost,

---

[125] Fox 2 "Detroit firefighter fired for bringing watermelon to station" by Taryn Asher (October 6th 2017)

[126] New York Post "CNN contributor jumps to conclusions and is left eating crow" by Max Jaeger (December 17th 2017)

she posted "Hey bacon-man. #Syracuse for the win. Bigots lose."[127] In reality, the kid in the costume has the last name of "Bakan" (pronounced *bacon*) and he liked dressing up and acting as the unofficial mascot for his team to help hype up the crowd.[128]

For "Pride Month" in 2017 (previously called "gay pride" month, but that's not "inclusive" enough for the ever-growing LGBT acronym), Skittles removed the "rainbow" colors from its candy, making them all white, saying "During Pride, only one rainbow matters. So we've given up ours to show our support."[129] As you can imagine, like everything the social justice warriors try to do to appease the Left, it backfired.

Idiots online raged that Skittles had put out a new "white supremacist" candy, and were "promoting white pride." "This is soooo fucking stupid. Why should whiteness mean equality?!" one woman tweeted.[130] Another said that "Skittles realized how [popular] white/capitalist pride was becoming and wanted to join in the efforts."[131] "If everyone was equal, they wouldn't be white," said another."[132]

---

[127] Ibid

[128] New York Post "CNN contributor jumps to conclusions and is left eating crow" by Max Jaeger (December 17th 2017)

[129] https://twitter.com/GroMarketingLtd/status/875042918477815808

[130] https://twitter.com/BlackMajiik/status/847680467939729408

[131] https://twitter.com/giaawoman/status/847665038319943682

[132] https://twitter.com/Takingover4da99/status/847626525172092929

Someone else said, "Shoulda been brown or black. I ain't eating no white Skittles."[133] The outrage went on, and on. Poor Skittles tried to virtue signal to the LGBT community and instead ended up being accused of being Nazis! Haha!

Dr. Seuss Books

After First Lady Melania Trump sent a box of books to an award winning elementary school in Massachusetts for National Read a Book Day, the librarian posted an open letter rejecting them, claiming that Dr. Seuss books are "steeped in racist propaganda, caricatures, and harmful stereotypes."[134] Someone should have told Michelle Obama this, because she read children Dr. Seuss books inside the White House at an event just a few years earlier.[135]

After word of this lunatic librarian getting triggered from the First Lady's gift began to spread, curious people started going through the Twitter feed for her school and noticed photos of this same librarian dressed up as a *Cat in the Hat* character at a Dr. Seuss themed event she hosted in the library![136]

---

[133] https://twitter.com/vivrantking_/status/847639169010515968

[134] The Horn Book "Dear Mrs. Trump" by Liz Phipps Soero (September 26th 2017)

[135] Washington Post "First lady reads Dr. Seuss to school children" via Associated Press (March 2nd 2011)

[136] Fox News "Librarian who rejected Melania Trump's Dr. Seuss books dressed as 'Cat in the Hat'" (September 29th 2017)

Some schools have actually banned books like *The Adventures of Huckleberry Finn*, written by Mark Twain and published in 1884 because of the way black people are depicted, and *To Kill a Mockingbird* because of its "racist" language.[137]

The American Library Association even renamed the Laura Ingalls Wilder Award which is given to authors who have made "substantial and lasting contributions" to children's literature, and is now called the Children's Literature Legacy Award because the author it was originally named after has been deemed a racist upon looking at her classic books in a new light.[138]

Her *Little House* series was written in the 1930s and 40s, and loved by children (and parents) for over 80 years, but are now considered racist for depicting American Indians as "savages," so after 64 years of giving out an award bearing her name, it was changed.[139]

The Library Association said in a statement, "This decision was made in consideration of the fact that Wilder's legacy, as represented by her body of work, includes expressions of stereotypical attitudes inconsistent with ALSC's core values of inclusiveness, integrity and respect, and responsiveness."[140]

---

[137] The Telegraph "To Kill a Mockingbird and Huckleberry Finn banned from schools in Virginia for racism" by Nick Allen (December 5th 2016)

[138] http://www.ala.org/alsc/awardsgrants/bookmedia/clla/about

[139] Washington Post "Laura Ingalls Wilder's name stripped from children's book award over 'Little House' depictions of Native Americans" by Meagan Flynn (June 25th 2018)

[140] http://www.ala.org/alsc/awardsgrants/bookmedia/clla/about

Pepe the Frog

As the 2016 presidential election got into full swing, a lot of tech-savvy Trump supporters began creating memes using Pepe the Frog, a cartoon character which was first used ten years earlier in a little-known online cartoon called *Boys Club*. For whatever reason, Pepe memes caught on and were used to troll Hillary supporters and depict reactions to certain events that unfolded throughout the campaign.

Being it's the Internet, of course some people created racist and anti-Semitic memes using the frog, as they do with just about any character or person, and the Leftist ADL [Anti-Defamation League], a social justice organization dedicated to amplifying anti-Semitism in order to justify their ongoing fundraising efforts, declared Pepe the Frog to be a "hate symbol" alongside the likes of the swastika and the KKK's fiery cross.   Pepe, they declared, was the mascot of the Alt-Right.[141]

Band-Aids

Band-Aids have also been called white supremacist because the "standard" color is a light tan that critics claim is designed to match "caucasian" skin. "Band-Aids are made for white people," vented one angry blogger.[142] And he's not alone. In the late 1990s an entrepreneur in

---

[141] Los Angeles Times "How 'Pepe the Frog' went from harmless to hate symbol" by Jessica Roy (October 11th 2016)

[142] Patheos "Why Is the Color of Band-Aids Caucasian?" by Rachel Marie Stone (November 26th 2012)

New York launched "Ebon-Aid" (short for ebony) "The bandage exclusively designed for people of color."[143]

A white man who adopted a few black children, apparently unaware that Ebon-Aids existed, felt uncomfortable when he had to put a Band-Aid on his four-year-old son because it "stuck out like a sore thumb," so he decided to start his own bandage company called True-Color Bandages. "I want them to see they were made just as authentic and just as beautiful and the bandage market needs to reflect that," he said.[144]

That's where we're at in society. Band-Aids are part of white privilege so black people need their own. Apparently they don't know that the Band-Aid brand sells clear bandages for those who are offended by not having a bandage that matches the color of the skin. Tolerance.org lists Band-Aids as a "perk" of white people's "skin privilege."[145]

They're also included on the "White Privilege Checklist" that a San Diego State University professor handed out to her sociology students.[146] And were recently used as an example of more "evidence" of white

---

[143] The Atlantic "The Story of the Black Band-Aid" by Sebastien Malo (June 6th 2013)

[144] Huffington Post "People Of Color Can Finally Wear Bandages That Match Their Skin" by Taryn Finely (October 7th 2015)

[145] Tolerance.org "On Racism and White Privilege"

[146] The College Fix "Students offered extra credit to determine their level of 'white privilege'" by Drew Van Voorhis (September 19th 2017)

privilege at a "cultural competency worship" held at the University of North Carolina at Chapel Hill.[147]

Santa Claus

Not even Santa Claus is safe from being called a white supremacist in our current political climate. A growing number of liberals are upset that he's white, and instead of making a bunch of different Santas (one for each race), the "solution" to this "problem," they think, is to depict him as a penguin, not a person.[148]

One activist was invited on CNN (as usual) to explain her absurd idea, where she said, "The world has changed a lot in the last fifty, one hundred years, and Santa Claus is a fictional character. He is nothing like the original historical character figure [Saint Nicholas] he was based off of anymore. We have kind of evolved him into this magical, mythical figure, and for kids I think it's important that they don't have to feel necessarily bogged down that Santa is always white."[149]   Bogged down!? Those poor children!

Ms. Magazine published an article written by a black woman complaining about her kid making the usual Christmas art projects at school using construction paper and gluing cotton balls together for Santa's beard. The

---

[147] Campus Reform "UNC diversity workshop says beige bandaids are white privilege" by Anthony Gockowski (March 29th 2016)

[148] Slate "Santa Claus Should Not Be a White Man Anymore" by Aisha Harris (December 10th 2013)

[149] CNN interview with Aisha Harris conducted by Brian Stelter on "Reliable Sources" (December 15th 2013)

mother ranted about having to teach her kid that Santa was an "able-bodied, heterosexual white guy."[150]

She went on to air her grievances as if it were Festivus, and concluded that, "In a society in which institutional racism and sexism exist, it's not enough to be non-prejudiced or an observer. We have to intervene and challenge institutional behaviors that perpetuate oppression."[151] So kids making Santa Claus arts and crafts is perpetuating "oppression"? I give up!

CNN's Don Lemon declared that by President Trump saying "Merry Christmas" instead of the new politically correct "Happy Holidays," that he is using a dog whistle (a secret code) to signal to white supremacists that he's on their side.[152] Christmas music is also now problematic. "Jingle Bells" was deemed racist by a Boston University professor because, "The legacy of 'Jingle Bells' is one where its blackface and racist origins have been subtly and systematically removed from its history."[153]

He says for most people the song, "may have eluded its racialized past and taken its place in the seemingly unproblematic romanticization of a normal 'white' Christmas, [but] attention to the circumstances of its performance history enables reflection on its problematic role in the construction of blackness and whiteness in the

---

[150] Ms. Magazine "White Christmas, White Santas, White Privilege" by Martha Pitts (December 21st 2010)

[151] Ibid.

[152] Real Clear Politics "Don Lemon: Is Trump's Use Of 'Merry Christmas' A Dog Whistle?" by Ian Schwartz (December 21st 2017)

[153] Fox News "'Jingle Bells' rooted in racism, Boston University professor says" by Caleb Parke (December 15th 2017)

United States."[154] The professor claims that the song was "originally performed" by white entertainers in blackface back in the 1850s, but there is no evidence of this.

In an experiment to see how much further the social justice warriors would go, a reporter for the Media Research Center asked students at George Mason University if they would sign a petition to support banning the song "White Christmas" from being played on the radio because it is "racist" since it, "perpetuates the idea that being white is automatically a positive attribute in our society."[155]   Many students eagerly signed the petition and supported the cause.

Police Body Camera Footage

Black Lives Matter activists have pressured police departments across the country to require their officers to wear body cameras, thinking it will catch cops on tape acting racist towards black suspects.   But what the cameras are capturing is an epidemic of black people lying about supposed racist interactions with white police officers.

In South Carolina the local NAACP [National Association for the Advancement of Colored People] president was pulled over for not using his turn signal and given a warning, despite not having the proper vehicle registration.   Instead of being grateful he didn't get a

---

[154] Ibid.

[155] National Review "College Students Sign 'Petition' to Ban 'White Christmas' Because It's Racist" by Katherine Timpf (December 22nd 2015)

ticket, he published a lengthy Facebook post alleging he was racially profiled and even fabricated racist statements he claimed the officer made to him.

The department then released the full unedited body camera footage of the incident, which proved it was not only a routine traffic stop, but the officer was actually very friendly.[156]

That same week a Virginia police department released footage of an officer's body camera after a black woman posted a video on Facebook crying about what she said was racial profiling and "bullying" from a white cop. The bodycam footage completely debunked her claims.[157]

A black woman arrested for driving while intoxicated in Texas claimed the white officer raped her before taking her to the police station, and so once again the department released the unedited (almost two hour long) footage showing exactly what happened from the moment the woman was pulled over to the time she arrived at the station in the cop car, and proved she was a liar and the officer conducted himself properly.[158]

A black city council member in McKinney, Texas was cited for speeding and then arrested for refusing to sign the ticket (which is required by law and not an admission of guilt), and so he claimed he was racially profiled and

---

[156] Fox 61 "Police body camera footage tells a different story from NAACP chapter president's claims" (May 20th 2018)

[157] WTVR "Body cam footage released after woman accuses deputy of racism: 'I was just bullied'" by John Burkett (May 7th 2018)

[158] Daily Wire "The department then release the unedited, almost two hour long footage, showing exactly what happened from the moment the women was pulled over to the time she arrived at the station in the back of the cop car." by Ryan Saavedra (May 23rd 2018)

got pulled over for "being black with dreadlocks."[159] So, once again, the department released the entire footage of the incident captured on the officer's bodycam which showed that he too was seeing "racism" where none existed. The city council then voted to censure him, officially reprimanding him for his behavior and false statements about his arrest.[160]

Milwaukee Bucks basketball player Sterling Brown made headlines after he was tazed and arrested by local police over a parking incident. He claimed they over-reacted, and when body camera footage was released it showed he was being argumentative with the officers and when ordered to take his hands out of his pockets, he refused, causing the officers to fear he was about to pull out a weapon, so they subdued him.[161]

With police body cameras showing so many black people to be liars who are fabricating their claims of racist encounters with white police officers liberals began complaining about the bodycams. *Newsweek* magazine actually claimed that they were contributing to black and

---

[159] Dallas News "McKinney councilman backpedals after accusing police of pulling him over for 'being black with dreadlocks'" by Nanette Light (May 9th 2018)

[160] Fox4News "City council votes to censure McKinney councilman after controversial arrest" (May 23rd 2018)

[161] Milwaukee Journal Sentinel "Sterling Brown case: What we know about the arrest of the Milwaukee Bucks rookie" by Ashley Luthern (May 24th 2018)

brown people having their "civil rights violated" and say that the cameras "distort evidence."[162]

Author's Note: Please take a moment to rate and review this book on Amazon.com or wherever you purchased it from to let others know what you think. This also helps to offset the trolls who keep giving my books fake one-star reviews when they haven't even read them. Almost all of the one-star reviews on my books are from NON-verified purchases which is a clear indication they are fraudulent, hence me adding this note.

These fraudulent ratings and reviews could also be part of a larger campaign trying to stop my message from spreading by attempting to tarnish my research through fake and defamatory reviews, so I really need your help to combat this as soon as possible. Thank you!

---

[162] Newsweek "Police Body Cameras Can Threaten Civil Rights of Black and Brown People, New Report Says" by Josh Saul (November 14th 2017)

Cultural Appropriation

A special kind of so-called "racism" that has been discovered in recent years is "cultural appropriation," which is described by the Thought Police as a white person "stealing" another race's "culture" or using their culture in an "offensive" way. Since everything offends liberals, it's hard to nail down a concise definition of what exactly cultural appropriation is, so in this chapter I'll cover a few examples that illustrate the concept and show how pervasive they think this "problem" is.

The most familiar example involves Halloween costumes, but the insanity is so much worse than these isolated incidences. It involves the names of sports teams and their mascots, music genres, hairstyles, and even food!

White rappers have often been accused of "stealing" black music, thus committing "cultural appropriation." Singer Halsey once ripped Iggy Azalea, calling her a "fucking moron" for her "complete disregard of black culture," simply for being a white rapper.[163] Singer Bruno Mars has also been accused of the "crime" because they say he "copies black music and profits off of his racial

---

ambiguity in a way that other black artists are not able to do."[164]   Bruno Mars (whose real name is Peter Hernandez) is half Puerto Rican and half Jewish.

In 2017 members of the World Intellectual Property Organization urged the United Nations to ban cultural appropriation by expanding international intellectual property regulations to protect "Indigenous designs, dances, words and traditional medicines."[165]

It's getting so bad that a school board in Toronto decided to stop using the title "chief" for various job positions and changed it to "manager" out of concern that "chief" was offensive to Indians.   No indigenous person or group even complained about the word "chief" being used for various titles, but some SJWs on the school board decided to take it upon themselves to make the change after imagining that calling people "chief" of a certain department is a "potential microaggression."[166]

Sports Mascots

A student at Bethel University in St. Paul, Minnesota wore a Chicago Blackhawks hockey team shirt to class one day and triggered a professor who vented on Facebook, writing, "So your college professor is a Native

---

[164] Complex "Bruno Mars Is the Center of Twitter's Latest Cultural Appropriation Debate" by Victoria Johnson (March 9th 2018)

[165] Yahoo "Cultural appropriation: Make it illegal worldwide, Indigenous advocates say" via CBS (June 13th 2017)

[166] CBC "Toronto District School Board to remove 'chief' from job titles out of respect for Indigenous communities" by Nick Boisvert (October 11th 2017)

American. A Native American who has spoken multiple times about the offensiveness of Indian Mascots. Yet you come to class with an Indian mascot sprawled across your shirt... Bold move sir."[167]

The student then met privately with the teacher and shortly after that he offered a public apology. So either out of fear or ignorance, or maybe succumbing to the liberal brainwash—instead of the student standing up for his right to wear a shirt supporting his favorite hockey team and ridiculing the snowflake professor for getting offended—he apologized! The professor then said, "They have truly matured and learned from this experience and we have taken big steps in the reconciliation process."[168]

The Adidas shoe company actually encouraged censoring the name "Indians" on sports jerseys during a commercial because they consider it to be cultural appropriation.[169] In an ad titled "Create Positivity" the person doing the voice over says "many teams are starting to change their names" as it showed what looked like a high school basketball team called the "Indians," but the players put a piece of tape over the name on their jerseys.

---

[167] The College Fix "Student apologizes for wearing Chicago Blackhawks sweatshirt to class" by Katheryn Hinderaker (May 16th 2017)

[168] https://www.facebook.com/jim.b.jacobs/posts/10154496470507227?pnref=story

[169] Adidas "Create Positivity" ad posted on their YouTube channel (March 5th 2018)

Adidas also offers financial assistance to high schools if they will change their logos or mascots from Native American imagery to something else.[170]

The Washington Redskins football team had their trademark canceled by the U.S. Trademark Office because they deemed it to be "racist" against Native Americans. The Redskins then waged a legal battle to keep the trademark, and after the U.S. Supreme Court ruled on a related case about a different "offensive" trademark, they were luckily able to keep the registration and prevent others from producing knockoff merchandise using the name.[171]

After President Trump launched a few Tomahawk missiles at a Syrian airbase in response to the Syrian Army using chemical weapons on the rebels in the ongoing civil war, the editor of *Mother Jones* expressed concerns that "a lot of Native Americans" were probably "outraged" because the missiles are called "Tomahawks."[172] Someone responded to her on Twitter saying, "Probably just Elizabeth Warren."[173] Another said, "Real journalists must be enraged that you call yourself one of them."[174]

---

[170] NPR "Adidas Offers To Help U.S. High Schools Phase Out Native American Mascots" by Laura Wagner (November 5th 2015)

[171] Washington Post "Washington Redskins win trademark fight over the team's name" by Ian Shapira and Ann E. Marimow (June 29th 2017)

[172] https://twitter.com/ClaraJeffery/status/850761684624982016

[173] https://twitter.com/rcno13/status/850791611411968000

[174] https://twitter.com/AussieAmerican2/status/850783984040759300

Food Appropriation

A burrito cart in Portland was forced out of business after some lunatic locals accused the two white women who ran it of "cultural appropriation" and said they stole Mexican "intellectual property" after the owners admitted that they "picked the brains" of taco stands in Mexico to find out what kinds of ingredients would taste the best in order to come up with their recipes.

The website "Mic" wrote a story with the headline, "These white cooks bragged about stealing recipes from Mexico to start a Portland business," and complained that, "The problem, of course, is that it's unclear whether the Mexican women who handed over their recipes ever got anything in return."[175] They later changed the headline to read that the white cooks "bragged about bringing back recipes" instead of "stealing them" after backlash over such an incendiary claim.

The local *Portland Mercury* newspaper posted a follow-up article covering their investigation into more "food appropriators" but later took it down, possibly after threats of a defamation lawsuit for such a ridiculous story. An editor's note reads, "Due to new information that has recently come to light, we have taken down our blog post, 'This Week in Appropriation: Kooks Burritos and

---

[175] Mic "These white cooks bragged about stealing recipes from Mexico to start a Portland business" by Jamilah King (May 19th 2017)

Willamette Week.' It was not factually supported, and we regret the original publication of this story."[176]

The story read, in part, "Week after week people of color in Portland bear witness to the hijacking of their cultures. Several of the most successful businesses in this town have been birthed as a result of curious white people going to a foreign country. Now don't get me wrong: cultural customs are meant to be shared. However, that's not what happens in this city."[177]

It went on to say that, "Because of Portland's underlying racism, the people who rightly own these traditions and cultures that exist are already treated poorly. These appropriating businesses are erasing and exploiting their already marginalized identities for the purpose of profit and praise."[178]

The food appropriation controversy in Portland got so big that it made national news. *The Washington Post* asked, "Should white chefs sell burritos?" and reported that a local resident had created a list of businesses that are committing "food appropriation," including one named Voodoo Doughnut which was accused of unethically profiting from African Voodoo![179]

The Washington Post writer struggled with the topic, saying, "Who can't identify with a campaign to support

---

[176] The Portland Mercury "This Week in Appropriation: Kooks Burritos and Willamette Week" by Jagger Blaec (May 22nd 2017)

[177] Eater - Portland, OR "Portland Burrito Spot Shutters Amid Claims of Cultural Appropriation" by Mattie John Bamman (May 22nd 2017)

[178] Ibid.

[179] Washington Post "Should white chefs sell burritos? A Portland food cart's revealing controversy." by Tim Carman (May 26th 2017)

the people whose voices are muffled in a culture still dominated by white males?" but then confessed he had trouble fully embracing the food police. He was, however, uncomfortable when, "a white person profits from the cuisine" or "becomes the leading authority on it, rather than a chef born into the culture," and pointed out that white chefs like Rick Bayless is known for his Mexican cuisine, Andy Ricker for Thai food, and Fuchsia Dunlop for her Chinese cuisine.

If you're white, I guess it's racist to cook food other than hotdogs and hamburgers.

Hoop Earrings

An RA [Resident Assistant] at Pitzer College in Claremont, California sent out a campus-wide email telling white students they can't wear hoop earrings because that too is "cultural appropriation." She had also painted a sign on a "free speech" wall in the dorm reading, "White Girl, Take Off Your Hoop Earrings."[180]

The email read that she and other "women of color" were, "tired and annoyed with the reoccurring theme of white women appropriating styles that belong to the black and brown folks who created the culture. The culture actually comes from a historical background of oppression and exclusion. The black and brown bodies who typically wear hooped earrings, (and other accessories like winged eyeliner, gold name plate necklaces, etc) are typically viewed as ghetto, and are not

---

[180] Claremont Independent "Pitzer College RA: White People Can't Wear Hoop Earrings" by Elliot Dordick (March 7th 2017)

taken seriously by others in their daily lives. Because of this, I see our winged eyeliner, lined lips, and big hoop earrings serving as symbols [and] as an everyday act of resistance, especially here at the Claremont Colleges."[181]

She went on, "Meanwhile we wonder, why should white girls be able to take part in this culture (wearing hoop earrings just being one case of it) and be seen as cute/aesthetic/ethnic. White people have actually exploited the culture and made it into fashion."[182]

A writer for *Vice News* echoed this woman's sentiments, saying that "Hoop earrings are my culture, not your trend" and cautioned white women to "think twice before you put them on" because "hoops are worn by minorities as symbols of resistance, and strength."[183]

Dreadlocks

A white student at San Francisco State University who wore his hair in dreadlocks was assaulted by a black student who claimed he was committing "cultural appropriation" because of his hairstyle.[184] The woman, who tried to physically stop him from walking away while she was lecturing him, asked her friend standing

---

[181] Ibid.

[182] Ibid.

[183] Vice "Hoop Earrings Are My Culture, Not Your Trend" by Anonymous (October 9th 2017)

[184] New York Post "Black woman goes off on white guy with dreads" by Associated Press (March 31st 2016)

nearby if he had any scissors, giving the impression she wanted to start cutting of his dreads right there!

"I felt that I didn't need to explain myself. It is my hair, my rules, my body," the white student said after video of the incident went viral.[185] But you can't expect a rabid SJW to understand personal freedom. He was more than polite when she accosted him, and when he finally broke free from her grip and walked away, the woman noticed someone was shooting video of the altercation, and then she assaulted them too, striking their phone.

After pop culture prostitute Kim Kardashian posted a selfie showing she got her hair braided into cornrows, the twits on Twitter erupted in anger and their idiocy made headlines about her supposed "cultural appropriation" violation.[186]

Pop star Katy Perry apologized for her past "cultural appropriation" during a sit down interview with Black Lives Matter leader Deray McKesson because she had previously worn her hair in cornrows for a music video and dressed up as a "Geisha girl" during a performance at the American Music Awards one year. "I've made several mistakes," she told McKesson. "I won't ever understand some of those things because of who I am. I will never

---

[185] The Independent "White San Francisco student Cory Goldstein defends his dreadlocks after he was harassed by black student" by Aftab Ali (March 31st 2016)

[186] Fox News "Kim Kardashian's braids called out as 'cultural appropriation'" by Alexandra Deabler (June 17th 2018)

understand, but I can educate myself and that's what I'm trying to do along the way."[187]

Let's make a deal with these critics. White people will stop braiding their hair or wearing dreads "like a black person," if black women stop bleaching their hair blond and stop straightening it too. That means you Beyonce!

Halloween Costumes

It used to be the only people who didn't like Halloween were a few far-right fundamentalist Christians who see it as a day celebrating the Devil and evil, but now people on the far-left have found problems with Halloween for completely different reasons. Certain costumes and characters that kids have enjoyed dressing up as for generations are now seen as problematic because they are "cultural appropriation" and thus "racist."

This idea isn't just something that a few fringe idiots on the Internet are espousing. Every year as Halloween approaches the chorus of complaints gets louder. Just before Halloween in 2016, Disney stopped selling the costume for Maui (a character voiced by Dwayne Johnson in their new film *Moana*), because people complained it was cultural appropriation.[188] The character is a muscular, tattooed Polynesian demigod who wears a grass skirt.

---

[187] Billboard "Katy Perry Apologizes For Her Past Cultural Appropriation During Livestream" by Peter Helman (June 12th 2017)

[188] USA Today "Disney pulls offensive 'Moana' Halloween costume" via AP (September 21st 2016)

To normal people, the character pays homage to the legends of Pacific Islanders, but some morons got upset and began venting on Twitter that, "culture is not a costume." Instead of just ignoring these lunatics, Disney pulled the costume from stores and apologized, saying, "The team behind 'Moana' has taken great care to respect the cultures of the Pacific Islands that inspired the film, and we regret that the Maui costume has offended some. We sincerely apologize and are pulling the costume from our website and stores."[189]

The Huffington Post cheered the move, saying "People shouldn't wear brown skin as a costume without understanding the experience of brown people."[190] The following year, the Disney costume controversy reared its ugly head again. *Cosmopolitan* magazine suggested to parents, "Maybe don't dress your kid up as Moana this Halloween" and said that, "It's on you to teach your kid not to be racially insensitive."[191]

USA Today issued a "guide" on the controversy titled, "Is it OK for a white kid to dress up as Moana for Halloween?"[192] Practically half of the Disney characters are now considered offensive. Pocahontas, Jasmine from *Aladdin*, the crows from *Dumbo*, King Louie from *The*

---

[189] Ibid.

[190] Huffington Post "Disney Pulled That Offensive 'Moana' Costume. Here's Why It Matters." by Clara Herriera (September 21st 2016)

[191] Cosmopolitan "Maybe Don't Dress Your Kid Up As Moana This Halloween?" by Redbook Editors (October 23rd 2017)

[192] USA Today "Is it OK for a white kid to dress up as Moana for Halloween?" by Alia E. Dastagir (October 23rd 2017)

Jungle Book, the Indians in *Peter Pan*, and the list goes on.

One blogger complaining about the Moana costume even criticized Elsa, the star of *Frozen*, saying that the character perpetuated "white beauty" because she's white with blonde hair and blue eyes.[193]

In 2016 when the war on Halloween costumes was really heating up, actress Hillary Duff and her boyfriend dressed up as a Pilgrim and an Indian for a party, and when photos of the couple were posted online the outrage began. She later tweeted, "I am SO sorry to people I offended with my costume. It was not properly thought through and I am truly, from the bottom of my [heart emoji] sorry."[194] Her boyfriend, Jason Walsh, also apologized on his Instagram, saying, "I meant no disrespect. I only have admiration for the indigenous people of America."[195]

Amazon.com has also removed certain costumes after complaints.[196] MTV News produced a segment titled "12 Racist Halloween Costumes For Kids" denouncing popular costumes ranging from an Indian chief to a "little

---

[193] RaceConcious.org "Moana, Elsa, and Halloween" by Sachi Feris (September 5th 2017)

[194] https://twitter.com/HilaryDuff/status/792813874923737088

[195] Hollywood Reporter "Hilary Duff Addresses Native American, Pilgrim Halloween Costume: "I Am So Sorry to People I Offended" by Ashley Lasimone (October 31st 2016)

[196] The Telegraph "Amazon withdraws 'sexy burka' fancy dress outfit following complaints" by Adam Boult (October 7th 2016)

amigo" Mexican, and even the popular "rasta" hat with fake dreadlocks![197]

An Elementary School in Massachusetts decided to cancel their annual Halloween costume parade to avoid any possible cultural appropriation. The school principal told parents in a letter, "During our conversations, we discussed how the costume parade is out of our ordinary routine and can be difficult for many students." He went on to say that, "the parade is not inclusive of all the students and it is our goal each and every day to ensure all individual differences are respected."[198]

Other elementary schools in Wisconsin and New Mexico did the same thing.[199] But it's not just elementary schools which are afraid of Halloween. This same stupidity has infected college campuses across the country, and many major schools are now fearful of the holiday.

A now famous incident happened at Yale University in 2015 when a mob of one hundred angry students surrounded a school administrator and berated him because he didn't support banning "offensive" Halloween costumes. He sent out an email explaining his position and was actually very sympathetic and supportive of

---

[197] MTV News "12 Racist Halloween Costumes for Kids" (October 21st 2015)

[198] Boston Globe "Walpole elementary school cancels Halloween parade" by Cristella Guerra dn Alyssa Meyers (October 19th 2017)

[199] SFGate "These elementary schools are banning students from wearing costumes on Halloween" by Susana Guerrero (October 30th 2017)

SJWs cultural appropriation concerns, but refused to ban certain costumes.

He encouraged students to, "actively avoid those circumstances that threaten our sense of community or disrespect, alienate or ridicule segments of our population based on race, nationality, religious belief or gender expression," but did say that students had a "right to express themselves."[200] Well, that triggered them.

One student literally shouted at him, "It is your job to create a place of comfort and home for the students that live in Silliman...Do you understand that!" When he started to respond, she shrieked, "Be quiet! Why the fuck did you accept the position? Who the fuck hired you?" When he started to reply, she interrupted him again, yelling at him to step down.

"If that is what you think about being a Master, then you should step down. It is not about creating an intellectual space! It is not! Do you understand that? It's about creating a home here! You are not doing that. You're going against that!"[201] Video of the bizarre incident went viral, and he later resigned.[202]

The Delta Sigma Phi fraternity at the University of Michigan was forced to cancel an Egyptian themed party after the president of the Egyptian Student Association complained about it and accused them of cultural

---

[200] Business Insider "Racial tensions are boiling over at Yale over Halloween costumes" by A.C. Fowler (November 9th 2015)

[201] New York Times "Yale Lecturer Resigns After Email on Halloween Costumes" by Anemona Hartocollis (December 7th 2015)

[202] New York Times "Yale Professor and Wife, Targets of Protests, Resign as College Heads" by Anemona Hartocollis (May 26th 2016)

appropriation on Twitter. "I am the president of the Egyptian student association and these whites don't know what they got themselves into," he warned them.[203]

An Egyptian Sphinx is incorporated into the fraternity's seal, along with a pyramid to symbolize stability and longevity, and a Facebook post for the party said it was to honor their Egyptian roots. Instead of denouncing their ridiculous critics, Delta Sigma Phi released a statement saying, "We sincerely apologize to anyone who was hurt by the theme choice. We have learned our lesson and will take more precaution in the future when deciding themes for events. We pride ourselves on being a diverse social fraternity with members from a wide variety of religions, races, backgrounds, sexual orientations, and other identities. It would never be the intention to make anyone from any group…feel unwelcome or uncomfortable."[204]

People need to stop apologizing to these idiots and either ignore them or mock them for their hyper-sensitivity and paranoid delusions that ruin everything. If you give them an inch, they will try to take a mile, so stop caving in to their demands!

Hawaiian Bobblehead Doll

A Lyft passenger videotaped herself berating her driver because he had a Hawaiian bobblehead doll

---

[203] The College Fix "University of Michigan frat cancels 'Nile'-themed party after student complaints" by Ben Decatur (August 22nd 2017)

[204] Ibid.

attached to his dashboard which had a grass skirt that swayed back and forth as the car drove around. The passenger deemed it "racist," and didn't shut up about it for over five minutes, ultimately calling the driver a "fucking dumbass idiot," causing him to pull the car over where he then asked her to get out multiple times before she finally complied.[205]

The woman said she was going to turn her video over to Gawker (before their bankruptcy) in order to "expose" the driver and "turn him into an Internet meme" because she was so disgusted by his "racist" bobblehead. The irony is, she herself became another SJW meme after it went viral and provided the world with one more piece of evidence that social justice warriors are nutjobs.

"I don't know why my beautiful Lady Lola is offending you," the driver said, and informed her that he is Asian. He was fired immediately after the passenger complained to Lyft, but was later re-hired after the woman's video went viral, showing what really happened. But the fact that someone could get fired from their job after one customer called them a racist without any evidence at all proves what dangerous waters we are in.

"Blackface"

White people painting their faces brown to look like a black person as a joke or as part of a Halloween costume is considered one of the most racist things a person can do in today's society. Black people lose their minds and feel

---

[205] Daily Caller "Video: Woman Becomes Unglued Over Lyft Driver's 'Racist' Hula Doll" by Blake Neff (August 30th 2016)

they need to give a history lesson on blackface and gripe about how offended they are by it and think it's the end of the world. But when black people dress up as white people, painting their faces peach color like the Wayans brothers in their film *White Chicks*, that's okay because life is a one-way street to liberals.

Plenty of comedians have done bits in blackface, including Howard Stern, Sarah Silverman, Jimmy Kimmel, and others (not to mention Robert Downey Jr.'s famous character in *Tropic Thunder*), but with the recent shift in society's sensibilities, most comedians would never risk doing such things today. But it's not just blackface comedy skits that trigger liberals. It's also face swap apps that digitally alter your face to make you look like someone else.

After Snapchat released a Bob Marley "face swap" feature on April 20th 2017 (4/20, the unofficial marijuana "holiday") allowing users to have their face replaced by Bob Marley wearing a rasta hat and dreads, it was immediately denounced as "racist." The Bob Marley estate, which controls the rights to his image and intellectual property, actually approved the face swap filter, and didn't see anything wrong with it.

The Washington Post took the craziness a step further by declaring, "It's not just Snapchat's Bob Marley lens: Every face-swap app has a 'blackface' option."[206]

---

[206] Washington Post "It's not just Snapchat's Bob Marley lens: Every face-swap app has a 'blackface' option" by Caitlin Dewey (April 20th 2016)

Girl's Prom Dress

A high school girl's prom picture went viral after SJWs freaked out because it was a Chinese design, and you guessed it — she's white. "My culture is NOT your goddamn prom dress," one Asian man responded, in a tweet that sparked the controversy causing it to explode into a worldwide news story. His tweet got over 172 thousand likes.[207] While most people shared word of his hateful comments to show how insane SJWs are, countless others supported him.

"Was the theme of prom casual racism?" asked one woman.[208] "This thread is funny because it's nothing but white people justifying her wearing this dress. That's like having a conversation with whites about them using the N-word. It shouldn't be a convo in the first place, don't do it," said another.[209]

If a white girl can't wear a Chinese prom dress because it's "cultural appropriation," then I guess Chinese people will have to stop wearing blue jeans. My culture is not your damn costume Jackie Chan! Unfortunately this is not the end of the Left's distorted views about racism. It's just the beginning.

---

[207] https://twitter.com/jere_bare/status/989981023076208640

[208] https://twitter.com/holdyourbutts/status/989999012865425409

[209] https://twitter.com/DesNotDesmond/status/990235291909873666

Anti-White Racism

While liberals claim to be adamantly against racism, the truth is they embrace and openly encourage racism against whites, while at the same time pretending that it doesn't exist or justifying it as "payback" for some white people owning slaves 150 years ago.

While white people's careers are often ruined for a joke that others find offensive (remember what happened to Roseanne Barr?), or for just pointing out certain undisputed facts; overt racism and hatred of white people is not only tolerated, it is celebrated.[210]

Many people refer to anti-white racism as "reverse racism," which is a deceptive and incorrect term because it implies that racism is just a one-way street, and something that's carried out by whites against blacks, Mexicans, and other minorities. Those who are intellectually honest acknowledge and understand that racism is something every ethnic group experiences because of humans' hard-wired tribal nature and the cultural differences between groups of people and the conflicts those differences cause.

---

[210] National Review "Yes, Anti-White Racism Exists" by David French (August 2nd 2018)

There's nothing wrong with people of any race preferring to date, marry, and live in communities consisting of people of their own kind — unless you're white of course, then it's considered "racist." Humans, and practically every creature on earth, usually feel more comfortable in a group of their own kind, which they share a common culture with, and have similar values, traditions, and backgrounds.[211]

Different subgroups within the same species tend to congregate together to harmonize their lives and minimize the conflicting motivations caused by variations within the species.[212] Animals on land, sea, and air all live and work primarily in groups consisting of the same kind. And humans are no different. The problems come in when one group hates another, or actively discriminate against them instead of peacefully and respectfully interacting with others who are "outside" of their own group. It's hard for most people to admit, but racial tensions are not caused by one particular race; they are a result of the inherent differences between the races, their cultures, customs, values, and histories.

And while racism of any kind should be equally denounced, it's very common for black people and the liberal media to accept anti-white sentiments as if that form of racism is somehow justified. One columnist for *Affinity* magazine wrote a whole article titled, "Why black

---

[211] Annual Review of Sociology - "Birds of a Feather: Homophily in Social Networks" by Miller McPherson, Lynn Smith-Lovin, and James M Cook (2001) pages 415–444

[212] The American Naturalist "Assortative Mating in Animals" by Yuexin Jiang, Daniel I. Bolnick, and Mark Kirkpatrick (June 2013)

people are allowed to be anti-white," and cited slavery (which was abolished 150 years ago) and insists "You [white people] have the privilege of saying 'two wrongs don't make a right' because you've never been targeted by centuries of systemic racism. You're a couple hundred years too late for that, so stop making yourself the victim. We have plenty of other things to worry about."[213]

Leftist trash website *Salon* even asked, "Is ending the so-called 'white race' the solution to the problem of white supremacy?"[214] Pop star Taylor Swift was attacked for being "aggressively white" by a critic at BuzzFeed after one of her new albums came out, even though her songs and persona have nothing to do with race at all.[215] Apparently the critic was just uncomfortable with the fact that Taylor Swift is white with blond hair and blue eyes, which I guess is now a crime in America.

Anti-white racism is increasingly being institutionalized with a disturbing number of college professors and entire courses dedicated to painting the white race as a problem.[216] Democrats are always adding fuel to this fire by labeling Republicans the "party of white men," and equating Trump supporters with neo-Nazis. When speaking at a women's conference Michelle Obama told her audience that many people "don't trust

---

[213] Affinity Magazine "Why black people are allowed to be anti-white" by Rihanna Martin (May 12th 2017)

[214] The tweet has since been deleted.

[215] Buzzfeed "Taylor Swift's Persona Is Not Built for 2017" by Alanna Bennett (November 10th 2017)

[216] CNN "University stands by 'Problem of Whiteness' course" by Amanda Jackson (December 23rd 2016)

politics" because the Republicans Party is "all men" and "all white."[217]

Anti-white racism is putting police officers' lives at risk because online activists perpetuate fake news that police departments across the country are filled with white supremacists who are looking for an opportunity to beat down black people. Such propaganda has sparked a rash of ambushes on random white police officers by unhinged black men who gun them down when they least suspected it.[218]

With the exception of a small fraction of white Americans, nobody supports discrimination against people of color. And while our country has a checkered past in regards to slavery and the treatment of non-whites, many liberals not only live in the past and blame injustices from hundreds of years ago on white people living today, but they have also embraced a radical form of anti-white racism and somehow think it's okay.

Thankfully for the most part we can all coexist alongside one another in America, despite our cultural differences, but in recent years we've seen a dramatic rise of racism against white people and new buzzwords have entered the lexicon like "white privilege" and "white normative," which are used to perpetuate this hatred.

Websites like the *Huffington Post* and *BuzzFeed*, along with CNN and MSNBC contributors take things

---

[217] Washington Times "Michelle Obama laments lack of diversity in 'all men, all white' GOP" by Jessica Chasmar (October 4th 2017)

[218] New York Times "Five Dallas Officers Were Killed as Payback, Police Chief Says" by Manny Fernandez, Richard Pena and Jonah Engel Bromwich (July 8th 2016)

even further by claiming that only white people can be racist,[219] and even blame white people for ruining America for everyone else.[220] They use mental gymnastics by claiming that non-whites "can't be racist" because they supposedly have no 'institutional power' and have redefined racism as a combination of power and prejudice. Blacks have no power, they say, despite a black man recently being president of the United States, so they can't be racist.

Liberals always say we need more "diversity" to help end racism, which is just a codeword for "less white people." Liberals want "people of color" to be the majority in the United States. They want to "take back the power" from white people, and if or when they do, they will wield that power in a way to "payback" the white man for all the injustices minorities have faced over the last several hundred years.

Liberals are now pushing the idea that all white people are beneficiaries of racism, even if they themselves are not racist. This results in "white privilege" they say, and whites are now encouraged to "check their privilege," meaning, "acknowledging the role those rewards play in your life and the lives of less privileged people."[221] Non-racist whites are given advantages in America because of *other* white people's

---

[219] RealClear Politics "Marc Lamont Hill: Black People Unable To Be Racist" by Ian Schwartz (July 12th 2016)

[220] BuzzFeed "37 Things White People Need To Stop Ruining In 2018" by Patrice Peck (December 27th 2017)

[221] The Atlantic "What the Origin of 'Check Your Privilege' Tells Us About Today's Privilege Debates" by Arit John (May 13th 2014)

racism, they claim. It's not an exaggeration to say that there is a cultural 'war on white people' and that whites are being systematically demeaned and blamed for the personal and cultural failures of black people and Latinos in America today.

We also see many minorities faking hate crimes in order to use the attention as leverage to further their cause of demonizing white people.[222] They're even seeing acts of "racism" where none exist, as if they're hallucinating like a schizophrenic as I covered in the previous two chapters. We see the same paranoia and hoaxes with regards to anti-Semitism,[223] which, as you know, is prejudice against Jews, but for some reason that form of racism has its own unique name.

It seems that no matter how hard some white people try not to be racist, they can't do enough. As one social justice warrior blogger wrote, "Sorry white people, but trying too hard not to be racist is low-key kind of racist."[224]

It's interesting that whites are seen as the "privileged" race in the United States, when Asians actually have the highest average income.[225] Liberals don't like facts though. Facts like black men make up only 7% of the

---

[222] FakeHateCrimes.org keeps a current database of hate crime hoaxes with links to local news reports for each instance.

[223] Syracuse.com "Jewish man arrested after spray painting swastikas on his own home in Upstate NY" by Ben Axelson (March 21st 2017)

[224] Babe.net "Sorry white people, but trying too hard not to be racist is low-key kind of racist" by Katie Way (December 1st 2017)

[225] Business Insider "American Median Incomes By Race Since 1967" by Steven Perlberg (September 17th 2013)

U.S. population but commit almost half of all murders.[226] And that the majority of black babies are born out of wedlock and grow up in homes without a father.[227] Conservative blacks like Sheriff David Clarke and Larry Elder have pointed out these uncomfortable facts, but facts hurt liberals' feelings.

Whites must not only ignore uncomfortable facts about black communities (or be labeled "racist"), but also put black people on a pedestal as special, and apologize and be ashamed for simply being white. If you're a white person and are attracted to white people of the opposite sex, then you are considered a racist as well for not engaging in interracial relationships.[228]

Meanwhile, many black men see dating white women as a "prize" and a way to "prove" that they're "more of a man" than white guys, but when a black woman is in a relationship with a white man, the women are seen as race traitors. For example, black people got so upset at Barack Obama's daughter Malia after a photo surfaced showing her kissing a white guy, that she trended on Twitter from so many people hating her.[229]

The Root, an online "magazine" for black people owned by Univision, declared that white women who date

---

[226] U.S. Department of Justice "Homicide Trends in the United States, 1980-2008" by Alexia Cooper and Erica L. Smith (November 2011)

[227] Washington Examiner "77% black births to single moms, 49% for Hispanic immigrants" by Paul Bedard (Mary 5th 2017)

[228] The Daily Beast "'No blacks' is not a sexual preference. It's racism" by Samantha Allen (September 9th 2015)

[229] Trending Views "Opinion: Black Twitter is Racist After Malia Kisses White Man" (November 30th 2017)

black men, or even have kids with a black man isn't proof enough that they're not racist. "Dear white women: interracial relationships and biracial children do not absolve you of racism," they claim.[230]

The article read, "There are many people who use their interracial relationships, both past and present, to prove that they can't be racist. There are parents of biracial children who are blind to racism because they believe that bearing half-black children means that they cured racism [but] news flash: sex with a black man doesn't earn you a get-out-of-racism-free card."[231]

This same outlet labeled Charles Barkley a "black white supremacist" after he spoke out against the crime problem plaguing black communities.[232]   Yes, they labeled a black man a white supremacist for urging his fellow black people to stop killing each other!

After rapper Kanye West tweeted support for Candace Owens, a black conservative YouTuber who had been making headlines for denouncing Black Lives Matter and supporting President Trump, the mainstream media went nuts. *The Washington Post* called him the new "alt-right darling."[233] BuzzFeed said "People Are Worrying That

---

[230] The Root "Dear White Women: Interracial relationships and biracial children do not absolve you of racism" by Kyla Jenee Lacey (October 31st 2017)

[231] Ibid.

[232] The Root "Charles Barkley Is a Great Example of a Black White Supremacist" by Michael Harriot (August 21st 2017)

[233] Washington Post "Kanye West, alt-right darling" by Molly Roberts (April 24th 2018)

Kanye West is Getting Radicalized by The Far Right,"[234] and Rolling Stone magazine said, "Kanye West's Pro-Trump Tweets Are a Real Threat."[235] Another rapper, one who was a member of Snoop Dogg's entourage, put out a "Crip Alert" for Kanye, urging members of the gang to find and attack him because of his support for President Trump.[236]

A *New York Times* Op-Ed recently written by a black woman asked, "Can My Children Be Friends with White People?" and went on to detail her reasons for teaching them they should avoid white people. "I will teach my boys to have profound doubts that friendship with white people is possible," she said.[237]

The tipping point for her "revelation" was the election of Donald Trump as president. "Donald Trump's election has made it clear that I will teach my boys the lesson generations old, one that I for the most part nearly escaped. I will teach them to be cautious, I will teach them suspicion, and I will teach them distrust. Much sooner than I thought I would, I will have to discuss with

---

[234] BuzzFeed "People Are Worrying That Kanye West is Getting Radicalized by The Far Right" by Ryan Broderick (April 23rd 2018)

[235] Rolling Stone "Kanye West's Pro-Trump Tweets Are a Real Threat" by Michael Arceneaux (April 26th 2018)

[236] CBS Los Angeles "Rapper Issues 'Crip Alert For Kanye', Warns West To 'Stay In Calabasas' After Supporting Trump" by April 30th 2018

[237] New York Times "Can My Children Be Friends With White People?" by Ekow N. Yankah (November 11th 2017)

my boys whether they can truly be friends with white people."[238]

The Leftists' rampage against "white America" keeps growing. They began demanding that historical statues be removed, and not just confederate monuments, but statues of the Founding Fathers! *Newsweek* magazine asked, "Should George Washington's statue be next?" after a bunch of confederate monuments had just been removed, and then activists in New York City started demanding that a statue of Christopher Columbus be torn down.[239]

CNN's Angela Rye said, "To me, I don't care if it's a George Washington statue or Thomas Jefferson, they all need to come down."[240] Notorious race-baiter Al Sharpton agrees.[241] Others joined in on the chorus, wanting to erase the history of our very own country.

Vice News published an article titled, "Let's Blow Up Mount Rushmore" and then after the growing backlash changed it to "Let's Get Rid of Mount Rushmore" hoping to deflect accusations they were trying to incite a terrorist attack on the monument. "Donald Trump says removing confederate statues is a slippery slope that could get out of

---

[238] Ibid.

[239] NBC News "Christopher Columbus statue in New York City could be considered for removal" by Daniella Silva (August 23rd 2017)

[240] RealClear Politics "CNN's Angela Rye: Washington, Jefferson Statues "Need To Come Down" by Ian Schwartz (August 18th 2017)

[241] National Review "Al Sharpton Puts Jefferson Memorial on Notice" by Kyle Smith (August 16th 2017)

control," it began, and concluded, "Maybe he's right—would that be such a bad thing?"[242]

It went on to suggest, "With the president of the United States basically justifying neo-Nazism, it seems unthinkable that we will ever see a day when there is a serious push to blow up Rushmore and other monuments like it. But if that moment ever arrives, I suspect I'd be onboard."[243]

Even before all this madness, I conducted a social experiment in 2015 for my YouTube channel where I asked random beachgoers to sign a petition to support issuing a new American flag design, telling them that since the stars and stripes are "synonymous with slavery" the country needed a "new" flag.[244] I recommended a rainbow pyramid to represent "diversity," and many gladly signed the petition and looked forward to replacing Old Glory.[245]

The Left's agenda of trying to erase history is straight out of *Nineteen Eighty-Four*, where George Orwell wrote, "One could not learn history from architecture any more than one could learn it from books. Statues, inscriptions, memorial stones, the names of streets— anything that

---

[242] Vice News "Let's Get Rid of Mount Rushmore" by Wilbert L. Cooper (August 17th 2017)

[243] Ibid.

[244] Washington Examiner "Millennials in San Diego sign petition to remove American flag" by Emilie Padgett (June 30th 2015)

[245] YouTube "Liberals Sign Petition to Ban the American Flag" by Mark Dice (June 29th 2015)

might throw light upon the past had been systematically altered."[246]

This topic (as with every chapter) could fill an entire book itself, so for sake of keeping this one to a manageable length, let's take a look at a few more of the countless examples of anti-white racism being perpetuated by the Left, so we can hopefully end this madness before it gets completely out of control.

MTV "Decodes" Hidden Racism

The MTV News YouTube channel posted a whole series titled "Decoded" where each week they uncovered the "hidden racism" that's supposedly everywhere. Of course, according to them, the only racists are white people, and just about every aspect of American culture is supposedly steeped in it. In 2015 MTV aired a documentary titled "White People" which consisted of the host (an illegal alien and open-borders activist named Jose Antonio Vargas) shaming white teenagers about their "white privilege."[247]

Just before New Years in 2016 MTV posted a YouTube video recommending New Years resolutions for white people which featured a montage of different minorities insulting whites for things they supposedly are doing wrong. "Try to recognize that America was never 'great' for anyone who wasn't a white guy," says a black man. "Just because you have black friends doesn't mean

---

[246] George Orwell's *Nineteen Eighty-Four* page 87

[247] The New Yorker "The Trouble with 'White People' by Hua Hsu (July 30th 2015)

you're not racist. You can be racist with black friends," says another one.

They also demanded that white people stop using the word "woke." While anti-white racism is a regular part of MTV's programming, this video got so much backlash they surprisingly deleted it 48 hours later.[248]

"Let Them Die"

A Trinity College sociology professor called white people inhuman assholes who should die after a gunman opened fire on Republican Congressmen practicing softball for their annual charity game in 2017, seriously injuring Congressman Steve Scalise.[249] "It is past time for the racially oppressed to do what people who believe themselves to be 'white' will not do, put an end to the vectors of their destructive mythology of whiteness and their white supremacy system. #LetThemFuckingDie," he posted on his Facebook page, appearing to endorse the assassination attempt. "The time is now to confront these inhuman assholes and end this now."[250]

He was placed on temporary leave, but not fired, and the college actually defended him. "Williams's actions and words were protected by academic freedom and did

---

[248] RealClearPolitics "'MTV News' Deletes YouTube Video Telling 'White Guys' What They Could Do Better In 2017 After Backlash" by Tim Hains (December 20th 2016)

[249] Washington Times "Trinity College professor calls white people 'inhuman': 'Let them f-ing die'" by Douglas Ernst (June 21st 2017)

[250] Mediaite "College Reinstates Professor Who Said To Let White People 'F***ing Die'" by Joe Bilello (August 2nd 2017)

not violate Trinity College policies," said President Joanne Berger-Sweeny.[251]

The "Problem" with Whiteness

The University of Michigan held a conference titled "Conversations on Whiteness" to "help" white employees become better social justice warriors by teaching them to "recognize the difficulties they face when talking about social justice issues related to their White Identity, explore this discomfort, and devise ways to work through it."[252]

A professor at Fairfield University in Connecticut who taught entire courses on "Black Lives Matter" and "Critical Race Theory" says that, "any critical investigation of race should devote some time to the problem that is whiteness."[253]   Just *being* white is a problem now.   The professor claims that, "Whiteness means a specific power apparatus that exists at the expense of the disempowerment of black people," and insists, "To be white in the U.S. is to be a perpetuator of the power apparatus unless one actively and consistently resists."[254]

---

[251] Ibid.

[252] College Fix "University teaches white employees how to overcome the 'discomfort' of being white" by Andrew Johnson (December 19th 2017)

[253] The College Fix "Professor teaches students about 'the problem that is whiteness'" by Nathan Rubbelke (July 5th 2017)

[254] Ibid.

Of course, the professor says that it is necessary for white people, "to acknowledge one's personal implications in the white power apparatus," which apparently means we're supposed to feel guilty about being white.

A sociology professor at CUNY [the City University of New York] declared, "Part of what I've learned is that the white-nuclear family is one of the most powerful forces supporting white supremacy."[255]   She went on to elaborate that, "I mean, if you're a white person who says they're engaged in dismantling white supremacy, but you're forming a white family [and] reproducing white children that 'you want the best for' — how is that helping [and] not part of the problem?"[256]

She made the statements on Twitter, and later put her account on private after her tweets started making headlines. She has a verified account, indicating that it wasn't a fake account set up by a student who was trying to get her in trouble. Her bio page on the university website claims she's "an internationally recognized expert on Internet manifestations of racism."[257]   Maybe they meant an expert on *creating* manifestations of racism.

---

[255] Fox News "Having 'white nuclear family' promotes white supremacy, says New York professor" (October 31st 2017)

[256] Ibid.

[257] http://www.hunter.cuny.edu/sociology/faculty/jessie-daniels/jessie-daniels

A Day Without White People

Students at Evergreen State College in Olympia, Washington came up with the idea for "A Day Without White People" on campus and demanded that all white students and professors not come to school on their special day so "people of color" could enjoy the campus without the presence of white people.[258] Bizarrely, many of the professors went along with the idea, but one who refused became the target of an angry mob of students who gathered outside of his classroom and demanded that he be fired! "Hey-hey, ho-ho, these racist teachers have got to go," they chanted.[259]

The president of the college later issued a statement, not denouncing the angry mob of students for their ridiculous (and racist) ideas and actions, but thanking them for their "passion and courage." His statement began, "I'm George Bridges, I use he/him pronouns," catering to the gender identity insanity that's sweeping across American campuses and making it clear that he too is infected with the liberal pathogen.[260]

---

[258] New York Post "A Day Without White People" by Jackie Salo (May 31st 2017)

[259] Washington Times "Students berate professor who refused to participate in no-whites 'Day of Absence'" by Bradford Richardson (May 25th 2017)

[260] Washington Times "Evergreen State College president expresses 'gratitude' for students who took over campus" by Bradford Richardson (May 29th 2017)

"Progressive Stacking"

A teaching assistant at the University of Pennsylvania named Stephanie McKellop tweeted about how she calls on white men *last* during classroom discussions. "I will always call on my black women students first. Other POC [people of color] get second tier priority. WW [white women] come next. And, if I have to, white men."[261] As you may expect, this kind of favoritism isn't just being practiced by this one random teaching assistant. Liberals have a name for choosing blacks and Latinos over whites in the classroom, in what they call "progressive stacking."[262]

The practice appears to have stemmed from the Occupy Wall Street protests in 2011, where people from "traditionally marginalized groups" were favored to speak at events over others (meaning over straight white men). The "Radical Teacher Journal" published an article in 2013 featuring an Occupy Wall Street-inspired course that incorporated the "progressive stack" which it described as, "calling on those who had not spoken (or rarely spoke), women, queer-identified students, and students of

261 The College Fix "White, male students called on last in some classrooms" by Nathan Rubbelke (November 6th 2017)

262 Inside Higher Education "A Pedagogy Questioned" by College Flaherty (October 20th 2017)

color before we called on regular talkers, white, straight, and/or male students."[263]

Ohio State University hosted a "Transnational Feminism" conference in 2014 which promoted the tactic as well.[264]   Other teaching assistants and academics have also supported it, saying that the progressive stack is an "established method of facilitating discussion."[265]

Reparations

A group of black students at the University of Chicago demanded that the school pay them reparations for slavery, and hoped to use the money to fund a new African American Studies department.[266]   They also complained about the "damages" that Capitalism has done to America, calling it a "monstrosity."   "Reparations promise us a monumental re-birthing of America," they said. "Like most births, this one will be painful. But the practice of reparations must continue until the world that

---

[263] Radical Teacher: A Socialist, Feminist, and Anti-Racist Journal on the Theory and Practice of Teaching By Cathy Borck, Jesse Goldstein, Steve McFarland, and Alyson Spurgas (Spring 2013) Issue 96

[264] The College Fix "White, male students called on last in some classrooms" by Nathan Rubbelke (November 6th 2017)

[265] https://twitter.com/KempoJesse/status/920726780465631233

[266] The Chicago Reporter "A case for reparations at the University of Chicago" by Reparations at UChicago Working Group (June 5th 2017)

slavery built is rolled up and a new order spread out in its place."[267]

A bar in Portland, Oregon hosted what they called "Reparations Happy Hour" for black people to gather and discuss their hopes of one day getting reparations passed while they enjoyed free drinks paid for by white people who donated to their cause.[268] If they don't have enough money to pay their bills and feel they need reparations to help, then going drinking at a bar is probably the last thing they should be doing, but common sense isn't something liberals are familiar with.

Many blacks still dream of getting reparations in the form of free money from the government, paid by white tax dollars. At a campaign event a few months before the 2018 midterm election, crazy congresswoman Maxine Waters was asked about it by a man from the National Coalition of Blacks for Reparations in America. "The global reparations movement is advancing mightily on the planet," he began, insisting that black people, "need someone to stand up and push this legislation forward."[269] He then asked her to sponsor H.R. 40, a ridiculous reparations bill proposed by Democrat Representative John Conyers in 1989.

"I'd be happy to do that. That's no problem," she answered. "But let me tell you this. In order to get where we need to go on this issue and other issues, we really got

---

[267] Ibid.

[268] Fox News "'Reparations Happy Hour' invites white people to pay for drinks" by Christopher Carbon (May 27th 2018)

[269] The American Mirror "Maxine Waters promises reparations if Dems retake House" by Kyle Olson (March 4th 2018)

to understand that 2018 [midterm election] is important in taking back the House and taking back the Senate. And of course, we've got to get the White House back."[270]

She went on to say, "If we want to get to the point where we can get reparations, we've got to have the power to do that, number one, by having a supportive president would be wonderful, but taking back the House would be absolutely wonderful, and so yes."

There is a simple solution for black people who are incessantly upset by whites dominating the culture and being the majority in the United States of America. They can go back to Africa. If their ancestors weren't brought here, as horrible of a process as it was, then the black people wanting reparations for it today may be living in a grass hut with dirt floors, no running water, and roasting snakes over a bonfire for dinner.

Charging a "White Tax"

A restaurant owner in New Orleans decided to charge white customers extra for their meals for a month in order to "raise awareness of racial wealth differences in the country."[271] A study done five years earlier alleged that black people earned 54% less money than whites in the city, so the owner (who is originally from Nigeria) figured he'd charge whites $18 more for a meal to make up the difference.

---

[270] Ibid.

[271] Indy100 "A restaurant is charging white customers more to highlight racial wealth inequality" by Greg Evans (March 11th 2018)

Whites were "encouraged" to pay the extra fee, but it wasn't mandatory (because that would get the business owner in trouble for violating federal discrimination laws), but he says that almost 80% of white customers that month chose to pay the extra fee!

Because I could see the progression of the anti-white racism liberals were promoting, I conducted an experiment in 2015 which you can view on my YouTube channel where I approached random people on the boardwalk in San Diego and asked them if they would support a new "White Privilege Tax" which would add an additional 1% tax onto the income of white people in order to fund social welfare programs for minorities.[272]

Plenty of people were happy to sign it. You can watch the video for yourself on my YouTube channel, and I hope you'll check it out regularly for new videos almost every day.[273]

"Too Many White People"

When President Trump nominated a judge for the U.S. District Court of South Carolina, Senator Chuck Schumer announced he wasn't going to vote for him because the judge is white.[274]   Schumer complained that his

---

[272] YouTube "New 'White Privilege Tax' for all White People Supported by Minorities in Shocking Racism Experiment" by Mark Dice (July 20th 2015)

[273] Ibid.

[274] Washington Examiner "Chuck Schumer will vote against this judicial nominee just because he's white" by Becket Adams (March 1st 2018)

nomination "speaks to the overall lack of diversity in President Trump's selections for the federal judiciary," and he was upset that the nominee would replace a black judge who President Obama appointed. Schumer went on to complain that the majority of the people Trump nominated for federal judges were also white.

Barack Obama did his best to appoint as many black and latino people to positions of power as he could, despite their lack of qualifications and there being a variety of other people more qualified for the job. People like Attorney General Eric Holder, Supreme Court Justice Sonia Sotomayor, along with many federal judges and cabinet secretaries, were all basically affirmative action hires and Obama's attempt to add more "diversity," favoring their race over their qualifications.

White People to the Back

A Canadian music festival called the Halifax Pop Explosion officially apologized for what they said was a racist white woman who refused to move to the back row when a performer demanded that all white people near the front give up their seats to non-whites before she began her show.

You read that correctly. The singer wanted all white people to give up their seats for non-whites and move to the back, and when one white woman refused, she was labeled a racist. The festival's vice chairman later apologized to the singer and the other attendees for the white woman "interrupting" the show and for being "aggressive and racist."[275]

Moving the white people to the back rows was a reference to black people being forced to sit in the back of the bus during racial segregation in the 1950s, and a way for the singer to "pay back" white people and "show them how it feels" by being racist herself. As I said before, liberals don't want to end racism, they want to use racism for their own ends.

We Need More "Diversity"

"Diversity" is a code word for less white people, or to be more specific, less straight white people. It's so over-used by social justice warriors that those of us who have a brain can't help but roll our eyes every time we hear it. But Illinois governor Bruce Rauner loves diversity so much, he demonstrated his commitment to it during Black History Month by drinking chocolate milk at an event. He had a glass of milk sitting on the table in front of him and said that it represented the white men who run businesses.

"This chocolate syrup represents diversity," he said, as he poured it into the glass, sinking to the bottom. "When you look at most organizations, diversity sits at the bottom of the organization [and] you don't get inclusion

---

[275] The Daily Caller "Canadian Music Festival Says Sorry For 'Racist' White Staffer Who Didn't Want To Move To The Back" by Ian Miles Cheong (October 29th 2017)

until you actually stir it up." He then stirred it, picked up the glass, and took a drink, proud of his idiotic analogy.[276]

Social justice warriors at a New York high school successfully pressured administrators to shut down the production of "The Hunchback of Notre Dame" play in the name of diversity because the lead role was awarded to a white student after the auditions. The school district released a statement saying the cancelation was part of an attempt to "be more inclusive and culturally responsive."[277]

An editor at the *Huffington Post* bragged on Twitter that their goals for the month were to publish pieces from "less than 50% white authors."[278] Uber's chief brand officer wants more "diversity" in the company, saying, "I want white men to look around in their office and say, 'Oh look, there's a lot of white men here. Let's change this.'"[279]

The Big Tech companies are obsessed with diversity, which flies in the face of federal discrimination laws that are supposed to prohibit companies from not hiring people based on their race, but when it comes to discrimination against white people, everyone seems to think that's okay.

---

[276] Newsweek "Watch: Illinois Governor Drinks Chocolate Milk to Show Diversity is 'Really Good'" by Greg Price (February 22nd 2018)

[277] Fox News "High school cancels musical after white student lands lead role" by Caleb Parke (February 6th 2018)

[278] https://twitter.com/ChloeAngyal/status/974031492727832576

[279] CNN "Uber exec: White men need to 'make noise' about diversity" by Sara Ashley O'Brien (March 13th 2018)

The Charity Commission, a nonprofit watchdog in the UK, encouraged charities to darken up so they "reflect the communities they serve," after they determined there were too many white people helping with local charities and felt they needed to "promote diversity"[280] Yep, too many white people helping out black communities! How racist!

The BBC thinks that the latest gun control movement in the United States involving the Parkland high school kids is "too white."[281] And some black people are apparently also upset that some of the protesters use the phrase "Don't Shoot," which was originally used by Black Lives Matter.

MSNBC's Chris Hayes complained that President Trump's proposed immigration reform plan would keep America predominantly white for 5 more years.[282] The Left are determined to overthrow the white majority in America as soon as possible and are furious that ending illegal immigration will slow down their agenda. During a speech denouncing Trump's plan and talking about how "great" immigrants are, Nancy Pelosi said that her

---

[280] Breitbart "UK Government Blasts Charities for Being 'Too White'" by Virginia Hale (November 14th 2017)

[281] BBC "Never Again: is gun control movement too white?" by Georgina Rannard (March 27th 2018)

[282] MSNBC's All In with Chris Hayes "Donald Trump Immigration Plan Would Keep America Whiter" Posted on MSNBC's YouTube Channel (February 6th 2018)

grandson wished he had brown skin and brown eyes because he sees people of color as special.[283]

Star Wars: Rogue One actor Riz Ahmed thinks that a lack of diversity in television shows is "alienating young people" and "driving them towards extremism and into the arms of ISIS."[284] He believes if young Muslims don't see characters who look like them on TV, they won't be able to connect with the show, and will, "retreat to fringe narratives, to bubbles online and sometimes even off to Syria."[285]

Liberals are even complaining about wanting more "diversity" in spin class at the gym. "Is your spin class too young, too thin and too white?" asked the *Washington Post*.[286] The story recounted the horrifying experience of a black woman who signed up for a class in New York, and on the first day found she was the only black person there. "I didn't have another woman who looked like me, who understood my struggles, [or] my insecurities, she cried.[287]

Another black woman interviewed for the article said, "The messaging is essentially: You're allowed in this space if you are white, slender, able-bodied and less than

---

[283] Town Hall "Pelosi Proud That Grandson Wishes He Wasn't White" by Chris Reeves (February 8th 2018)

[284] The Guardian "Riz Ahmed warns lack of diversity on TV will drive young to Isis" (Hannah Ellis-Petersen (March 2nd 2017)

[285] Ibid.

[286] The Washington Post "Is your spin class too young, too thin and too white?" by Lavanya Ramanathan (March 18th 2018)

[287] Ibid.

45, cis-gender and heterosexual. And if you're not, then you're not welcome."[288] This lady doesn't need a spin class, or a personal trainer. In my opinion, she needs a psychiatrist.

Racist "Microaggressions"

It's getting harder to spot (actual) racism in America these days since thankfully we've made amazing progress over the last several decades learning to live alongside one another despite our differences. But since incidents of racism have dramatically shrunk and racism is a business for liberals, they have invented a new term to describe the microscopic racism they say still remains —"microaggressions." And like bacteria too small to see with the naked eye, racist microaggressions are supposedly everywhere.

Psychology Today defines them as, "the everyday verbal, nonverbal, and environmental slights, snubs, or insults, whether intentional or unintentional, which communicate hostile, derogatory, or negative messages to target persons based solely upon their marginalized group membership."[289] And apparently every white person is still racist, whether they know it or not, because "most well-intentioned white Americans have inherited the racial biases of their forebears; [and] the most harmful

---

[288] Ibid.

[289] Psychology Today "Microaggressions: More than Just Race" by Derald Wing Sue (November 17th 2010)

forms remain outside the level of conscious awareness."[290]

An example of this is when, "A white man or woman clutches their purse or checks their wallet as a black or latino man approaches or passes them," they say.[291] Even telling a black person that you don't see them as a "black person" is considered a racist microaggression because now you're ignoring the supposed struggles they face because of their race.[292]

Being surprised that a Mexican-American doesn't speak Spanish is also a "microaggression." And so is being wrong about an Asian person's heritage, for example, when you think someone is Chinese, but they're Korean. Expecting an Asian person to be smart is one too, because that's a "stereotype" as well, they say.

The librarians at Simmons College in Boston published a guide to "help" students stop committing "Islamophobic microaggressions" and listed greeting someone with "Merry Christmas" and saying "Happy Easter," as inappropriate. Even saying "God bless you" after someone sneezes is on their list of microaggressions because that might offend an atheist.[293]

Liberals say Christians are especially averse to "committing" microaggressions because of our "Christian

---

[290] Ibid.

[291] Ibid.

[292] BuzzFeed "21 Racial Microaggressions You Hear On A Daily Basis" by Heben Nigatu (December 9th 2013)

[293] Campus Reform "Librarians warn 'Christian fragility' causes microaggressions" by Toni Airaksinen (March 1st 2018)

Privilege" and believe that, "Within this dominant social environment, Christians come to expect social comfort and a sense of belonging and superiority," and "when this comfort is disrupted, Christians are often at a loss because they have not had to build skills for constructive engagement with difference."[294]

The Air Force Academy apologized for committing a "racist microaggression" after they sent out a campus-wide email about maintaining a good personal appearance and used Michael Jordan as an example of portraying a positive image. "He was never seen with a gaudy chain around his neck, his pants below his waistline, or with a backwards baseball hat on during public appearances," the email noted.[295] But that was "offensive" to black people.

The Air Force later sent out an apology, saying in part, "Microaggression such as these are often blindspots/ unintentional biases that are not often recognized, and if they are recognized they are not always addressed."[296] So telling Air Force cadets not to walk around with their pants sagging and their underwear showing like some thug on his way to the corner liquor store in the ghetto is now considered to be "racist."

---

[294] Huffington Post "Christian Fragility" by Susan M. Shaw (July 2nd 2015)

[295] Fox News "Be like Michael Jordan? Not at Air Force Academy" (February 17th 2018)

[296] Washington Examiner "Air Force Academy apologizes for 'microaggressions' after making Michael Jordan reference in email" by Katie Leach (February 17th 2018)

#VerifiedHate

To highlight the double standards of Twitter's enforcement of their terms of service, a conservative using the account @Meme_America started the #VerifiedHate campaign which consisted of doing searches on Twitter for racist, anti-white, and violent threats posted against white people by users with verified accounts (the ones with the little blue checkmarks next to their names).

"Verified Hate" uncovered hundreds of racist and threatening tweets from BuzzFeed employees,[297] writers for the *Huffington Post*,[298] *The New Yorker*,[299] *The Daily Beast*,[300] Vice News,[301] and other mainstream publications which had often remained online for years, skirting past the moderators.

The campaign brought attention to countless calls to murder random white people, support for white genocide, assassination threats to President Trump, and all kinds of hate speech which was ignored by moderators and allowed to stay up on the platform. Screen shots were taken of the tweets which were also labeled with their accompanying URL from Archive.is to prove they are real

---

[297] http://archive.fo/uwdcA

[298] http://archive.fo/pJYNz

[299] http://archive.fo/4EMzS

[300] http://archive.fo/hRTVN

[301] http://archive.fo/mmgiz

in the event that users delete them after having attention called to them and try to claim they were photoshopped.

In the ultimate ironic twist, about a week after the #VerifiedHate campaign was started by @Meme_America, the account was permanently suspended for supposedly violating Twitter's terms of service.[302]

Facts are "Racist"

When black people complain about white people in general, the liberal Establishment embraces the criticism as necessary and frames it as an important issue that white people need to address, no matter how wildly inaccurate or exaggerated their claims are. But when whites simply point out basic facts about black people, such as the murder rate, the high percentage of fatherless homes, or that according to the Center for Disease Control half of black women (48% to be exact) have genital herpes,[303] then those facts are labeled "racist" no matter the context or the purpose of pointing them out.

Like I said before, black men make up only about 7% of the U.S. population but commit almost *half* of all murders.[304] Facts are "racist" though. Facts like three

---

[302] Twitter.com/Meme_America shows the status of the account is suspended.

[303] NPR "CDC: Genital Herpes Among Black Women High" (March 12th 2010)

[304] U.S. Department of Justice "Homicide Trends in the United States, 1980-2008" by Alexia Cooper and Erica L. Smith (November 2011)

quarters of black children are born out of wedlock.[305] Or the fact that most black children don't have a father in the home.[306]   Or the fact that 59% of black women have children by two or three different men, none of whom they've ever married.[307]

Since the black community in America has largely embraced thug culture and view gangster rappers as role models, it's not surprising that crime, STDs, and poverty is a major problem for them. *The Los Angeles Times* even says that the reason sexually transmitted diseases are so prevalent among blacks and Mexicans is because of "racism."[308]

Hopefully the black community can break their self-defeating behavior patterns and cycle of poverty by leaving the liberal plantation they have been tricked by Democrats to continue living on, but it's an uphill battle because so many of them have been improperly raised in broken homes and born to drug abusing mothers so it's going to be very difficult, if not impossible, for some of them to become fully productive citizens or even self-sufficient.

---

[305] Washington Examiner "77% black births to single moms, 49% for Hispanic immigrants" by Paul Bedard (Mary 5th 2017)

[306] National Center for Fathering "The Extent of Fatherlessness" 56.6% of black children are living absent their biological fathers.

[307] Forbes "Multiple Baby Daddies Can Make You Poor" by Kiri Blakeley (April 1st 2011)

[308] Los Angeles Times "STDs in LA county are skyrocketing. Officials think racism and stigma may be to blame" by Soumya Karlamangla (May 7th 2018)

It's Okay to Be White

As a result of the growing anti-white racist sentiments on school campuses and on social media, some creative members of 4Chan decided to print fliers that simply read "It's Okay To Be White" and posted them around various schools to see how others would react. As you can imagine, instead of ignoring the flyers or agreeing with such an innocuous statement, they made national headlines and were denounced as "racist," which proved the very point that those who posted them were trying to make.

The Washington Post reported that the flyers were found at over a half dozen different schools across the country and that the schools were "investigating."[309] One student at UC Davis who is on the Black Leadership Council said, "Whoever is posting these photos, I don't think they're realizing how triggering these posters are for people."[310]

One resident of East Grand Rapids, Michigan said, "With the kind of world that I'm trying to build for my son, I'm deeply offended, the outrage knows no bounds."[311] The city officially condemned the flyers, and

---

[309] Washington Post "'It's okay to be white' signs and stickers appear on campuses and streets across the country" by Janell Ross (November 3rd 2017)

[310] CBS San Fransisco "Anonymous 'It's OK To Be White' Flyers Posted At UC Davis, Other Campuses" (November 11th 2017)

[311] Fox 17 East Grand Rapids commissioners condemn 'It's okay to be white' fliers" by Michael Dupre (November 6the 2017)

of course the Southern Poverty Law Center launched an "investigation" of their own.[312]

The backlash to such a harmless statement only proves there is war being waged by liberals against white people in America today and those daring to just disagree with the rampant anti-white agenda are labeled "white supremacists" and cited as more evidence of the "problem" with whiteness.

Author's Note: Please take a moment to rate and review this book on Amazon.com or wherever you purchased it from to let others know what you think. This also helps to offset the trolls who keep giving my books fake one-star reviews when they haven't even read them. Almost all of the one-star reviews on my books are from NON-verified purchases which is a clear indication they are fraudulent, hence me adding this note.

These fraudulent ratings and reviews could also be part of a larger campaign trying to stop my message from spreading by attempting to tarnish my research through fake and defamatory reviews, so I really need your help to combat this as soon as possible. Thank you!

---

[312] Huffington Post "'It's Okay To Be White' Signs Appear In Schools, Cities Across The U.S." by Taryn Finley (November 9th 2017)

Gender Identity

It used to be pretty easy to determine who was a man and who was a woman, even from a distance or if you have bad eyes and didn't have your glasses on. Not just from the shape of people's faces and bodies, but also from the way they dress, walk, and even sound. The different styles of clothes that men and women wear and use of makeup grew out of the basic biological differences between the two sexes.

For example, women want to emphasize youth and health, so they use makeup to cover-up flaws in their skin. Eye shadow gives the impression of larger eyes, which gives the appearance of youth, while foundation smooths the skin and covers up imperfections, aging spots, and wrinkles.[313]

Women wear high heels because they cause them to stick out their butts and walk in a sexually provocative way in hopes of more easily influencing men to give them what they want.[314] They show cleavage for the same reason, and this is also why women wear sleeveless shirts and skirts in the middle of winter, while men dress appropriately for the cold weather. They know we're

---

[313] Psychology Today "5 Research-Backed Reasons We Wear Makeup" by Theresa E. DiDonato (February 6th 2015)

[314] Psychology Today "Why high heels make women more attractive" by Raj Persuad and Peter Bruggen (August 28th 2015)

suckers for a beautiful woman so they show off "the goods" as much as possible.

Because of our biological differences, men and women not only dress differently, but we think different, and act different, because we *are* different. We tend to work different kinds of jobs, we have different demeanors, and we fulfill different roles in society. Men work dangerous and dirty jobs, while women tend to prefer safer and cleaner jobs indoors.

Historically men would venture into the wilderness to hunt for food, while women would stay home to raise the kids and cook meals. Since a pregnant woman can't chase down a wild animal to kill for dinner as easily as a man for obvious reasons, hunting was something men did. And we are physically stronger which suits us for such a grueling task.

But in the backwards world of liberalism, every tradition and social norm is being turned upside down, and so men are encouraged to wear lipstick and skirts, and women are pressured to not shave their legs and armpits as a symbolic rejection of the traditional gender roles.[315] But it's even worse than that, as you're probably already aware.

There is a growing trend of people completely rejecting the fact that they are a man or a woman, and are demanding we refer to them by "gender neutral" pronouns in place of the usual "he" or "she." Instead, they want to

---

[315] New York Post "To shave or not: Female armpit hair is getting its moment" by Associated Press (June 16th 2015)

be called "they," "them," or "ze."[316] And instead of being called Mr., Mrs, or Miss, they now want to use the "gender neutral" title of "Mx." (pronounced mix).[317]

Many ridiculous social trends start with kids because they can be easily manipulated and convinced of almost anything in the name of "rebelling" against society, but it's not just high school and college kids who are getting confused about whether they are a man or a woman. A growing number of parents are deciding to raise their children "gender neutral," meaning they refuse to even acknowledge a boy as a boy or a girl as a girl.[318]

A 10-year-old boy in New York who goes by the name "Desmond Is Amazing" has an Instagram account (even though the minimum age requirement is thirteen) where his parents post photos of the boy dressed in drag, and he has (at the time I'm writing this) over 80,000 followers.[319]

Many liberal media outlets have done features on the boy, giving him glowing reviews. Media reports brag that he (in reality his lunatic parents) launched the "first and only drag club for kids" called Haus of Amazing. He's

---

[316] New York Times "She? Ze? They? What's In a Gender Pronoun" by Jessica Bennett (January 30th 2016)

[317] Time "This Gender-Neutral Word Could Replace 'Mr.' and 'Ms.'" by Katy Steinmetz (November 10th 2015)

[318] NBC News "'Boy or girl?' Parents raising 'theybies' let kids decide" by Julie Compton (July 19th 2018)

[319] https://www.instagram.com/desmondisamazing/

also marched in New York City's gay pride parade and appeared in a music video with RuPaul.[320]

Clickbait factory *Mashable* did a feature on him, saying, "At only 10 years old, Desmond has already immersed himself with a handful of LGBTQ youth advocacy projects and is making one thing clear: Desmond Is Amazing is the future and we're here for it."[321] Immersed *himself?* More like brainwashed by his parents, who are in my opinion, committing child abuse.

Another 10-year-old boy named Jack Bennet has almost a half million Instagram followers on his @MakeuupByJack account, where his parents post photos of him with his face painted up like a drag queen. *The New York Times* did a feature on him titled, "His Eye Makeup is Way Better Than Yours," and gloated, "He is the latest evidence of a seismic power shift in the beauty industry, which has thrust social media influencers to the top of the pecking order. Refreshingly, they come in all shapes, sizes, ages and, more recently, genders."[322]

Even if you've been watching in horror as this gender-bending craze is spiraling out of control, I'm sorry to tell you that it's far worse than you can imagine. Just keep reading, if you dare, and I'll show you how deep the rabbit hole goes.

---

[320] The Daily Mail "'You can just do you': Boy, 10, founds a drag club for KIDS so they can express themselves in a 'positive, encouraging, and safe' space" by Aoibhinn McBride (January 2nd 2018)

[321] Mashable Watercooler (YouTube) "Meet The 10-Year-Old Drag Kid Shaping The Future Of Drag Youth" May 1st 2018)

[322] New York Times "His Eye Makeup is Way Better Than Yours" by Bee Shapiro (November 22nd 2017)

58 Different Genders

When you first signed up for Facebook, you may recall, that the site asked for your name, birthdate, where you went to school, and your gender — giving you the standard two choices of male or female. But they later increased those two "old fashioned" options in 2014 to fifty-eight different options, including "gender fluid," "neither," and "gender questioning."[323] But fifty-eight still wasn't "inclusive" enough, and in order to not leave anybody out, they later decided to just let users enter whatever word or made-up word they wanted (or even a number) in the blank box as their gender.[324]

The hookup app Tinder also increased their gender options in 2016 to thirty-seven different gender "identities."[325] The state of New York now legally recognizes thirty-one different genders, including "gender fluid" (meaning sometimes male and sometimes female), "androgynous" and "gender-nonconforming" (which means neither male nor female), and even more insane-sounding options like "pangender," "two spirit," and "gender gifted."[326]

---

[323] ABC News "Here's a List of 58 Gender Options for Facebook Users" by Russell Goldman (February 13th 2014)

[324] Mashable "Facebook's new gender options let you choose anything you want" by Karissa Bell (February 26th 2015)

[325] USA Today "Tinder update includes 37 new gender identity options" by Carly Mallenbaum (November 15th 2016)

[326] Daily Caller "New York City Lets You Choose From 31 Different Gender Identities" by Peter Hasson (May 24th 2016)

In fact it's now illegal in the city of New York for an employer or even a landlord to call someone by the "wrong gender" if they identify as one of these insane characters. "Refusal to use a transgender employee's preferred name, pronoun, or title may constitute unlawful gender-based harassment," reads the New York City Legal Enforcement Guide on Gender Identity.[327] Fines of up to $250,000 may be issued for willfully "mispronouning" someone.[328]

In California, Democrat governor Jerry Brown signed a similar bill into law in 2017 which now makes it a crime for healthcare workers to "willfully and repeatedly" refuse to call a patient by their "preferred name or pronouns."[329] Workers can be fined $1000 or even sent to jail for up to one year.[330] Similar laws will likely be put in place for schoolteachers, business owners, or maybe everyone, if we don't reverse this madness soon.

The same craziness is happening in Canada. In June 2016 Canada's Senate passed a bill into law (C-16) which essentially criminalizes calling someone by a pronoun

---

[327] The Washington Post "You can be fined for not calling people 'ze' or 'hir,' if that's the pronoun they demand that you use" by Eugene Volokh (May 17, 2016)

[328] New York City Gender Identity/Gender Expression: Legal Enforcement Guidance (June 28th 2016)

[329] Fox News "New California law allows jail time for using wrong gender pronoun, sponsor denies that would happen" by Brooke Singman (October 9th 2017)

[330] Ibid.

that's not their "preferred" pronoun.[331]   Liberal media, including outlets in the United States claimed, "Arguments about free speech and pronoun criminalization have been debunked," but in the details they admit that fines may be issued and other punishments (like being fired from your job), but "jail time is not one of them."[332]

An NBC contributor recommended that the FCC fine anyone who calls a transgender person by a pronoun other than their "preferred" pronoun (like calling Caitlyn Jenner a "he").   "We need to stop misgendering people in the media, and there needs to be some type of fine that's put into place for outlets, for media outlets — that could be print, online, radio or what have you — that decide they're just not going to call people by their name," she said. "There are guidelines that have been put in place by GLAAD that have been put out to all press outlets, and if you don't follow them, you should be fined by the FCC. It should be that serious."[333]

---

[331] NBC News "Canadian Lawmakers Pass Bill Extending Transgender Protections" by Julie Monreau (June 16th 2017)

[332] Mark S. Bonham Centre for Sexual Diversity Studies "Bill C-16 – No, Its Not about Criminalizing Pronoun Misuse" by Brenda Cossman

[333] The Daily Caller "MSNBC Guest: FCC Should Fine People For Using Biological Pronouns To Describe Transgender People" by Christian Datoc (July 28th 2015)

What is Cisgender?

While it would be impossible to understand (or even list) all the different "genders" liberals have invented, you should know what "cisgender" is since it's a new term they're throwing around a lot to describe "people of privilege." Cisgender (pronounced "siss") means a person whose biology matches their "gender identity," or in other words, a normal man or woman.

But, since it's not "inclusive" to say that boys have a penis and girls have a vagina, or to call them "normal" boys or girls if they're normal, the Leftists have invented yet another term we're supposed to waste our brain cells remembering and get punished if we don't use it.

If you're a normal person and refuse to call yourself a "cisgender" male or female, and instead insist that you're just a normal man or woman, that is now seen as bigotry and "trans-exclusionary."[334]

Terms "Boy" and "Girl" are "Wrong"

There is increasing pressure on parents and teachers to stop referring to children as boys or girls, and instead raise them "gender neutral," meaning no gender at all! *The Independent* in London argued, "We should reconsider assigning babies as 'boys' or 'girls' at birth," and said with transgender celebrities like Lavern Cox and Caitlyn Jenner raising 'awareness' of gender dysphoria,

---

[334] Pluralist "Female Singer Slammed for Not Wanting to be Called a 'Cis' Woman" (July 11th 2018)

maybe it's time to stop raising children as either boys or girls.

The writer wonders, "why do we still assign gender to children at birth? People are accepting that the gender the midwife assigns us at birth after taking a look at our genitals doesn't always match up with how we feel inside. That's why some people identify as trans, gender non-binary and queer."[335]

At the beginning of the 2016 school year, teachers in Charlotte, North Carolina were told to stop addressing their students as either boys or girls, and instead just refer to them as "students" or "scholars" because some of them may be transgender or gender non-conforming and maybe aren't comfortable being raised as a boy or a girl.[336]

In August 2017, Planned Parenthood, best-known for being the largest killer of babies in the history of the human race, published their recommendations for parents on how they should teach their preschoolers about gender in a guide titled, "How do I talk with my preschooler about their body?" and want parents to teach their kids that, "your genitals don't make you a boy or a girl."[337]

It says, "While the most simple answer is that girls have vulvas and boys have penises/testicles, that answer isn't true for every boy and girl. Boy, girl, man and woman are words that describe gender identity, and some

---

[335] The Independent "Why we should reconsider assigning babies as 'boys' or 'girls' at birth" by Kashmira Gander (September 7th 2017)

[336] Fox News "NC school to teachers: Don't call students 'boys and girls'" by Todd Starnes (August 16th 2016)

[337] PlannedParenthood.org "How do I talk with my preschooler about their body?"

people with the gender identities 'boy' or 'man' have vulvas, and some with the gender identity 'girl' or 'woman' have penises/testicles."[338]

Why parents should be talking about sex and gender with children still learning their ABCs is a mystery to normal people, but we're talking about Planned Parenthood, an organization that murders several hundred thousand babies each year.[339]

Many celebrities have jumped on the gender-bending bandwagon since they're always at the forefront of moral decay. Charlize Theron adopted a son in 2012 from her home country of South Africa and on several occasions has been photographed with him wearing dresses and other girl clothes.[340]

Before they divorced, Brad Pitt and Angelina Jolie were also seen in public with their daughter Shiloh wearing boy's clothes, causing many to wonder if they were raising her as a boy.[341] Will Smith's teenage son Jaden proudly wears women's clothes in order to "challenge" gender norms and hopes to make others

---

[338] Ibid.

[339] Washington Examiner "Planned Parenthood annual report: An increase in revenue and abortions" by Jeremy Beaman (May 30th 2017)

[340] BET "Is Charlize Theron's 5 Year-Old Son Transitioning Into a Female?" (January 20th 2017)

[341] OK Magazine "Shiloh Jolie-Pitt 'Only Wears Boys' Clothes' After Questioning Gender Identity To Brad & Angelina" (August 4th 2016)

"more comfortable" to do so.[342] Singer Pink is reportedly raising her child gender neutral as well.[343]

The largest gay lobbyist organization in the United States, calling themselves the "Human Rights Campaign" (whose symbol is the yellow "equal" sign over a blue background you've probably seen on bumper stickers), published a "Back to School Guide" encouraging school administrators to, "Avoid using gender to divide and address students," and recommends, "Instead of addressing your class using 'boys' and 'girls,' try something new. Words like 'friends,' 'students' or 'scholars' allow all students to feel included, expand student vocabulary and model inclusive language and behavior for other students and teachers."[344]

It also discourages schools from including the words "mother" or "father" on any paperwork or questionnaires. "Make sure that forms do not have specific spaces for 'mother' and 'father.' If a form requires the name(s) of legal caregivers(s), the form can just say 'parent,' 'guardian,' or 'caregiver.'" It also suggests to, "avoid asking students to identify as male or female unless it is absolutely necessary."[345]

---

[342] Entertainment Tonight "Jaden Smith Opens Up About Wearing Skirts: 'I Don't See Man Clothes and Woman Clothes'" by Alex Ungerman (March 14th 2016)

[343] Newsweek "Pink Says She's Raising Her Children in a Gender Neutral 'Label-Free' Household" by Emily Gaudette (December 4th 2017)

[344] Human Rights Campaign "Four Ways To Make a Classroom Gender-Inclusive" by HRC Staff (August 13, 2015)

[345] Ibid.

The ADL (Anti-Defamation League), a Jewish "civil rights" organization, issued identical recommendations to make classrooms "inclusive for all families," saying, "As a school, evaluate the messages you convey through language, policies and procedures. Re-think forms, permissions slips and other procedures that explicitly ask for 'mother' and 'father' identifying information. Instead, change these designations to parent/guardian across the board. In talking with children, use terms like parents and guardians or adult family members rather than mothers and fathers."[346]

The University of Dayton, Ohio includes an "educational resource" on their website recommending students and teachers use "gender neutral language" and gives several examples, such as saying "workforce" instead of "manpower" and "go-between" instead of "middleman." They even advise using the terms "spouse" or "partner" instead of "husband" or "wife."[347]

A graduate student in Canada at Wilfrid Laurier University was investigated by school authorities after she played a clip of University of Toronto Professor Jordan Peterson discussing his stance on gender pronouns. Peterson refuses to use pronouns other than "he" or "she" and doesn't care which of the fifty-eight different gender identities a student wants to be called, he'll call them the one that corresponds to their biological sex.

---

[346] ADL.org "We Are Family: Making Classrooms Inclusive for All Families" (April 27th 2015)

[347] Campus Reform "Saying 'husband/wife' violates Christian 'dignity,' school says" by Kassy Dillon (February 14th 2018)

Refusing to bow down to the requests of the gender benders is now considered to be "hateful" and "dehumanizing" and may even get you banned from social media platforms.[348]

Raising "Genderless" Children

A "non-binary transgender" person in Canada wanted it's baby to be listed on the birth certificate as having no sex, or a "U" for "undetermined" or "unclassified" instead of male or female. She (or "it" - or whatever) told CBC News, "I'm raising Searyl in such a way that until they have the sense of self and command of vocabulary to tell me who they are, I'm recognizing them as a baby and trying to give them all the love and support to be the most whole person that they can be outside of the restrictions that come with the boy box and the girl box."[349]

The child was born at home, not in a hospital, to the literal bearded lady mother, and when she filed for a birth certificate British Columbia authorities refused to issue one because there was no sex listed. A group of transgender advocates called the Gender Free I.D. Coalition is representing eight different transgender or intersex plaintiffs who are suing the government,

[348] Politifact "Why Infowars' Alex Jones was banned from Apple, Facebook, Youtube and Spotify" by Manuela Tobias (August 7th 2018)

[349] Canadian Broadcasting Corporation "Parent fights to omit gender of B.C. child's birth certificate" by Maryse Zeidler (June 30th 2017)

attempting to have the gender classification removed from birth certificates.[350]

Many media outlets that reported on this "genderless baby" story were confused, and reported that a "couple" wanted to raise "their" baby gender neutral, but it appears that this bearded lady is a single mother and has no partner. The confusion was a result of the idiotic pronouns she uses, such as "they" to refer to herself, since she refuses to identify as either a woman or a man. Of course referring to her as "they" is grammatically incorrect since "they" and "their" is plural, but we can't expect these people to do anything that makes sense.

So when outlets reported that "*they* want their child to form *their* own sense of identity, not conform to one assigned to them at birth," people assumed the story meant the mother and father, but there doesn't appear to be a father in the picture, and it is unclear where the sperm came from to fertilize the mother's egg. I assume she purchased it from a sperm bank.

There is a YouTube mini documentary about the mother and her "genderless baby" that shows her feeding and cuddling the poor thing and there is no father to be seen. One can only begin to imagine how messed up this child is going to be from being raised by such a deranged mother.[351]

Inspired by this bearded lady's quest to raise a "genderless" baby, a Brooklyn couple decided to follow in her footsteps. They instructed hospital staff in the

---

[350] Ibid.

[351] Rebecca Poulin YouTube Channel "Non Binary Baby" (April 25th 2017)

delivery room not to "announce" whether it was a boy or a girl when their child was born, because that, "would have fucked us up," they said.[352] "At minimum, do not describe the anatomy, or what you think the anatomy means, when this baby's born."[353]

It's not just two or three weirdos (who, in my opinion shouldn't be anywhere around children, let alone raising them) who are doing this. There is a growing trend of these whack jobs raising "theybys" (get it, *they*, as in the gender neutral pronoun) who don't refer to their babies as boys or girls, but instead "they" and "them."[354]

When the Brooklyn couple found a Facebook group of fellow nutcases raising their children like this, it "empowered" them to do it. "It was my favorite place to go on the Internet. It was just like, 'Wow, there's something that we can do parenting-wise that completely goes with our value system," they said.[355] As the delivery date approached, the soon-to-be mother thought, *"Why isn't everybody doing this?"*

Another woman raising her child "Zoomer" as non-binary, actually "corrects" the child for "perpetuating gender stereotypes." The mother says, "So they [meaning

---

[352] The Cut "It's a Theyby! Is it possible to raise your child entirely without gender from birth? Some parents are trying" by Alex Morris (April 3rd 2018)

[353] Ibid.

[354] Washington Examiner "The disturbing rise of genderless babies" by Nicole Russell (April 9th 2018)

[355] The Cut "It's a Theyby! Is it possible to raise your child entirely without gender from birth? Some parents are trying" by Alex Morris (April 3rd 2018)

the child] have picked up on the differences between their dad and me and are recognizing similarities that I have with other women and their dad has with other men," (as any normal child would. But that's upsetting to this mother.)[356]

"I will typically say something like, 'That person does have a beard like Dada,' but I'm not going to say, 'Yup, that's a dad,' because that would be assuming the person's gender identity. We're laying the foundation for having more complex conversations in the future. All I can do now is narrate the world how I want them to experience it."[357] It's a tragedy people like this are allowed to raise children, but this is what the liberals are doing.

BuzzFeed interviewed two lesbians who are raising "their" son after one of them got artificially inseminated, and one of the women appeared to be uncomfortable that the boy likes doing boy things, and said she is "constantly trying to queer her relationship with him and get him to wear [ballerina] tutus."[358]

She also expressed frustration with the child because when looking at books he'll point to a picture of a boy or a girl and say, "boy" or "girl" so she "corrects" him, saying that they're not boys or girls, but instead it's a gender neutral "child," because, "This is where he starts learning what things are. And so I hate the idea that he's getting it imprinted on him that people who look like this

---

[356] Ibid.

[357] Ibid.

[358] BuzzFeedVideo "I Am A Gender Non-Conforming Parent" on YouTube (June 14th 2016)

are boys, and people who look like that are girls. Everyone needs to be reconsidering the way that they're presenting gender to their kids."[359]

One woman in California named Lori Duran, wrote a book in 2013 titled *Raising My Rainbow: Adventures in Raising a Fabulous, Gender Creative Son*, detailing how she was raising her son to be gender neutral, and said he preferred wearing girls clothes and would rather sew than play soccer. Actor Neil Patrick Harris (a homosexual) wrote the foreword for her book. Bravo talk show host Andy Cohen (who is also gay) called it, "A powerful book at the right time."[360] It has a four and a half star rating on Amazon from liberals who love it and call her a "wonderful mother" who gives readers "an inside look into the struggles and joys of raising a child who goes against the norms of society."[361]

Gender Neutral Baby Names

If you thought the Cultural Marxist liberals would be satisfied once boys were wearing makeup and dresses, you are wrong. Not only do they have disdain for the traditional gender roles in the family, styles of dress, and differentiating between boys and girls because of their genetics, but they are upset about the very names that boys and girls are given. They want a world where girls are named Frank, and where boys are named Tiffany.

---

[359] Ibid.

[360] Amazon.com Official "Review" section for *Raising My Rainbow*

[361] Amazon Customer Reviews for Raising My Rainbow

Since celebrities largely shape the social fabric of society in our Media Age, now many Millennials are following their lead and naming their children gender-neutral baby names. *Dead Pool* star Ryan Reynolds and his wife Blake Lively named their daughter "James."[362] Hillary Duff's sister, who is a lesser-known actress named Haylie Duff, named her daughter "Ryan," and was praised for defying gender conventions.[363]   Other, lesser-known actors are also doing the same.[364]

The parenting website BabyCenter, which is a large forum of parents, said there are more conversations today supporting "unisex" names.[365] And as the gender-bending fetish continues to spread we'll likely see baby girls named Bob, and boys named Brooke. There is literally no end to the depths of depravity these people are trying to unleash on society. And the damage being inflicted on these innocent children is immeasurable.

Gender Reveal Parties

Cosmopolitan magazine wants all children raised gender neutral too. In the summer of 2017 they published

---

[362] Eonline "Ryan Reynolds Worries About Daughter James' Future, But for Now, "There Is No Problem That a Breast Won't Fix"" by Rebecca Macatee (April 1st 2015)

[363] US Magazine "Haylie Duff Gives Birth to a Baby Girl: Find Out What She's Named!" by Sophia Vokes-Dudgeon (May 12th 2015)

[364] Parents Magazine "6 Celebrity Parents Raising Kids Without Gender Stereotypes" by Libby Ryan

[365] Washington Times "Millennial parents embracing gender-neutral baby names" by Associated Press (March 21st 2018)

an article titled "Dear Parents-to-Be: Stop Celebrating Your Baby's Gender," complaining about soon-to-be parents having "gender reveal parties" that were created by the "baby industrial complex." The writer, a proud feminist, said she "cannot stomach" them and, "Cutting into a pink or blue cake seems innocent enough—but honestly, it's not."[366]

She went on to say that the parties were "potentially damaging" to the children and continued on into the usual diatribe about how "gender is different from sex," whining, "For starters, gender-reveal parties don't actually reveal gender—they reveal anatomy. Gender is a wholly different thing, inextricably tied to the social constructs around it." She then went on to say that the reason we associate pink with girls is because of Adolf Hitler. "Hitler—yes, Hitler—feminized the color pink by forcing gays to wear triangles in that shade during World War II," she writes.[367]

Yes, she really blamed Hitler for pink being feminine, and argued that since there are people who identify as transgender or neither gender (or one of the other 500 they've come up with by now) gender reveal parties aren't "inclusive" enough because they leave out a cross-section of the population.

The article quotes an intersex baker who gets "queasy" from parents-to-be coming into the bakery and ordering gender reveal cakes for their parties. "The popularity of gender-reveal parties speaks to how

---

[366] Cosmopolitan "Dear Parents-to-Be: Stop Celebrating Your Baby's Gender" by Diane Stopra (July 9th 2017)

[367] Ibid.

powerful and central this binary is to our sense of identity," she says. "Still, they make me a little queasy. By collapsing gender expression, gender identity, and sex, you're doing everyone a disservice, because no one buys into the whole package all the time."[368]

Another feminist blog ranted against gender reveal parties, calling them a sham. "They're a reinforcement of binary gender. Despite the mainstream trans visibility and gay rights movements, gender reveals show that we are traditionalists who are eager to amplify dominant cultural narratives. It still belies an obsession with fitting people into one of two neat categories—Pistols or Pearls — and imposes gendered traits and behaviors before a child has even left the womb."[369]

The misfit goes on to say, "Celebrating that your baby is destined to either experience a lifetime of emotional suppression while being encouraged to be violent and self-serving or be treated as a second-class citizen with avenues of opportunity withheld, strikes me as a tad macabre—but maybe I'm just bad at getting into the spirit of these things."[370]

She concludes, "Catering to this hope, or rather fear, is profitable. Between the baked goods, party favors, and event planning that goes into these affairs, capitalism is supporting cisnormative narratives as usual while making money off the whole thing. It's a nice, symbiotic

---

[368] Ibid.

[369] Bitch Media "Gender Reveal Parties Are a Sham" by Rae Gray (November 6th 2017)

[370] Ibid.

relationship between data-mining social media, bakers with blue-and-pink frosting, and jittery cis parents wishing with all their hearts that their baby's gender comes down to a simple coin flip that will remain unchallenged throughout the child's life. Ultimately it boils down to just wanting the best for your baby, in a particularly trans-antagonistic way."[371]

Boys Don't Wear Dresses

A Formula One race car driver named Lewis Hamilton posted a brief video of his three-year-old nephew on Christmas morning wearing a "Princess Dress" where he asked the boy why he was wearing it and told him that boys don't wear princess dresses. He wasn't mean, or yelling at the kid, he was genuinely confused as to why his nephew was wearing a dress.

The PC police went nuts, claiming he was "bullying" the kid. *The Huffington Post* ran the headline, "Lewis Hamilton Mocks Nephew For Wearing A 'Princess Dress' On Christmas,"[372] and other Leftist websites jumped on the story. He quickly deleted the video and issued an apology, saying, "Yesterday I was playing around with my nephew and realized that my words were inappropriate so I removed the post. I meant no harm and did not mean to

---

[371] Ibid.

[372] Huffington Post "Lewis Hamilton Mocks Nephew For Wearing A 'Princess Dress' On Christmas" by Curtis M. Wong (December 26th 2017)

offend anyone at all. I love that my nephew feels free to express himself as we all should."[373]

He went on to say, "My deepest apologies for my behavior as I realize it is really not acceptable for anyone, no matter where you are from, to marginalize or stereotype anyone,"[374] and "I have always been in support of anyone living their life exactly how they wish and I hope I can be forgiven for this lapse in judgment."[375]

In January 2018 Abercrombie announced they were releasing a gender-neutral clothing line for kids called the "Everybody Collection" consisting of pink clothes for boys and camouflage designs for girls.[376] There's even a company selling "lingerie for men" and Milan Fashion Week in 2018 featured men wearing miniskirts.[377]

Many schools in England have introduced gender-neutral uniforms after some parents and students became upset that girls had to wear skirts while boys wore trousers (pants), so now all students wear pants and skirts are banned.[378] Other schools are now allowing girls to

---

[373] https://twitter.com/LewisHamilton/status/945718243511144448

[374] https://twitter.com/LewisHamilton/status/945718655949602823

[375] https://twitter.com/LewisHamilton/status/945718744680206336

[376] Fox News "Abercrombie Kids debuts unisex collection" by Janine Puhak (January 18th 2018)

[377] New York Post "New York Post: Men are wearing mini skirts now" by Nicole Zane (June 19th 2018)

[378] The Independent "40 secondary schools across England have banned pupils from wearing skirt" by Rachel Hosie (July 2nd 2018)

wear pants and boys to wear skirts if they want, in order to "end gender stereotypes."[379]

Boys and Girls Toys

In 2015, Target eliminated the "boys" and "girls" aisles in its toy department and bedding section to support the "gender neutral" movement.[380]   Leftists are also complaining to McDonalds because their Happy Meals offer different toys for girls and boys. "I remember my mother being asked whether the Happy Meal was for a boy or a girl when I was a child," says one activist. "Are we really still so far behind on this gender stereotyping thing?"[381]

Another activist decided to "investigate" her local McDonalds to see what kinds of toys customers were offered.   She then filed a complaint with the state's Commission on Human Rights and Opportunities, claiming McDonalds was discriminating against people based on their sex![382]

---

[379] The Daily Mail "Now 150 schools introduce gender neutral uniforms so pupils can experience 'equality' by wearing either skirts or trousers" by Sarah Harris (September 19th 2017)

[380] Time "Target Will Stop Separating 'Girls' Toys From 'Boys' Toys in Stores" by Victor Luckerson (August 8th 2015)

[381] Stuff.co.nz "When we gender toys, we hold kids back - that's why I complained to McDonald's" by Imogene Burgess (May 30th 2017)

[382] Slate "McDonald's Gave Me the 'Girl's Toy' With My Happy Meal. So I Went to the CEO." by Antonia Ayres-Brown (April 21st 2014)

The Huffington Post celebrated her activism, writing, "It might be the end of gendered toys at McDonald's, and you have a teen to thank for it."[383] Someone even started a petition on Change.org urging them to "Stop Promoting Gender Stereotypes with Happy Meal Toys."[384]

Samsung recently released a commercial encouraging people to "do" what others said they can't, which featured a series of inspirational scenes of children trying to walk for the first time and learning to ride a bike, and athletes playing sports trying to show how people can break through their perceived limitations and accomplish great things. But included in the commercial is a brief clip of a young boy in a toy store with his dad, and he is shown holding a doll so the dad snaps at him, "You can't get a doll. Just get this one," as he holds up something else.[385] The message is that the father is an old fashioned bigot for not wanting his son to play with Barbie.

National Geographic did a report on the "harm" toys are doing to girls saying that, "The long history of separate toys for girls and boys shows that marketing by gender has a profound impact on children."[386] They

---

[383] Huffington Post "It Might Be The End Of Gendered Toys At McDonald's, And You Have A Teen To Thank For It" by Jessica Samakow (April 21st 2014)

[384] https://www.change.org/p/mcdonald-s-stop-promoting-gender-stereotypes-with-happy-meal-toys

[385] Samsung ad "'Human Nature': Samsung Brand Philosophy - Do What You Can't" available on their YouTube channel (February 6th 2018)

[386] National Geographic "How Today's Toys May Be Harming Your Daughter" by Natalie Daly (January 2017 Issue)

complained that girls are marketed toys about homemaking and motherhood, while boys are marketed toys that involve building things (like Legos) and being strong protectors (such as action figures and super heroes).

Terms "Ladies" and "Gentlemen" is Offensive

Since 2017, the subway system (known as the Underground or the Tube) in London has placed a ban on greeting passengers as "ladies and gentleman" over the loudspeaker because it was "discriminatory" against people with "other" genders. They now greet passengers with the gender-neutral "hello everyone."[387]

The Transportation Department said, "We have reviewed the language that we use in announcements and elsewhere and will make sure that it is fully inclusive, reflecting the great diversity of London."[388] A few months later the same change was implemented by the New York City Metropolitan Transit Authority for the subway system there.[389] Now they refer to people with terms like "passengers" or "riders," so they don't offend

---

[387] The Telegraph "London Tube scraps 'ladies and gentlemen' to make announcements gender-neutral" by Danny Boyle (July 13th 2017)

[388] The Washington Post "London's tube drivers aren't allowed to say 'ladies and gentlemen' anymore" by Amanda Erickson (July 13th 2017)

[389] The Daily Caller "New York Subway Operators Banned From Saying 'Ladies And Gentlemen'" by Nick Givas (November 10th 2017)

people who identify as any of the dozens of other "genders."

Gender Neutral Honorific

In April of 2016, the Merriam-Webster dictionary added the "honorific" *Mx*, which gender benders are now using instead of Mr., Mrs., or Miss. "The gender-neutral Mx. is used as a title for those who do not identify as being of a particular gender, or for people who simply don't want to be identified by gender," the dictionary reads. It is pronounced *mix*.

Dictionary.com has also added "Mx." as a real word, and *Time* magazine reported, "If you don't feel like labeling yourself a Mr. or a Ms. and would rather leave your gender unknown or undeclared, Mx. is a gender-neutral option."[390]

In an article from the *Washington Post* trying to popularize this new title, they quoted a transgender person saying, "I prefer Mx. because I'm transgender and don't identify as either male or female. . . . I use Mx. because that says exactly what I am — a mix of all genders."[391]

The Church of Sweden announced in 2017 that their pastors would stop referring to God as "He" and even "Lord" because God is "beyond our gender

---

[390] Time magazine "This Gender-Neutral Word Could Replace 'Mr.' and 'Ms.'" by Katy Kteinmetz (November 10th 2015)

[391] Washington Post "Civilities: Is it time to include 'Mx.' in the mix with 'Ms.' and 'Mr.'?" by Steven Petrow (August 3rd 2015)

determinations."[392]   Apparently this church hasn't bothered to read the Bible.

"Mankind" is Sexist

Purdue University's writing lab has a handout titled "Stereotypes and Biased Language" that encourages students to not use the word "man" in their writing, because, "although MAN in its original sense carried the dual meaning of adult human and adult male, its meaning has come to be so closely identified with adult male that the generic use of MAN and other words with masculine markers should be avoided."[393]

A student at the University of Florida had his grade reduced for referring to mankind as "Man" instead of "humankind" in a paper for his history class. The professor gave him a B minus, and wrote, "Thoughtful paper, although the writing-mechanics errors are killing you."[394]

An anthropology museum in San Diego's Balboa Park called "The Museum of Man," which was created in 1915, is now under fire by critics who are demanding the city change its name "to be more inclusive."[395] The board

---

[392] The Guardian "Church of Sweden to stop referring to God as 'he' or 'Lord'" by Associated Press in Stockholm (November 24th 2017)

[393] Campus Reform "Purdue writing guide: Words with 'MAN' should be avoided" by Adam Sabes (February 20th 2018)

[394] The College Fix "Student penalized for using word 'man' on his essay" by Rebecca Downs (May 1st 2017)

[395] KUSI "New Name for The Museum of Man" by Dan Plante (July 30th 2018)

agrees and is considering new names, and will likely settle on changing it to the "Museum of Humankind."

Canadian Prime Minister Justin Trudeau "corrected" a woman during a town hall event when she referred to the future of mankind, interjecting, "We like to say 'peoplekind,' not necessarily 'mankind' because it's more inclusive."[396]

The term "founding fathers" is also deemed sexist and gender bias, and SJWs demand it be replaced with "the founders" instead. The terms "freshmen" and "upperclassmen" are also now offensive, and are being replaced with "first year student" and "upper-level students."[397] Yale University officially dropped the terms in exchange for "more modern" and "gender inclusive" language to describe the students.

What's next, is building a snowman sexist? Are kids supposed to call it a "snowperson?" Instead of saying something is "man-made" are we supposed to say it's "people-made?" One cafe in Melbourne, Australia sells "vegan genderless gingerbread figures" in what some people called the most world's politically correct snack. A picture of the "gingerbread person" made it onto Reddit and then went viral.[398]

It's unknown whether they sell it tongue-in-cheek, or if they are so hypersensitive to modern liberalism that

---

[396] The Guardian "Justin Trudeau tells woman to say 'peoplekind' not 'mankind'" by Anna Livsey (February 6th 2018)

[397] Fox News "Yale Replaces 'Freshman,' 'Upperclassman' With Gender-Neutral Terms" (September 16th 2017)

[398] BBC "#BBCtrending: The organic genderless gingerbread debate" (October 22nd 2014)

they think they are being innovative and "helping the cause" of gender "equality," but judging by some of the other social justice stupidity that's come out of Melbourne, the owner probably thinks the gingerbread *person* is a genius idea.

Homecoming King and Queen Banned

In 2015 San Diego State University ended the time-honored tradition of naming a homecoming king and queen, and decided to instead call them the "royals" in order to be gender-neutral and not "discriminate" against same-sex couples. The school's paper, *The Daily Aztec*, explained, "During the application process, candidates were allowed to select gender-neutral pronouns to identify themselves. These gender-inclusive pronouns aim to dispel the common gender binary of categorizing people as solely masculine or feminine."[399]

This is far from an isolated incident. The same thing is happening in colleges across the country. Appalachian State University's homecoming king and queen are now called the "homecoming royals,"[400] the University of

---

[399] The Daily Aztec "Homecoming court goes gender-neutral" by Maria Del Carmen Huerta (November 10th 2015)

[400] The College Fix "Appalachian State U. goes 'genderless' at homecoming — no more king and queen" (October 23rd 2016)

Minnesota is doing the same thing,[401] as well as the University of Nebraska at Omaha,[402] and many more.

It's not just colleges which are doing this, many high schools are doing away with having a homecoming king and queen as well.[403] Now it's not "inclusive" to elect a guy as the homecoming king and a girl as the queen, and the Leftists are pressuring high schools to stop the tradition of choosing a prom king and queen as well so that same-sex couples can be the "royals" there too.[404]

Students Triggered by Biological Facts

Several students walked out of a Portland State University event featuring James Damore, an engineer who was fired by Google for writing an internal memo explaining some of the problems with Google's goals of increasing gender "diversity" in the company.[405] The panel discussion included Evergreen State College biologist Heather E. Heying, and when she began pointing

---

[401] Twin Cities Pioneer Press "UMN Homecoming will crown gender-neutral 'royals,' not king and queen" by Josh Verges (February 27th 2017)

[402] CBS News "No king nor queen: gender-neutral school homecoming may be trend" (November 6th 2016)

[403] The Washington Post "School adopts gender-neutral homecoming court, so there might be no 'king' or 'queen'" by Donna St. George (September 27th 2016)

[404] KRCR "Same-sex couple fights to be prom king and queen" by Christina Davies (April 27th 2016)

[405] CBS News "James Damore lawsuit: Fired engineer sues Google" by Alain Sherter (January 8th 2018)

out basic biological differences between men and women, some people in the audience got triggered and threw a temper tantrum.

The moderator asked her to help explain the validity of the arguments Damore made in his memo, and she responded, "James argues, accurately, that there are differences between men and women. This is a strange position to be in, to be arguing for something that is so universally and widely accepted within biology. Let's look at differences between men and women that are explicitly anatomical and physiological; are men taller than women on average? Does anyone take offense at that fact? I would say you could be irritated by it; you could be irritated by the fact that women have to be the ones who gestate and lactate; you could be irritated by a lot of truths…"[406]

It was at this point that a fat woman with green hair got up from her seat and headed for the exit, joined by a small group of others. The biology professor continued, "So, men and women are different on height; they're different on muscle mass; they're different on where fat is deposited on our bodies. Our brains are also different. So there are some binaries…"[407]

At this point another student walked out and yanked some of the cords loose from the sound system, disabling the microphones of the panelists. Security came in and grabbed the perpetrator (who had purple hair) as she

---

[406] RedState "Watch: SJWs Destroy Microphone System, Label Biologist a Nazi After She Says Men and Women are Different" by Brandon Morse (February 26th 2018)

[407] Ibid.

shouted "He's a piece of shit," meaning James Damore, and "That is not okay. Even the women in there have been brainwashed!" As she exited the room she raised her fist and said "Fuck the police! Power to the people."[408]

A feminine-looking sissy who also walked out told the camera, "You should not listen to fascism. It should not be tolerated in civil society. Nazis are not welcome in civil society."

"There Are Only Two Genders" is Hateful

A student at Indiana University of Pennsylvania was kicked out of his Christianity: Self, Sin, and Salvation class by the professor after he pointed out the fact that there are "only two genders."[409] His comments came after the students were made to watch a TED Talk by a transgender "pastor" who was espousing their unhinged ideas on gender. The feminist professor claimed the student was engaging in "disruptive behavior" for verbalizing his "there are only two genders" comment.

The student appealed the professor's decision to the Academic Integrity Board, but before they ruled on whether he would be allowed back in the class after several weeks of not being allowed to attend, the university president decided to overrule the professor, and let the student back in. He was a senior, and if he had not been able to finish the course it would have forced him to

---

[408] Ibid.

[409] Fox News "College student kicked out of class for telling professor there are only two genders" by Caleb Parke (March 12th 2018)

postpone his graduation because he would have been a few credits short.[410]

I used to sell a t-shirt in my online store at MarkDice.com that simply said "There Are Only Two Genders," but the printer later refused to print the shirt anymore, claiming that the design violated their terms of service for being "discriminatory." I've also had my Twitter account locked after I said there are only two genders and the rest are mental illnesses, because that's considered "hate speech." I had to "acknowledge" that I violated their rules and was forced to delete the tweet before I could use Twitter again.

Mother's Day

Now even Mother's Day is being targeted by the Left and has been deemed offensive to gay couples who have adopted children because their "families" consist of "two dads."[411] Liberals are also upset that Mother's Day isn't "inclusive" enough because the term "mother" refers to a *woman* who has given birth to a child, and since the Left believe in dozens of different genders, they say that the word "mother" ostracizes gender non-conforming people who have children but don't identify as women.

A popular supermarket chain in England is now selling "gender-neutral" Mother's Day cards to make the

---

[410] Ibid.

[411] Washington Post "For some gay parents, Mother's Day (or Father's Day) is awkward" By Gail Cornwall (May 8th 2017)

holiday "transgender inclusive."[412]   Other chains have been selling cards for lesbian couples which read, "Two Mums Are Better Than One."   Another reads, "Dad, thanks for being the most amazing mom," which was designed for a transgender "man" who gave birth to children when they identified as a woman.

One activist has even called for Mother's Day to be renamed "Guardian's Day."   The London *Guardian* newspaper reported that, "Mother's Day is a minefield for two-dad families," and is concerned about it because the holiday makes gay men who have adopted children feel uncomfortable and left out.   One elementary school in Canada sent a letter home to parents in 2017 informing them that they were canceling Mother's Day arts and crafts because of these same fears.

"In an effort to celebrate diversity, inclusivity and also nurture our students who are part of non-traditional families, we have decided to encourage those celebrations to take place at home," it began.   "Due to this, the children will not be making gifts at school to give on Mother's Day and Father's Day.   We feel each family knows the best way to celebrate with their own family."[413] One of the stunned parents posted the letter on their Facebook page which got shared so many times it caught the attention of the local, and then national media.

---

[412] The Sunday Times "Mothers day cards go gender-netural" by Andrew Gilligan and Vincent Wood (March 11th 2018)

[413] Washington Times "Elementary School respects non traditional families by axing mothers and fathers day" by Jessica Chasmar (May 9th 2017)

The Jewish ADL encourages elementary schools that commemorate Mother's Day by having the kids make cards during arts and crafts time to instead, "consider making the day more general like 'Family Day' or 'Parent/Guardian Day.'"[414]

Some people are even offended that Mother's Day marginalizes non-mothers! "There's no need to feel left out on Mother's Day just because you don't have children," one columnist wrote.[415] "The qualities we traditionally associate with motherhood—love, selflessness, wisdom—are things all women can use for the benefit of others and their own fulfillment."[416]

"If you don't have children, Mother's Day must be a teensy bit difficult. Amidst the flowers and cards, even the most saint-like woman would find it hard not to feel overlooked if she's not a mother herself. Which is a trifle hard on the non-mothers on two counts."[417]

Others are echoing this psychotic sentiment. "Let's Make Mother's Day More Inclusive," is another headline from a feminist blog.[418] "In this day and age of diversity and inclusivity, it is about time that we made Mother's Day more inclusive too," the author pleads, and also

---

[414] ADL.org "We Are Family: Making Classrooms Inclusive for All Families" (April 27th 2015)

[415] Daily Mail "Mother's Day is for All Women" by Elizabeth Wilson (March 16th 2007)

[416] Ibid.

[417] Ibid.

[418] Blasting News "Let's Make Mother's Day More Inclusive" by Naina Bhardwaj (December 3rd 2018)

praises the decision of supermarket chains which, "made a conscious effort to reduced the use of the word 'mother' on its Mother's Day cards."[419]

One conservative commentator responded to this madness, saying, "I mean, my mom is dead, and I'm sick of getting advertising e-mails asking me if I've bought her anything for Mother's Day yet, but I'm not going to expect the whole damned thing to be canceled or renamed just because of my feelings. I just, you know, deal with it — which is really something that more people should be encouraged to try more often."[420]

Father's Day is a Problem

Since those infected with the liberal pathogen have a problem with Mother's Day, you can guess they also hate Father's Day as well, for "perpetuating toxic masculinity," "gender stereotypes" and "heteronormativity" (meaning heterosexual couples are seen as the standard or normal, while the LGBT-whatevers are seen as "unusual" or abnormal).

On Father's Day 2018, NBC News published an op-ed titled, "This Father's Day, men are experiencing a crisis of masculinity. The solution? More feminism." It went on to say, "Men experience violence and oppression because

---

[419] Ibid.

[420] National Review "School Cancels Father-Daughter Dance Over Complaints It Wasn't 'Inclusive'" by Katherine Timpf (May 6th 2016)

gender norms are not changing. In other words, feminism isn't killing men — toxic masculinity is."[421]

The Sydney Morning Herald published an article titled, "How Father's Day and Mother's Day Teach Gender Stereotypes to Kids," that was written by a man who says, "I try to teach my two boys to challenge these traditional male roles, to question what it means to be masculine, and to not pigeonhole members of any gender. But I can see they already have an aversion to pink and the only recent superhero film they have not been excited about is *Wonder Woman*. The sexist crap is leeching in, no matter how hard I try."[422]

He went on to suggest, "Perhaps the whole thing [Father's Day] needs a rethink. Especially given the growing diversity of families, whether it be single parents, blended families, same-sex parents or grandparents that are steering the parental ship...What would be wrong with just one Parents' Day where we celebrate keeping our kids alive together in our myriad forms?"[423]

An activist named Dr. Red Ruby Scarlet (who insists that's her real name) is trying to get Father's Day renamed to "Special Person's Day" so children without a father around won't feel left out.[424] "We have single parent

---

[421] NBC News "This Father's Day, men are experiencing a crisis of masculinity. The solution? More feminism" by Noah Berlatsky (June 17th 2018)

[422] Sydney Morning Herald "How Father's Day and Mother's Day Teach Gender Stereotypes to Kids" by Paul Chai (August 31st 2017)

[423] Ibid.

[424] News.com.au "Activist pushes politically correct plan to rename Father's Day 'Special Person's Day'" (August 25th 2017)

families, satellite families, extended families, lesbian and gay families," she said, and feels Father's Day isn't "inclusive" enough for them.

Snopes, the Internet "hoax" debunking website, posted an article "debunking" the claim that radical feminists were calling for an end to Fathers Day, and used a meme someone created showing two women holding large signs   that read "Father's Don't Deserve a Day" and "End Father's Day."[425]

While the photos were photoshopped and that's not what the signs in the original picture said, the idea behind the meme was true because it was ridiculing the radical feminists who really do want Father's Day abolished. In fact, the *Huffington Post* published an article in 2017 explicitly titled, "Three Reasons Why Father's Day Should Be Abolished."[426]

Leftist activist group GLAAD, the Gay and Lesbian Alliance Against Defamation, released a "Father's Day Resource Kit" for the media, where they complain that, "The lives of gay, bisexual and transgender parents and their families are often absent in Father's Day coverage since print and electronic press reports often focus solely on straight parents. GLAAD encourages journalists to include gay and transgender families in their coverage of Father's Day.   This toolkit provides story ideas and suggestions on how to make coverage of Father's Day

---

[425] Snopes "Protests Seek to #EndFathersDay?"

[426] Huffington Post "Three Reasons Why Father's Day Should Be Abolished" by Jeremy Davies (June 14th 2017)

more inclusive."[427] They sent their "resource kit" to all major television studios and advertising agencies hoping to get their ideas incorporated into the plots of shows and commercials.

The ADL published a "guide" for schools and teachers to make "classrooms inclusive for all families," which recommends, "In discussions about family, actively discourage the concept of a 'traditional,' 'average' or 'normal' family," and says, "If you are going to commemorate Mother's and Father's Day, consider making the day more general like 'Family Day' or 'Parent/Guardian Day.' If you decide to go ahead with the language of Mother's and Father's Day, be more inclusive and allow children to include other female and male family members or friends such as aunts, uncles, grandparents, family friends, etc. If children have two moms or two dads, allow them to create two cards/gifts for these occasions."[428]

The feminist magazine *Everyday Feminist* recommends "Practicing Feminism for Father's Day" and says that, "we embrace feminist struggle against patriarchy as key to creating healthy families."[429] Of course, creating healthy families is the exact opposite of what liberalism does and it is the root cause of creating *dysfunctional* ones! And the traditional family is literally

---

[427] https://www.glaad.org/publications/fathersdaykit

[428] ADL.org "We Are Family: Making Classrooms Inclusive for All Families" (April 27th 2015)

[429] Everyday Feminism "Practicing Feminism for Father's Day" by Chris Crass, Tomas Moniz, and The Rad Dad Community (June 14th 2014)

enemy number one of liberalism, which is why we have to preserve and protect it at all costs.

Gender-Bending at the Local Library

Public libraries are now encouraging small children to become gender benders. The Brooklyn Public library hosted an event called "Genderful" that was organized by a nonprofit group called "If You Want It" that's dedicated to "expanding the definition of gender." The event included a performance by a transgender "woman" who looks like a Harley Davidson biker in drag, who says, "For kids, I feel that gender is a lot more fluid. It's just something that's not as a part of your daily existence or your interaction with friends and if you withdraw them from certain gender coding situations, kids are just kids when it comes down to it."[430]

Marie McGwier, the cofounder of "If You Want It" says, "There's a lot of conversation around the difference between someone who grows up in a world where they're made to be this or that, compared to a world where we can just kind of offer kids the opportunity to explore their gender on their own and to land where they want to land."[431]

Public libraries in San Francisco, New York, and Los Angeles are now holding "Drag Queen Story Hour" where, you guessed it, drag queens read books to young children. There are videos of these events on YouTube

---

[430] https://twitter.com/nowthisnews/status/934173036747436033

[431] Ibid.

where you can see dozens of young children, aged three to ten who are brought in by their "progressive" parents to have them listen to drag queens read them books.[432]

And they don't just read the children any old book. They read them books about gay and transgender children (or other characters) like *Worm Loves Worm.* One drag queen asked the children, "Who wants to be a drag queen when they grow up," and started singing a song and dancing: "The hips on the drag queen go swish, swish, swish. Swish, swish, swish. Swish, swish, swish."[433]

"Drag Queen Story Hour is fantastic because it addresses all these issues of gender fluidity and self-acceptance, and all of these topics that are real. They're very, very real," said Kat Savage, who works at the Brooklyn Public Library and supports the events.[434]

On the Drag Queen Story Hour official website they explain that, "DQSH is just what it sounds like—drag queens reading stories to children in libraries, schools, and bookstores. DQSH captures the imagination and play of the gender fluidity of childhood and gives kids glamorous, positive, and unabashedly queer role models. In spaces like this, kids are able to see people who defy rigid gender restrictions and imagine a world where people can present as they wish, where dress up is real."[435]

---

[432] Associated Press Archive YouTube Channel "NY Library Brings Drag Queens to Kids Story Hour" (May 21st 2017)

[433] Ibid.

[434] Ibid.

[435] Dragqueenstoryhour.org (About Page)

Austin, Texas hosts the annual International Drag Festival that not only features drag performers with names like "Poo Poo Platter," "Maci Sumcox" (get it, may see some cocks) and "Eaton Johnson," but also includes child drag queens as well (called "drag kids"). One of them goes by "E! the Dragnificcent," and is a 12-year-old boy.[436] Another child drag queen performer goes by the name "Lactacia," and is an 8-year-old boy whose parents dress him up in drag and parade him around at different drag queen festivals across the country.[437]

The website for the Austin International Drag Festival says that "This is an ALL AGES festival," thus encouraging parents to bring children to participate in their drag fetish.[438] ("ALL AGES" is in all caps on their website to emphasize that they want children there) Video footage of the event, which you can see on YouTube, shows children walking up to the adult drag queens and tipping them with dollars for their risqué performances.

Alex Jones was banned from YouTube, Facebook, iTunes, and most streaming apps (Spotify, Stitcher, TuneIn Radio, etc) for calling the festival an "abomination" and a "freak show" because the Big Tech

---

[436] Pittsburgh City Paper "12-year-old drag artist E! The Dragnificent wants people to change the way they view gender" by Meg Fair (November 1st 2017)

[437] The Advocate "Meet 8-Year-Old Drag Queen Lactatia" by Neal Boverman (May 6th 2017)

[438] https://austindragfest.org/

overlords deemed his commentary was "hate speech" and "transphobic."[439]

I wonder if Amazon.com and the major ebook stores (Kindle, Google Play, and iBooks) will ban this book for the same reason, claiming my analysis of modern liberalism is "hate speech" and too offensive for people to read, and thus it "violates" their "terms of service."

"Queering Up" Schools

A Leftist organization in the UK is encouraging nursery schools and elementary schools to "queer up" the education system by reading the children books that encourage them to question or experiment with their gender.[440] One of the books is titled *Introducing Teddy*, which is about a teddy bear named Thomas who decides he's a girl instead of a boy. "In my heart, I've always known that I am a girl teddy, not a boy teddy. I wish my name was Tilly, not Thomas," the book reads.

The organization promoting this is the same one that began pressuring schools in 2016 to refer to the boys and girls as "zie" instead of he or she.[441] The group's founder wants to "break the binary" and says, "We need to educate adults to speak a common language because we grew up

[439] Politifact "Why Infowars' Alex Jones was banned from Apple, Facebook, Youtube and Spotify" by Manuela Tobias (August 7th 2018)

[440] Breitbart: British Nursery Age Toddlers Given Picture Books Encouraging Transgender Questioning of Gender by Oliver JJ Lane (December 3rd 2017)

[441] Ibid.

in a generation with no prior experience about the [LGBT communities]... It's a new language that's absolutely needed in schools. We have, of course, restrictions within the English language but the more we use these pronouns the more they become part of the language."[442]

Child psychotherapist Dilys Daws says, "There's this idea that's sweeping the country that being transgender is an 'ordinary situation.' It's getting so much publicity that it's getting children thinking that they might be transgender, when it otherwise wouldn't have occurred to them."[443]

Young children, as you know, believe that a fat man in a red suit magically climbs down their chimney into their house with a sack of toys every Christmas, and then flies away on a sleigh pulled by magic reindeer. At a young age they can be taught to believe anything, and the reason that normal parents shield their children from certain ideas and images when they're young is because they are too little to understand them, and if exposed to things too soon they will end up engaging in inappropriate, unhealthy, and dangerous behavior because they won't understand the ramifications of what they are doing.

Transgender Cartoons for Kids

In 2013, liberals celebrated the first "transgender cartoon superhero" named *SheZow* which aired in Canadian and Australian television markets. The cartoon

---

[442] Ibid.

[443] Evening Standard "'Transgender lessons' to be given to nursery children as young as two" by Ella Wills (November 12th 2017)

was geared towards children aged 2 through 11. The storyline revolves around a boy who inherited a magic ring from his dead aunt that when activated using the words "You go girl," it turns him into a transvestite super hero.[444]

In an episode of Disney's *Star vs. The Forces of Evil*, a character disguised himself as a princess to help save a group of girls at a reform school run by the evil "Ms Heinous." At the end of the show, when she exposes him as a boy thinking the girls will all turn on him, instead they embrace him. "Why does it matter if he's a boy?" said one character. "Yeah, we believe in you, Turdina," said another. "Turdina is a state of mind," and, "He can be a princess if he wants to!"

The show's creator and executive producer Daron Nefcy posted on her Tumblr page (a social network similar to Instagram but for weirdos) to thank everyone who helped make the show possible.

The Huffington Post praised the cartoon saying that Disney sent a "beautiful message" with the first "boy princess, complete with chest hair."[445] The show also aired an episode titled "Just Friends" where the characters attend a concert, and in the background of one scene it

---

[444] Newsbusters "Transvestite Superhero Cartoon to Debut on Children's Network The Hub" by Randy Hall (May 29th 2013)

[445] Huffington Post "Disney Sends Beautiful Message With First 'Boy Princess,' Complete With Chest Hair" by Noah Michelson (November 22nd 2017)

shows a bunch of couples kissing, including several same-sex couples.[446]

In 2018, an animated series called *Drag Tots* was launched, featuring voices from RuPaul and several other contestants from "her" drag queen competition show *Drag Race,* who all play baby drag queens.[447] *Entertainment Weekly* called the show "adorable."[448]

Removing Children from Parents

In Canada, a law was passed in 2017 that gives the government authority to remove children from their parents if they don't approve of their child's "gender expression," and now considers it child abuse.[449] Parents now have to, "direct the child or young person's education and upbringing in accordance with the child's or young person's creed, community identity and cultural identity."[450] The law also allows the government to remove children from their parents if a child doesn't want to be raised in accordance with their parent's religion.

---

[446] http://daronnefcy.com/post/158636399265/proud-of-the-team-for-everything-we-do-with-the

[447] Hollywood Reporter "Watch the Politically Charged Trailer for RuPaul's 'Drag Tots'" by Evan Real (May 10th 2018)

[448] Entertainment Weekly "RuPaul gives tiny *Drag Tots* a shady reading lesson in adorable clip" by Joey Nolfi (June 27th 2018)

[449] Christian Post "Ontario Passes Law Allowing Gov't to Seize Children From Parents Who Oppose Gender Transition" by Anugrah Kumar (June 4th 2017)

[450] Ibid.

One critic said the law now allows the government to "bust down your door, and seize your biological children if you are known to oppose LGBT ideology and the fraudulent theory of 'gender identity,' if for instance, some claim is made that your child may be same-sex attracted or confused about their 'gender.'"[451]

This isn't just something happening in Canada. It's already happening in the U.S. as well. In February 2018 a court in Ohio removed a 17-year-old girl from her Christian parents after they refused to call her by her "preferred" (male) name or allow her to get hormone injections and begin transitioning into a "male."[452] Child protective services sought temporary custody of the child and she was later turned over to her grandparents who support her decision to live as a "man."

MTV Awards Go "Gender Neutral"

The 2017 MTV Movie Awards decided to go "genderless" and eliminated the usual categories of best actor and best actress, and bragged that it was the first "gender-neutral" awards show in history.[453] The first presenter was a little-known actress named Asia Kate Dillon who appears in *Orange is the New Black* on

---

[451] Lifesitenews "Ontario passes 'totalitarian' bill allowing gov't to take kids from Christian homes" by Lianne Laurence (June 1st 2017)

[452] The Washington Times "Religious parents lose custody of transgender teen for refusing hormone treatment" by Bradford Richardson (February 20th 2018)

[453] Variety "The MTV Movie & TV Awards: A New Gender Revolution?" by Owen Gleiberman (May 7th 2017)

Netflix, and in the Showtime series *Billions*, where she plays a gender-nonbinary character.

She herself identifies as a "gender non-binary" person, and goes by the pronoun "they." ("They" has a shaved head, and as you might expect.)

After the *New York Times* wrote about the award show referring to Asia Kate Dillon as "she," they issued an apology and said that "American culture is outpacing the language to describe it," and they were very sorry for being "out of touch" for using the "wrong" pronoun.[454]

Another outlet that covered the award show later changed all pronouns in their story referring to Asia Kate Dylan as "she" and "her" to "they" and "their" and added an editor's note reading, "This article has been updated to reflect Asia Kate Dillon's preferred gender pronoun usage."[455]

Emma Watson won the first "gender-neutral" award that night for her role in the live-action *Beauty and the Beast,* and as expected gave a speech about how "progressive" the new format for the show was. "The first acting award in history that doesn't separate nominees based on their sex says something about how we perceive the human experience," she began. "MTV's move to create a genderless award for acting will mean something different to everyone, but to me, it indicates that acting is about the ability to put yourself in someone

---

[454] The New York Times "Vague Guidelines Lead to a Misstep on Gender Pronouns" by Liz Spayd (May 25th 2017)

[455] Refinery 29 "Asia Kate Dillon Just Made History At The MTV Movie & TV Awards" by Morgan Baila (May 17th 2017)

else's shoes. And that doesn't need to be separated into two, different categories."[456]

Instead of the usual awards for acting, directing, and screenwriting; the MTV Movie Awards gives a trophy for unique categories like Best Villain, Best Fight, and Best Cameo. The Best Kiss award was given to two men for the "gay coming-of-age" film *Moonlight*. In previous years it had been given to normal on-screen couples like Rachel McAdams and Ryan Gosling for *The Notebook*, and Robert Pattinson and Kristen Stewart for the *Twilight* series, but it's no surprise that with the media pushing the LGBT agenda every chance they get, that they would give the "Best Kiss" award to two men.

Teen Magazines

The editor of *Teen Vogue* made an announcement in 2016 that the magazine would stop portraying heterosexual people as the norm. "For the past year or so, we've made a concerted effort to limit (and, eventually, banish) heteronormativity from all of our content," the statement said. Adding, "we use gender neutral pronouns in almost all contexts. Our readers have appreciated the shift, and often help police our language."[457]

This is the same magazine that published "A Guide to Anal Sex" for teens, writing that, "Anal sex, though often stigmatized, is a perfectly natural way to engage in sexual

---

[456] Washington Post "Emma Watson takes first major gender-neutral movie award" by Travis M. Andrews (May 8th 2017)

[457] Vice News "Why Teen Magazines Have Gone Queer" by Melissa Kravitz (September 29th 2016)

activity."[458]   *Seventeen* magazine also decided to stop treating cis-gender and heterosexual people as the norm, and released a statement saying, "We want *Seventeen* to be a magazine where all girls feel represented and included, regardless of their sexual identities."[459]

The announcement was accompanied by a video titled, "Trans Students Explain Why Pronouns Are Important," featuring a bunch of trans kids complaining about people using "gender restrictive" pronouns like "he" and "she."

Men Wearing Makeup

Makeup giant Maybelline hired a man to be the face of a mascara ad campaign in January 2017. They chose a male "beauty blogger" named Manny Gutierrez who has over 4 million Instagram followers that enjoy his selfies showing his bearded face adorned with lipstick and eye shadow. The decision was celebrated by the Leftist media with *Glamour* magazine praising the idea, saying "Now this is exactly how we should be ringing in 2017."[460]

The previous year, Cover Girl hired their first male model, a YouTuber named James Charles who posts videos of himself doing makeup tutorials and painting himself up like a transvestite. Yes, they now have a male

---

[458] Teen Vogue "A Guide to Anal Sex" by Gigi Engle (July 7th 2017)

[459] Vice News "Why Teen Magazines Have Gone Queer" by Melissa Kravitz (September 29th 2016)

[460] Glamour "Manny Gutierrez Is the First Man to Star in a Maybelline Campaign, and It's a Huge Deal" by Erin Reimel (January 4th 2017)

"Cover Girl."[461]   Fellow makeup giant L'Oreal followed suit and hired a male YouTuber as a spokesmodel for their brand as well.[462]

Gender Neutral Driver's Licenses

In 2014 a gender non-conforming teen in South Carolina sued the DMV after they refused to allow him to take his driver's license photo wearing makeup, accusing them of discrimination.[463]   He won the case, setting the precedent for more craziness to come. The following year a man in Portland won the right to wear a "silly fox hat" in his driver's license photo after he sued for "religious discrimination" claiming he is a member of the Seven Drums, a Native American religion whose adherents sometimes wear ceremonial animal totems, and claimed his was a fox.[464]

In 2017 California began to legally recognize a third gender option on driver's licenses, which is strange because there is no "gender" listed on California driver's

---

[461] Advertising Age "Teen Makeup Star James Charles Is the First Male CoverGirl" by Ann-Christine Diaz (October 12th 2016)

[462] Business Insider "L'Oreal just hired this YouTube star to be its male spokesmodel" by Rachel Lubitz (February 9th 2017)

[463] NPR "Transgender Teen Wins Case To Wear Makeup In DMV Photo" by Kate Parkinson-Morgan (April 22nd 2015)

[464] New York Daily News "Portland man wins right to wear 'silly fox hat' in Oregon license photo after claiming religious exemption" by Keri Blakinger (Marchy 14th 2016)

licenses, instead it lists the person's sex. "Non-binary" is now allowed and is listed as an "X" instead of M or F.[465]

Oregon also passed the same law, allowing residents to choose "X" for their sex.[466]   New York has similar legislation in the works, and may be law by the time you're reading this.[467]   Washington D.C. began issuing gender neutral driver's licenses in 2017 as well.[468]   Other states are expected to follow.

After the DMV in Vermont revealed they would be allowing people to choose a third option other than male or female in January of 2018, an editor of the *Burlington Free Press* tweeted out sarcastically, "Awesome!   That makes us one stop closer to the apocalypse," and was soon fired for "hate speech."[469]

One response to his tweet read, "As a gender fluid person, I demand an apology, particularly for the children and adults in our beloved city who suffer under the oppressive hell of binary gender privilege."[470]   Maybe

---

[465] USA Today "Female, male or non-binary: California legally recognizes a third gender on identification documents" by Mary Bowerman (October 19th 2017)

[466] The Oregonian "Oregon becomes first state to allow nonbinary on drivers license" by Casey Parks (June 15th 2017)

[467] NBC News "Lawmakers in New York, D.C. Propose Third Sex on Driver's Licenses" by Mary Emily O'Hara (June 20th 2017)

[468] Washington Post "Meet the first person in the country to officially receive a gender-neutral driver's license" by Perry Stein (June 30th 2017)

[469] New York Post "Newspaper editor fired for 'poisonous' tweets on gender" by Joshua Rhett Miller (January 9th 2018)

[470] Ibid.

that person was just trolling with a sarcastic response, mocking the social justice warriors, or maybe they were serious—again, it's impossible to tell the difference anymore. There is no requirement for an evaluation by a doctor to get a driver's license listing your sex as "neither." All someone needs to do is check whatever box they feel like.

When this gender identity tornado was just getting started, a Canadian YouTuber named Lauren Southern—a beautiful blonde-haired blue-eyed woman in her early twenties—decided to see how easy it would be for her to be declared legally a man. At the time, in Canada if you got a doctor's note saying you were a certain gender, then you could then get a driver's license listing whatever it was.

Her "examination" consisted of simply telling the doctor what gender she wanted to be, and without looking at her genitals or giving her a DNA test, she was given a doctor's note that simply read, "To whom it may concern (for application for ID card) this is to certify that the above should be identified as male."[471]

She then took the doctor's note to Canada's equivalent of the DMV and got a new government ID card which identifies her as male. Canadian Prime Minister Justin Trudeau later changed the law so that nobody would even need a doctor's note, and now anyone can have whatever

---

[471] YouTube "Lauren Southern Becomes a Man" by Rebel Media (October 3rd 2016)

they want listed on their driver's license, including an
"X"[472]

Ads with "Gender Stereotypes" Banned

In England, the Advertising Standards Authority
(which is basically Britain's equivalent of the Federal
Trade Commission in America) banned advertisements
which they feel portray or reinforce, "outdated and
stereotypical views on gender roles in society." The
agency told the BBC, "While advertising is only one of
many factors that contribute to unequal gender outcomes,
tougher advertising standards can play an important role
in tackling inequalities and improving outcomes for
individuals, the economy and society as a whole."[473]

This is the same organization that banned a "fat-
shaming" billboard from a company called Protein World
which was encouraging people to get "Beach Body
Ready" for the summer.

The BBC reported, "Advertisements that show men
failing at simple household tasks and women left to clean
up are set to be banned by the UK advertising
watchdog."[474] The move was made after idiots
complained about various "sexist" advertisements,
including one from the Gap which depicted a boy

---

[472] Huffington Post "Ontario Driver's Licences To Offer Gender-
Neutral Designation" via The Canadian Press (June 30th 2016)

[473] New York Times "Britain Cracking Down on Gender Stereotypes
in Ads" by Iliana Magra (July 18th 2017)

[474] BBC "Advertising watchdog to get tough on gender
stereotypes" (July 18th 2017)

growing up to be an "academic" and a girl growing up to be a "social butterfly."

Another advertisement cited as the cause for the new policy was one for baby formula that depicted a baby boy growing up to be an engineer and a baby girl growing up to be a ballerina, because that's too "sexist" to be allowed on TV in the UK now.[475]

The United Nations has even launched a campaign called "Unstereotype" which has been backed by consumer product giants like Procter & Gamble, and Johnson & Johnson, along with Google, Facebook, Microsoft and other tech titans who all aim to use their advertising as propaganda in order to "fight stereotypes."

"No country in the world has achieved gender equality, even though we have big initiatives and laws passed," says the executive director of the UN Women organization, which is part of the campaign. "Changing laws didn't do much to change cultural norms [and] advertising has skill in behavior change."[476]

Microsoft's vice president of advertising praised the plan, saying, "Advertising is a reflection of culture and sometimes can be ahead of the curve and help effect change. We are proud to be a founding member of this UN sponsored initiative to "unstereotype" through the power and breadth of our messaging. We are all in."[477]

---

[475] Ibid.

[476] AdAge "The UN Believes Ads Can Turn the Tide in Long-Losing War for Gender Equality" by Jack Neff (June 23rd 2017)

[477] Unilever Press Release "Launch of Unstereotype Alliance set to eradicate outdated stereotypes in advertising" (June 20th 2017)

Their mission statement reads, "The Unstereotype Alliance is a thought and action platform that uses advertising as a force for good to drive positive change. It seeks to eradicate harmful gender-based stereotypes. The alliance is focused on empowering women in all their diversity (race, class, age, ability, ethnicity, religion, sexuality, language, education, etc.) and addressing harmful masculinities to help create a gender equal world."[478]

No-Shave November

Every November millions of men in America quit shaving for a month, or grow a mustache or a goatee, for what has been dubbed "No-Shave November" or "Movember" (Mustache November). It's not just a catchy name and an excuse to let loose for a few weeks and free one's self of the daily burden of shaving, but it's also to raise awareness for men's health issues like prostate cancer.

Feminists and sissy-boys are upset about this because it "perpetuates toxic masculinity" and think growing a mustache is a "sexist microaggression" and is "exclusionary" because it "celebrates masculinity."[479] One blogger even said, "I hate Movember so much, on

---

[478] http://www.unstereotypealliance.org/en

[479] Slate "Movember Is a Misguided Cancer Awareness Campaign" by Jacob Brogan and Christina Cauterucci (November 12th 2015)

Halloween, I shaved my scruffy beard-in-progress so no one would think I was participating."[480]

He also downplayed the dangers of prostate cancer, saying, "I also think it's important not to scare people by overstating their risks. And that's *exactly* what I think is happening here."[481] So, I guess raising awareness for breast cancer is also "fear mongering" and "scarring people." And speaking of cancer, this moron must have it growing in his brain.

One feminist triggered by Movember said, "Women are mostly the ones who get breast cancer, and men are mostly the ones who get prostate cancer, but gendering the *fight* against these cancers does far more to solidify gender norms and stratification than it does to further any noble cause. Sporting a mustache doesn't raise awareness about anything—and besides, everybody already knows about prostate cancer. If someone didn't, what's a mustache going to do about it, anyway?"[482]

Feminists on Tumblr (which is basically Instagram for the insane) get so upset about men having some fun and forgoing shaving for a month that they decided to try and hijack the cause to promote feminism by not shaving their armpits or legs for a month!

One of them wrote about it in her local college newspaper, saying, "My purpose in doing this experiment and in writing this column is not to condemn any woman who chooses to remove hair from her legs, pits or any

---

[480] Ibid.

[481] Ibid.

[482] Ibid.

other part of her body; I myself choose to do that, too. My purpose, however, is to prove to myself that it really is something I choose to do, and not just something I feel pressured into in order to feel like a normal human being. And perhaps my more important purpose is to try to convince others (women and men) that choosing not to do these things does not make you disgusting and aberrant."[483]

"Toxic" Masculinity

Being a strong and confident man is now considered to be a bad thing to liberals. It's "toxic" they say. Doing "manly" things like knowing how to fix a leaking faucet, or being able to change a flat tire is only "perpetuating the patriarchy." Liberals don't want young boys to build ramps out of scraps of wood and have fun jumping their bikes off them, or building forts in the woods like most kids in small Midwestern towns. Instead they want them painting their nails and putting on makeup.

"Hyper-masculine" men in movies are truly evil to liberals because they not only reinforce "gender stereotypes" but set an "unrealistic" and "unachievable" standard which boys are encouraged to strive for. In reality, it's good to have role models like Arnold Schwarzenegger, Hulk Hogan, Sylvester Stallone, and other fitness icons.

These men inspired an entire generation of young boys to hit the gym and develop the self discipline needed

---

[483] Doanne Line "No Shave November - A history of hair" by Hannah Nauer (November 14th 2012)

to build up their muscles, knowing they would never be as buff as the movie stars, but they provided something to work towards, and inspired skinny and weak kids that they could dramatically change their bodies with hard work, diet, and dedication.

Today, liberals embrace sissy boys whose arms are atrophied from lack of movement and poor diets, and whose only "exercise" is playing with their phone or their PlayStation. After President Trump addressed the Boy Scout Jamboree, an international meeting of scouts from around the world, *Time* magazine was worried that the president was "spreading toxic masculinity to future generations."[484]

They complained that he focused on his "victories" and his "power and wealth" and claimed that, "only privileged white men can follow in his footsteps," and, "We all must call on the Boy Scouts to do a better job of guiding our boys into adulthood."[485]

Sadly, the Boy Scouts have completely given in to the Leftist agenda. First in 2015, when they lifted their long-held ban on gay scout leaders.[486] Since their creation in 1910, their policy was that, "a known or avowed homosexual is not an appropriate role model of the Scout

---

[484] Time "How to keep Donald Trump from spreading his toxic masculinity to future generations." (July 27th 2017)

[485] Ibid.

[486] Reuters "Boy Scouts lift blanket ban on gay adult leaders, employees" (July 27, 2015)

Oath and Law,"[487] but now they allow gay men to "lead" the young boys.

Then, three years later they changed their name to just the "Scouts," and now include girls. What's next, skirts for everyone as the new uniform? Or maybe merit badges for the best speech about the "benefits" of fifty-eight different "genders?"

Boys need male role models so they can learn how to grow up and be men. Having girls in the "Scouts" causes boys to act differently then they would if they were in just a group of boys. Now that it's coed they'll try to impress the girls, and sometimes they'll be afraid to ask certain questions about life because they don't want to be embarrassed in front of the girls, or they may be shy because they have a crush on one of them, and can't be themselves.

College campuses across the country are also trying to emasculate men by combating "toxic masculinity."[488] A new program at the University of Texas, Austin aims to fight against manliness by working to, "increase acceptance of gender diversity."[489]

Duke University launched a "Men's Project" inviting men to join a nine-week training program to "destabilize masculine privilege" and combat "toxic masculinity," calling it a, "great way for men and masculine-of-center

---

[487] BSALegal.org "Morally Straight" (February 6, 2010)

[488] Fox News "Princeton University's 'men's engagement manager' to battle aggressive masculinity" by Christopher Carbone (July 25th 2017)

[489] Houston Chronicle "Is a new 'masculinity' program at UT wrong about men?" by Chris Ferguson (May 9th 2018)

people on campus to engage with issues of gender equity on campus and beyond."[490]

The March 2018 edition of *The Hollywood Reporter* celebrated what they called the "Triumph of the Beta Male" because the editors are uncomfortable with men doing manly things and being men.[491] The new brand of "sexy" Hollywood is trying to promote is emaciated-looking effeminate soy boys who don't know which way to turn a screwdriver in order to tighten a screw and who struggle to carry a gallon of milk from the refrigerator to the breakfast table because they are so weak.

Actually, let me correct that. Social justice warriors don't like milk anymore because it's very production includes cruelty to animals. Consuming animal products is too masculine, so instead they drink soy "milk" which is helping rid them of what little manhood they have remaining.

Soy Boys

I'm sure you've noticed the plague of scrawny, effeminate "males" roaming the streets, particularly Millennials. They look so weak they probably couldn't even do ten push-ups and likely struggle to put away the groceries because they are too heavy. Many are afraid to eat meat because it perpetuates "toxic masculinity," and

---

[490] Campus Reform "Duke 'Men's Project' recruits 'masculine-of-center' students" by Toni Airksinen (January 25th 2018)

[491] The Federalist "Triumph of the Beta Male" by Bre Payton (March 8th 2018)

have opted for soy instead.[492] Lots of soy, which is why we call them "soy boys."

The *Urban Dictionary* defines soy boy as being slang for, "males who completely and utterly lack all necessary masculine qualities. This pathetic state is usually achieved by an over-indulgence of emasculating products and/or ideologies."[493]

Calling someone a soy boy is like calling them a pussy, except the term soy boy is so much more accurate because it describes one of the scientific causes for their weakness and femininity. The term is so precise and self-explanatory that it hurts the feelings of those with soy syndrome so bad that Leftists have deemed the term one of the most vile insults in the English language.

A writer for *The New York Times* claimed that if you call someone a soy boy, you're basically a Nazi. In an Op-Ed about how "America's Boys are Broken" the writer claimed, "Too many boys are trapped in the same suffocating, outdated model of masculinity, where manhood is measured in strength," and worried that they, "don't even have the language to talk about how they feel about being trapped, because the language that exists to discuss the full range of human emotion is still viewed as sensitive and feminine."[494]

The writer then uses a "case in point" that a few days earlier when he brought up his concerns on Twitter he got

---

[492] Fox News "Eating meat promotes toxic masculinity, academic journal says" (December 5th 2017)

[493] UrbanDictionary.com definition of "soy boy"

[494] The New York Times "The Boys Are Not All Right" by Michael Ian Black (February 21st 2018)

dozens of "hateful" replies, many of them calling him a "soy boy" which he described as, "a common insult among the alt-right that links soy intake to estrogen."[495]

The Los Angeles Times ran the headline "'Soy boy' is the alt-right's new most biting insult," and said that, "in the imaginations of many among the alt-right, the Asian-native soybean has apparently come to symbolize creeping multiculturalism as well as the demise of the meat-and-potatoes man's man."[496]

Actually, it has nothing to do with "soybean symbolism." Instead, studies show that consuming soy boosts estrogen levels, which is why for decades personal trainers have warned against drinking soy protein shakes, and instead recommend whey protein.

Some of the beta males at BuzzFeed called the "Try Guys" decided to test their testosterone levels in one of their YouTube videos, and the results confirmed the obvious, that they shouldn't really be considered men. The average T-score for an adult male between the age of 25-34 is around 600 ng/dL.[497]

The four "men" at BuzzFeed who tested their levels came back with results ranging from a low of 212 to a high of 363.[498] For a frame of reference, a typical 85-year-old man has an average T-score of 376 ng/dL, which

---

[495] Ibid.

[496] Los Angeles Times "'Soy boy' is the alt-right's new most biting insult" by Jeremy Rose (November 8th 2017)

[497] EliteMensGuide.com "Testosterone Levels by Age"

[498] BuzzFeedVideo "The Try Guys Test Who is The Most Attractive" (October 28th 2017)

is higher than the highest score any of the "men" at BuzzFeed had, who are all in their late twenties and early thirties.

In recent years, sperm counts in western men have been dropping dramatically, down by more than 50% over the last 40 years.[499] Scientists say they don't know why, but maybe they're just afraid to admit the truth. Men are consuming too much soy, along with a variety of other chemicals finding their way into our food and water which are having adverse effects on our bodies and minds.

Men's Health magazine published an article looking into the "dark side" of soy titled, "Is This The Most Dangerous Food For Men?" and warned that it "has the power to undermine everything it means to be male."[500] Their investigation detailed the case of a retired U.S. Army officer whose estrogen levels were eight times higher than normal for a man from simply using soy milk in his cereal every morning.

He went to see a doctor because he was developing breasts (gynecomastia) and had no sex drive any more and after going to several different doctors looking for answers, one of them suspected soy after examining his diet. Once he quit consuming it, his estrogen levels immediately began dropping back down to normal.

Alex Jones, the founder of Infowars, is often mocked for a rant he did about how the government or

---

[499] NPR "Sperm Counts Plummet In Western Men, Study Finds" by Rob Stein (July 31st 2017)

[500] Men's Health "Is This the Most Dangerous Food For Men?" by Jim Thornton (May 19th 2009)

corporations are "putting chemicals in the water that turn the fricking frogs gay," but the evidence shows that's exactly what's happening.[501] A study at the University of California, Berkeley showed that the pesticide atrazine causes 10% of male frogs to mutate from males into females and chemically castrates 75% of the others.[502]

Some fish are now mutating because of chemicals in the water and changing sex, and the males are becoming so feminized they can't successfully breed. The London *Independent* reported, "In some rivers, all the male roach [fish] were found to have been feminized to a degree because of high levels of estrogen, which is used along with progestin in birth-control pills to prevent ovulation and is also present in other drugs."[503]

A professor involved in the study said, "We're starting to establish not just effects on gender, but that they can also affect other physiological processes in the fish as well," adding, "If they are moderately to severely feminized, they are compromised as individuals and they really struggle to pass their genes on."[504]

It should be no surprise that chemicals in our food and water are having dramatic effects on our health, but it's just too politically incorrect to even ask questions about whether they may be responsible for causing so many

---

[501] Berkeley News "Pesticide atrazine can turn male frogs into females" by Robert Sanders (March 1st 2010)

[502] Ibid.

[503] The Independent "Male fish mutating into females because of waste chemicals, expert warns" by Ian Johnston (July 3rd 2017)

[504] Ibid.

boys to be such sissies and for an alarming number of people to be confused about their gender or turning them into homosexuals.

The Gay Agenda

We as a society have to admit the fact that homosexual behavior is abnormal, whether the result of a birth defect or a mental disorder, or as some psychiatrists believe — a disruption in the Oedipal phase of children's psychosexual development when they're growing up.[505] Something is wrong with gay people and to call their behavior normal is like saying someone born with feet on the ends of their arms has a "normal" human body. They don't. And trying to tell them that there's nothing wrong with them, hoping to make them feel better, is disingenuous.

Obviously we shouldn't hate people who have birth defects, whether physical or mental, but we shouldn't have to pretend they don't exist in the name of being politically correct. And thinking science should search for a way to prevent more people from being born with the defect isn't "hateful" either.

Because heterosexual people are normal people, the gays and bisexuals feel that society as a whole is "discriminating" against them and have coined the term "heteronormative" to describe this pervasive "oppression" they believe they are subjected to by straight people. Gays and bisexuals feel they shouldn't be treated as an alternative to the norm, in a way that someone with

---

[505] Basic Freud: Psychoanalytic Thought for the 21st Century by Michael Kahn, Ph.D page 77 - on the negative resolution of the Oedipus complex.

blonde hair shouldn't be treated as abnormal from someone who has brown hair.

But in the case of sexuality, there is a clear distinction because God (or mother nature, or whatever you want to call the "thing" that created every living creature on earth) clearly and intricately designed males and females to have intimate relations with members of the opposite sex.

To claim that heterosexuality isn't normal or not the way that humans were designed to be would be like claiming that having 10 fingers and 10 toes isn't "normal." Sure, some people are born missing limbs, or with six fingers on one hand, but it's certainly not normal, and is a birth defect. And to claim that homosexuality is "normal" would be saying it's "normal" to ride a bike by sitting on the handlebars. Some people do, but that doesn't mean it's normal. That's not how a bike was designed to be used. Sure it *can* be used that way, but that is a perversion, which by definition means using something in an abnormal or unnatural way.[506]

Liberal extremists want everyone to be gay or bisexual, because they are hoping to shatter the basic structure of human relationships that has been in place since the beginning of our species. They want gender to be erased, and all children to be treated as the same, instead of as boys and girls, and they're upset that children are taught that men marry women and that boys date girls.

They are trying to brainwash children that "people date people" and that there is no distinction between a heterosexual person and a homosexual. Not teaching

---

[506] Dictionary.com - Definition of "perversion"

children that heterosexuality is normal would be like not giving them peanut butter and jelly sandwiches because an extremely small fraction of kids might be allergic to the peanuts.

Liberals even have an ideology called "political lesbianism" in which they encourage all female feminists to embrace lesbian lifestyles, believing that sexual orientation is a social construct, not a biological drive. This, they believe, will help them to "fight" against sexism, which they see as being perpetuated by men and heteronormativity.

In the 1970s, a group called the "Revolutionary Feminists" published their "manifesto" in a booklet titled *Love Your Enemy?* where they declared, "all feminists can and should be lesbians. Our definition of a political lesbian is a woman-identified woman [cisgender] who does not fuck men."[507] They hate men so much they encourage women to rid men "from your beds and your heads."[508] Perhaps many feminists' deep hatred of men causes the attraction mechanism in the brain to rewire itself, diverting the natural functions of sexuality into abnormal channels.

The acronym representing LGBT people keeps getting longer and longer with more letters being added onto it seemingly every few months. First it was LGBT, then LGBTQ, then LGBTQI, and that was just the beginning! Conservatives sometimes mock the acronym additions by

---

[507] *Love Your Enemy? The Debate Between Heterosexual Feminism and Political Lesbianism* by Onlywomen Press Collective (1984)

[508] The Guardian "My Sexual Revolution" by Julie Bindel (January 29th 2009)

referring to it as "LGBT-ABCDEFG," but in a strange turn of events, the Leftists keep adding so many letters that it's approaching the length of the entire alphabet. One popular Leftist organization declared the "official" acronym is now LGBTQQICAPF2K+.[509] (This is not a joke)

It stands for: "Lesbian," "Gay," "Bisexual," "Transgender," "Queer," "Questioning," "Intersex," "Curious," "Asexual," "Agender," "Ally," "Pansexual," "Polysexual," "Friends and Family," "Two-spirit" and "Kink." The plus sign is meant to signify that there are even *more* letters and types of people in their community, and they don't want them to feel left out.

One outlet reported that more letters kept getting added since the original LGBT acronym was coined in the 90s, "out of a need to move away from the limiting gay community," and because they are trying to "encompass any community that defines itself as anything but heterosexual or cisgender."[510]

Others are using the acronym: LGGBDTTTIQQAAPP, which stands for: Lesbian, Gay, Genderqueer, Bisexual, Demisexual, Transgender, Transsexual, Twospirit, Intersex, Queer, Questioning, Asexual, Allies, Pansexual, Polyamorous.[511] To say that these people are confused is a dramatic understatement.

---

[509] The Gay UK "There is now a K in LGBTQQICAPF2K+ This is a new one for us but welcome the Ks" (January 23rd 2018)

[510] Washington Times "K is for 'Kink': Some gay-rights activists push to add letter to expanding LGBTQ acronym" by Bradford Richardson (February 1st 2018)

[511] Ibid.

Not long ago the Left said that all they wanted was for gay marriage to be legal and they would be happy, but that was just them getting their foot in the door so they could later burn the house down. Instead of being satisfied that same-sex marriage is now legal, they are getting increasingly hostile and litigious as they continue to pursue their radical agenda.

Christian Mingle, the popular online Christian dating website, was sued by gays for "discrimination" because the only options for searching for people to date were of the opposite sex.[512] The website should have the Constitutional protection of the freedom of assembly, because contrary to popular beliefs there are exemptions to discrimination statutes for various businesses to protect their members' rights to assemble with whoever they want to under the first amendment, but Christian Mingle settled the lawsuit and now includes options for men seeking men.[513]

One man even sued a popular Bible publisher, claiming that by simply publishing the Bible with its anti-gay verses, that they were somehow harming him.[514] After Los Angeles Clippers owner Donald Sterling was forced to sell his basketball team when a secretly recorded audio clip revealed he made racist statements about black

[512] Wall Street Journal "ChristianMingle Opens Doors to Gay Singles Under Settlement" by Jacob Gersham and Sara Randazzo (June 30th 2016)

[513] The Washington Post "ChristianMingle now allows gay dating, after a lawsuit" by Julie Zauzmer (July 7th 2016)

[514] Christian Post "Gay Man Files $70M Suit Against Bible Publishers Over 'Homosexual' Verses" by Elena Garcia (July 10, 2008)

people, some called for team owners who are Christians to be forced out of the NBA next if they didn't support gay marriage.[515]

After the owner of a small mom and pop pizza restaurant in Indiana named Memories Pizza was interviewed on the news about a pending religious freedom law that would protect businesses from being forced to participate in activities that violate their religious convictions (such as catering a gay "wedding"), social media mobs organized a smear campaign and flooded their Yelp page with fake one-star reviews, and forced them to temporarily close down due to terrorist threats and the ongoing harassment.[516] Gays could eat in their restaurant, they didn't care. The owners just didn't want to be forced to attend a same-sex "wedding" by having to cater it.

Gays had already bullied multiple high profile people out of their jobs for not supporting gay "marriage." Brandon Eich, the founder and CEO of Mozilla (the company behind the popular Firefox Internet browser) was the target of a coordinated outrage mob after it was discovered that he donated a few thousand dollars of his own personal money to the Proposition 8 campaign in California in 2008 (which passed, and became law until the Supreme Court overruled it) defining marriage as only

---

[515] Huffington Post "What About NBA's Homophobe Owner?" by Craig Crawford (June 30th 2014)

[516] USA Today "Indiana pizza shop that won't cater gay weddings to close" by Mary Bowerman (April 1st 2015)

182

between a man and a woman.[517] He was forced out of his own company for having the same position on the issue that Barack Obama did at the time (who later flip flopped after his election).[518]

Actually, to be clear, Obama lied to his supporters when first running for president in 2008 after his advisor David Axelrod warned him early in the campaign that he would lose support from the black community and moderate Democrats if he publicly supported gay "marriage" so he claimed to be against it until after he was elected, and then said his position had "evolved" and came out for it.[519]

The Benham Brothers (not to be confused with 'The Property Brothers' on the same channel) had their deal with HGTV canceled after it was revealed that they attended church and one of them had dared say that homosexuality was a sin.[520] BuzzFeed even started a smear campaign against HGTV stars Chip and Joanna Gaines who hosted a "fixer upper" show because they're

---

[517] Washington Post "Mozilla exec out of job for gay rights intolerance. Some think that's intolerant." by Gail Sullivan (April 4th 2014)

[518] Politifact "President Barack Obama's shifting stance on gay marriage" (by Becky Bowers (May 11th 2012)

[519] Time "Axelrod: Obama Misled Nation When He Opposed Gay Marriage In 2008" by Zeke Miller (February 10th 2015)

[520] Hollywood Reporter "Benham Brothers, Dumped by HGTV Over Anti-Gay Remarks, Could Land at 'Traditional Values' Network INSP TV" by Paul Bond (May 12th 2014)

Christians and attend a church where the pastor doesn't support gay marriage.[521]

LGBT extremists want to ruin the lives of anyone who doesn't support them, and they are systematically infiltrating schools, city councils, and the media to do it.[522] They are also getting increasingly hostile to those who don't embrace their agenda. Boxer Manny Pacquiao was assaulted by a gay extremist after he posted a Bible verse on his Instagram about sexual perversion.[523] Pac was then banned from the popular L.A. shopping mall The Grove because the owners consider him a "homophobe."[524]

One of the dirty secrets of Barack Obama lifting the ban on gays in the military is the frequency of gay soldiers raping other men.[525] It's not just straight men who commit rape. The sexual predators liberals don't want to talk about are homosexuals who rape other men when they're drunk and passed out, or after drugging them, or simply over-powering them with threats of

---

[521] Washington Post "BuzzFeed's hit piece on Chip and Joanna Gaines is dangerous" by Brandon Ambrosino (December 1st 2016)

[522] Desert Sun "An all-LGBT council in Palm Springs takes charge" by Jesse Marx and Barrett Newkirk (November 8th 2017)

[523] LGBTQ Nation "Boxer Manny Pacquiao attacked outside restaurant for antigay comments" (April 4th 2016)

[524] Los Angeles Times "Manny Pacquiao is banned from L.A.'s Grove for anti-gay comments" by Churck Schilken (March 18th 2016)

[525] Washington Times "'Gay' rape in military underreported by Pentagon" by Rowan Scarborough (November 3rd 2015)

mayhem.[526]   Men getting raped by fellow male soldiers in the U.S. armed forces are dramatically under-reported because the victims are too embarrassed to come forward.[527]

Gays feel that the entire world revolves around them and should cater to their every desire because they're "special."   For example, gays were furious when they weren't given a spot in the Saint Patrick's Day Parade in New York City in 2014.   Mayor de Blasio was so upset, he broke the decades-old tradition of the city's mayor attending, and instead boycotted the parade.[528]

The mayor and the gays failed to understand that it's a parade about *Saint Patrick's Day*, not a gay pride parade. The following year, however, the event organizers caved into pressure and allowed a 'Pride' group to march.

One of the stars of an HBO vampire show called *True Blood* was labeled "homophobic" after he disagreed with the new direction the show's writers took his character when half-way through the series they decided to depict him as bisexual and wanted him to do gay sex scenes. Rather than shoot the scenes, he decided to quit the show

[526] New York Times "Men Struggle for Rape Awareness" by Roni Caryn Rabin (January 23rd 2012)

[527] Washington Times "'Gay' rape in military underreported by Pentagon" by Rowan Scarborough (November 3rd 2015)

[528] New York Daily News "Mayor de Blasio breaks tradition, boycotts St. Patrick's Day Parade over gay-pride ban" by Erin Dunkin and Corinee Lestch (February 5th 2014)

and was denounced by his fellow cast members for being "homophobic."[529]

Hollywood is always on the forefront of promoting perversion. Singer "Halsey," who is bisexual, is on a mission to end what she calls "bi-phobia" or the "fear of bisexuals."[530] Yes, she is trying to glamorize bisexuality as normal, and encourages her young teenage fans to sexually experiment with each other. Katy Perry's claim to fame was her bisexual-themed anthem "I Kissed a Girl" which kicked off her career in 2008.

Demi Lovato's 2015 song "Cool for The Summer" is about having a lesbian fling. During the 2014 Grammys, Macklemore performed his LGBT anthem "Same Love" while 33 same-sex couples were "married" on stage during the show.[531] (When talking about gay "marriage" I always put it in quotes because it's not really a marriage. A marriage is between a man and a woman.)

Bill Maher, host of HBO's *Real Time,* surprisingly admitted how powerful and sensitive the LGBT extremists are, calling them a "gay mafia" after they forced Mozilla CEO Brendan Eich out of his job for not

---

[529] *New York Daily News* "'True Blood' star Nelsan Ellis on Luke Grimes quitting show because he didn't want to play gay: 'I'm over him'" by Kirthana Ramisetti (July 24th 2014)

[530] Rolling Stone "Halsey on Duetting With Bieber, Hating 'Tri-Bi' Label" by Brian Hait (February 10th 2016)

[531] New York Post "33 couples wed in emotional Grammys climax" by Gregory E. Miller (January 26th 2014)

supporting gay "marriage." "I think there is a gay mafia. I think if you cross them, you do get whacked," he said.[532]

While hosting the 2016 Oscars, Chris Rock admitted that he was afraid to make a joke about singer Sam Smith who had just won an Academy Award for the soundtrack to the latest James Bond movie, which he dedicated to the LGBT community. "Congratulations. No jokes there. Don't want to get me in trouble," Rock said after Sam Smith's acceptance speech and odd connection between his James Bond song and his sexuality.[533]

They're treated by the mainstream media as so special and cool that in 2016 I decided to conduct an experiment where I asked people walking along the boardwalk next to the beach if they would sign a petition to give all LGBT people $1000 a month for "gay reparations," and the petition quickly filled up with signatures. You can see the video on my YouTube channel (at YouTube.com/MarkDice provided they haven't removed it yet for "violating their terms of service.")

The Father of "Gay Rights" Movement

The man who is considered to be the father of the "gay rights" movement is a creep named Harry Hay, who marched in the Los Angeles Gay Pride Parade in 1986 while carrying a banner reading "NAMBLA Walks With Me," referring to the North American Man Boy Love

---

[532] RealClear Politics "Maher: 'There Is A Gay Mafia -- If You Cross Them, You Do Get Whacked'" by Ian Schwartz (April 4th 2014)

[533] New York Daily News "Chris Rock's best jokes from Oscars night" by Don Kaplan (February 29th 2016)

Association, a pedophile advocacy group that wants to legalize pedophilia.[534]

The parade organizers that year had banned NAMBLA from participating because they didn't want to be associated with them, but Harry Hay denounced this "discrimination" and said that by not accepting pedophiles, the LGBT community was "pandering to our heterosexual dominated society."[535]

Later when he was asked about his support for the pedophile group, he said, "If the parents and friends of gays are truly friends of gays, they would know from their gay kids that the relationship with an older man is precisely what thirteen, fourteen, and fifteen-year-old kids need more than anything else in the world."[536]

This is basically the same thing that Milo Yiannopoulos said, which caused his speaking invitation to CPAC [the Conservative Political Action Conference] to get rescinded, his book deal with Simon and Schuster canceled, and many of his supporters to distance themselves from him in 2017.[537]

Decades earlier when Harry Hay was younger, he created a gay secret society inspired by Freemasonry and

---

[534] Timmons, Stuart —*The Trouble with Harry Hay: Founder of the Modern Gay Movement* page 295 Alyson Publications (1990)

[535] The Phoenix "The Real Harry Hay" by Michael Bronski (July 7th 2002)

[536] The American Spectator "When Nancy met Harry: Nancy Pelosi Winks at Man-Boy Love" by Jeffry Lord (October 5th 2006)

[537] New York Times "Milo Yiannopoulos's Pedophilia Comments Cost Him CPAC Role and Book Deal" by Jeremy W. Peters, Alexandra Alter and Michael M. Grynbaum (February 20th 2017)

Communism to promote the gay agenda back in the 1950s. It was called the Mattachine Society, named after a medieval French secret society which worked to undermine the monarchs. Harry Hay formed the group using a cellular structure modeled after the Communist Party and had new members swear oaths of secrecy and then began infiltrating schools, the media, and government.

Hay admired Communism's revolutionary ideologies aimed at "freeing" so-called oppressed minority groups, a Leftist tradition that has been carried on by the disciples of Saul Alinsky.

They're Coming for the Children

We're seeing an alarming number of new children's books depicting gay storylines in order to teach kids that it's perfectly "normal" and that they shouldn't be expected to marry a member of the opposite sex when they grow up. In *King and King*, a would-be prince decides he wants to marry a man instead of a princess. In *Worm and Worm*, two male worms get married. *And Tango Makes Three*, which was released in 2005, tells the story of two gay penguins who adopt a baby penguin and live as a "family." In *Santa's Husband*, Santa Claus is depicted as gay with a black boyfriend.

A kindergarten teacher in Sacramento, California read her class *I Am Jazz*, a book about a biological boy who transitions into a girl, (based on the true story of "Jazz Jennings" who had a reality show on TLC.) The teacher also read a book titled *Red: A Crayon's Story* which is

189

about a blue crayon that "identifies" as red. She read the books to the kids to coincide with introducing them to one of their fellow students who had "transitioned" from a boy into a girl at the age of five. The parents were not told about the books and some said the teacher made their kids fear that they might "change" into the opposite sex because they were so confused by the stories.[538]

A sixth grade teacher in Texas gave her 12-year-old students a questionnaire titled "How Comfortable Am I," which asked the kids to rate on a scale of 1 to 4 how comfortable they were with a variety of situations involving race, ethnicities, and sexual orientation. One of the questions asked the kids how comfortable they would feel at a gay bar.[539]

After one of the students' parents were made aware of the questionnaire and confronted the school, "disciplinary action was taken," according to the school's spokesman. What that action was, they would not say, which probably means the teacher was given a week suspension, and was not fired.

A middle school teacher in Florida gave a similar questionnaire to his students which included one scenario in which they were asked how comfortable they would feel if their mother "came out" as a lesbian. That teacher

---

[538] Washington Times "Teacher who taught kindergartners about transgenders named 'teacher of the year'" by Bradford Richardson (March 27th 2018)

[539] WFAA "6th graders receive 'gay bar' questionnaire at Birdville ISD campus" by David Goins (February 14th 2018)

was thankfully fired.[540] Of course, one parent interviewed by the local news thought the questionnaire was a good idea, saying, "I think the school could do it a lot better than we could. It'd be a lot more comfortable. It's weird talking to your kids about this."[541]

Gays Adopting Children

Gay "marriage" was just a red herring and a distraction to divert attention away from their true agenda. It wasn't really about "marriage" it was about getting ahold of children. Gay couples are legally allowed to adopt children and lesbians can buy sperm from a sperm bank and impregnate themselves, and then are legally awarded custody of the child.

Despite all the debates about the gay "marriage" issue before the Supreme Court ruled on it in 2015, you never heard a word about gay adoption, because it flew under the radar. Why there isn't a national outrage over two gay men being allowed to adopt children is beyond me.

A 24-year-old woman who was conceived by a lesbian after she and her "wife" decided to allow a man to have sex with one of them, spoke out against same-sex couples having children because of the unnatural environment they're forced to be raised in. She said voices like hers are rarely heard because, "nobody wants to hear about the other side of the rainbow. The side that is not catered for,

---

[540] WFLA "Florida teacher fired after assignment asks students controversial questions" by WFLA Staff Reporters (April 6th 2017)

[541] Ibid

that don't grow up happy and grow up with a dissenting idea of what a family structure should be."[542]

The victim said, "I knew that I loved both of my parents but I could not place my finger on what it is I was missing inside myself," adding, "When I hit school I started to realize through observing other children and their loving bonds with their fathers that I really was missing out on something special."[543]

She said she was lied to by the lesbians who raised her about where she came from. "I was lied to throughout school, I was told that I didn't have a father or that perhaps they didn't know who he was."[544]

"We [children of same-sex couples] want our mothers and fathers," she pleaded. "I don't understand why society is so fiercely rejecting such a natural concept that is acceptable in every other family structure."[545]

The woman who wrote a book titled *Raising My Rainbow* documenting her insane ideas about bringing up genderless children has a son who felt he needed to "come out" to her as straight! "Mom, I'm straight. It's time you faced the facts," he told her. "I know what you're doing.

---

[542] Daily Mail "Nobody wants to hear about the other side of the 'rainbow': Australian woman conceived by sperm donor who grew up with two Lesbian mums reveals how unhappy she was to not have a father" by Brianne Tolj and Anneta Konstantinides (August 30th 2017)

[543] Ibid.

[544] Ibid.

[545] Ibid.

You always leave it open, like I could be gay. But I'm not."[546]

She later admitted, "By trying to eliminate the need for a gay son to come out, I created an environment where a straight son felt the need to come out."[547] So it appears she did everything she could to try "gay up" her kids, but the oldest one at least, was still in tune with his biological drives and had to finally tell her to stop treating him like he should be gay.

Movie Characters

When Marvel's new *Captain America: Civil War* film came out in 2016, liberals took to Twitter to complain that Captain America was straight. *Vanity Fair's* review of the movie said it was great, except for what they called "the one flaw" of not including a subplot of Captain America and his friend Bucky being gay lovers.[548]

In earlier versions of the film they were depicted as chasing girls and having girlfriends, but the Leftists had a fantasy that Captain America (played by Chris Evans) would hook up with his best friend Bucky and when he didn't, they were upset about it.

The same type of hysteria spread when Disney announced they were making part two of their hit *Frozen*, causing "Give Elsa a Girlfriend" to trend on Twitter from

---

[546] Huffington Post "What Happened When My Son Came Out... as Straight" by Lori Duron (February 2nd 2016)

[547] Ibid.

[548] Vanity Fair "Is This the One Flaw in the Otherwise Great *Captain America: Civil War*?" by Joanna Robinson (May 8th 2016)

so many people tweeting that they wanted Disney to depict her as a lesbian in the sequel.[549]

When the new *Star Wars* film *The Force Awakens* was about to be released in 2015, the same thing happened when they wanted Luke Skywalker to be gay. Mark Hamill who plays the character said fans kept asking him, "Could Luke be gay?" and he said, "If you think Luke is gay, of course he is. You should not be ashamed of it."[550] This is particularly strange because those familiar with the franchise know that before he learned Princess Leia was his sister, he had a crush on her as both he and Han Solo competed for her affection.

Just before *Solo: A Star Wars Story* was released in the summer of 2018, the writer said that Han Solo's friend Lando Calrissian is a "pansexual," meaning not only is he bisexual, but he doesn't have a preference for gender identity either (meaning he would have sex with transgender "men" or "women").[551]

"I would have loved to have gotten a more explicitly LGBT character into this movie," said Johnathan Kasden, who wrote the screenplay. "I think it's time, certainly, for that, and I love the fluidity — sort of the spectrum of

---

[549] Time "The Internet Is Rooting for the *Frozen* Sequel to Give Elsa a Girlfriend" by Megan McClurskey (March 1st 2018)

[550] Vanity Fair "'Of Course' Luke Skywalker Is Gay, Confirms Mark Hamill, Echoing Thousands of Fan-Fiction Prayers" by Charles Bramesco (March 5th 2016)

[551] Hollywood Reporter "'Solo' Writer Says Lando Is Pansexual" by Ryan Parker (May 17th 2018)

sexuality that [he] appeals to and that droids are a part of."[552]

When *Beauty and the Beast* was made into a live-action film in 2017, they included a same sex couple in a dance scene. When Marvel's *Black Panther* came out in February 2018 it was widely celebrated for portraying a black "super hero," but that wasn't progressive enough. Liberals were upset there were no gay characters included.[553]

When the production of the Harry Potter spinoff *Fantastic Beasts Part 2: The Crimes of Grindelwald* was announced, liberals were furious that Dumbledore wouldn't be depicted as "explicitly gay" despite J.K. Rowling claiming years earlier that the headmaster of Hogwarts was a homosexual.[554]

After Marvel's *Infinity War* came out, it caused the same reaction by the crazies. One critic denounced the film, saying, "The total lack of queer characters in 'Infinity War' indicates a problem in the comic book industry."[555] It wasn't just one disgruntled critic. Social media was flooded with disappointment, including a "queer cartoonist" named Kate Leth who tweeted that even though there were so many different super heroes in

---

[552] Ibid.

[553] Washington Times "Black Panther packed with action, diversity - but no gays" by Bradford Richardson (February 20th 2018)

[554] Vanity Fair "Dumbledore Won't Be Explicitly Gay in *Fantastic Beasts 2*—but Why?" by Laura Bradley (January 31st 2018)

[555] Hornet.com "The Total Lack of Queer Characters in 'Infinity War' Indicates a Problem in the Comic Book Industry" by Matt Keely (April 23rd 2018)

Infinity War, she was upset because not a single one was queer.[556]

The LGBT lobbying group GLAAD is pressuring movie studios to include major gay characters in 20% of their films by the year 2021 and 50% of all films by the year 2024.[557] Gay people only make up about one and a half percent of the population (although they'd like you to believe it's around 30%) so why does such a small group of people need to be depicted in *half* of the movies?

It's not enough to just include them, they want them to be major parts of the plot, saying, "Studios must do better to include more LGBTQ characters, and construct those stories in a way that is directly tied to the film's plot…Far too often LGBTQ characters and stories are relegated to subtext, and it is left up to the audience to interpret or read into a character as being LGBTQ."[558]

Emojis

Soon after emojis became popular and smartphones started including them on the keyboard, Leftists were upset that all of the ones featuring families consisted of a man and a woman with children, so they demanded "gay emojis" and of course Apple was more than happy to oblige.

---

[556] https://twitter.com/kateleth/status/986274776296517632

[557] GLAAD.org "2018 Studio Responsibility Index" by Megan Townsend (May 22nd 2018)

[558] Ibid.

In 2012 they released their "diversity emojis" including lesbians and gays with children.[559] That wasn't "diverse" enough though, so a few years later they released androgynous and gender non-conforming emojis too.

In 2016 Apple also changed the gun emoji from a realistic looking revolver to a fluorescent green squirt gun, a move that was later followed by Samsung, Facebook Twitter, Google, and Microsoft. People were upset that the gun was included in the emoji keyboard because they considered it a "symbol of violence," and so they pressed Apple to change it by tweeting the hashtag #DisarmTheiPhone.[560]

Microsoft made the announcement on Twitter by saying, "We are in the process of evolving our emojis to reflect our values and the feedback we've received. Here's a preview," and included a photo of the new green water gun.[561]

Valentine's Day

Liberals' hatred of Valentine's Day goes far beyond the typical complaints about the commercialization of the day, or the social pressures to buy candy and flowers, or even the "poor single people" who feel left out. Many are

---

[559] Gizmodo "Apple Adds Gay and Lesbian Couple Icons to iOS 6" by Jesus Diaz (June 14th 2012)

[560] Business Insider "Apple made a controversial change in 2016 — but now all of Silicon Valley is playing catch-up" by Kid Leswing (April 25th 2018)

[561] https://twitter.com/Microsoft/status/989269615887900673

now upset that it's a holiday which celebrates heterosexual couples and armed with one of their new buzzwords, Leftists are waging war against the "heteronormative" holiday.

'Heteronormative,' in case you're having a hard time wrapping your mind around this insanity, means that heterosexuals are considered normal (which we are), but that's seen as a problem to the LGTB-whatevers, since they are not.

The "Everyday Feminism" website published a story complaining that, "Heteronormativity and gender roles also rear their ugly heads on Valentine's Day," and went on to say that, "Gifts for 'him' or 'her' are clearly divided and marked and it's almost impossible to find cards that represent queer couples."[562]

The student newspaper at California State University, San Marcos published a story titled, "Heteronormative Valentine's Depictions Marginalize LGBTQIA+ Community," which whined about how "The holiday perpetuates a fixed depiction of couples and romance as primarily held between a man and a woman."[563]

The author went on to blame "the media" for the "acceptance of heteronormative relationships" as being normal and complained that there aren't enough portrayals in movies and TV shows of those in the LGBTQIA+ community.

---

[562] Everyday Feminism "Valentine's Day: What's A Feminist To Do?" by Sara Alcid (February 14th 2013)

[563] The Cougar Chronicle "Heteronormative Valentine's depictions marginalize LGBTQIA+ community" by Samantha Carrillo (February 7th 2018)

A student group at Yale University hosted an "Anti-Valentine's Day" event to fight "capitalism" and "heteronormativity." The group's flyer read, "Are you going out this Wednesday out of respect to a tradition rooted in capitalism and heteronormativity? Or have you slipped through the cracks to suffer the awkward, social consequences of aloneness on Valentine's?"[564] The event was started by a group called Engender, which wants to force fraternities to accept women (but of course, leave sororities as they are, for women only).

An elementary school in Saint Paul, Minnesota canceled Valentine's Day arts and crafts and banned the children from bringing any cards or candy to the school. The principal sent a letter to the parents saying, "My personal feeling is we need to find a way to honor and engage in holidays that are inclusive of our student population."[565]

He went on to say, "I have come to the difficult decision to discontinue the celebration of the dominant holidays until we can come to a better understanding of how the dominant view will suppress someone else's view."[566] I wish I could say this is just a joke, but it's not.

---

[564] Campus Reform "Yale group hosts 'Anti-Valentine's' to fight 'capitalism'" by Toni Airaksinen (February 13th 2018)

[565] Star Tribune "St. Paul school kisses Valentine's Day, other 'dominant holidays,' goodbye" by Paul Walsh (January 29th 2016)

[566] Ibid.

Bake the Cake, Or Else!

Leftists won a major legal victory in 2017 when a judge ordered a small bakery in Oregon to pay a lesbian couple $135,000 for "discriminating" against them after the owners refused to make them a custom "gay" cake for their "wedding."[567] It sparked a serious debate about what potential customers could force businesses to do or face similar lawsuits. This was different than refusing "service" to them because they're gay.

They could have purchased any of the pre-made cakes, but the bakers wouldn't use their artistic talent to create a custom cake for something that went against their religious beliefs. This is not a case of a business turning away customers because they're gay. It wouldn't matter if a straight customer wanted the gay cake made. It's the design of the requested product, not the sexual orientation of the customer that's the problem.

If an artist (and a pastry chef is an artist) feels uncomfortable with a design that a customer wants them to create, whether they're a pastry chef, a painter, or a t-shirt printer, that person should be able to legally refuse to make the product. This is completely different than a customer wanting to purchase pre-made products already on the shelf in a store. It's about not being forced to build something that fundamentally goes against someone's religious or personal convictions.

Should a black pastry chef be forced to design a special cake depicting KKK members hanging an African

---

[567] KATU "Final order: Sweet Cakes bakery must pay $135,000 to lesbian couple" via Associated Press (April 24th 2015)

American from a noose? Should a Jewish bakery owner be forced to make a special cake with a giant swastika on it for a neo-Nazi's birthday party? Should a photographer be forced to take nude pictures of a client? What about a videographer being forced to shoot porn for someone? When it comes to hiring an artist, no potential customer should be able to force them to use their talent or equipment to create something that they don't feel comfortable creating.

Liberals just can't seem to understand how this is completely different than flat-out refusing to allow gay people into a store or restaurant. They're free to buy anything that's on the shelf available for anyone, but they shouldn't be allowed to force someone to make them a custom product that violates that person's values.

A man in New Mexico figured if same-sex couples can now get "married" and force Christian bakeries to bake them a custom cake, then he could marry his laptop. He then sued the same bakery that was sued by a lesbian couple for refusing to bake a cake for them, demanding the bakery make a cake for him and his laptop "bride."[568]

He was just doing this to prove a point, taking the liberal position of "equality" to the next step. He then sued the state of Utah to officially recognize his "marriage" to his laptop, which he labeled a man-object marriage for "machinists" like him.

---

[568] Washington Times "Man 'marries' his laptop, sues for state recognition and a wedding cake" by Alex Swoyer (July 30th 2017)

It's Not "Normal"

If a child is born with Type 1 Diabetes, we wouldn't say that the child is "normal." We would admit that the child has a birth defect — that their pancreas is malfunctioning. Same thing is true with a child born with a cleft lip. We wouldn't celebrate the fact that the child's lip is deformed. And we wouldn't ignore reality and say that it's normal. The child undergoes surgery to fix the deformity and doctors do their best to prevent other children from being born with deformities and diseases.

But what we're seeing today with regards to gays and bisexuals is the liberal media and tech giants celebrating them as if they're special, and denying that they have a malfunction. It's like the Bible prophecy that predicted in the End Times what is right will be considered wrong, and what is wrong will be considered right.[569]

Comedian Adam Carolla has stated that in the future teenage boys may be bullied if they *aren't* bisexual. Speaking as a hypothetical teen in the future, he said sarcastically, "You don't suck dick? What's wrong with you?"[570] He also wondered, "The way things are going, my son will probably get his ass kicked for *not* being gay."[571]

Carolla is a rare conservative in Hollywood, who owes much of his success to *The Man Show* which aired

---

[569] Isaiah 5:20 "Woe to those who call evil good and good evil, who put darkness for light and light for darkness, who put bitter for sweet and sweet for bitter."

[570] The Adam Carolla Podcast

[571] Adam Carolla - *In 50 Year's We'll All Be Chicks* page 12

on Comedy Central from 1999 to 2004, a show that would likely not be allowed on a major network today due to it's "sexist" themes. In 2011 he published a book titled *In 50 Years We'll All Be Chicks*, and it seems his prediction may come true to a large extent, in half that time.

Avoiding a Cure for Homosexuality

Since simply calling homosexuality a disease, a birth defect, or a mental disorder, is considered to be a cardinal sin by the PC police; getting academic institutions or medical research facilities to invest their time and resources into looking for a cure would be blasphemy. Lack of folic acid in a woman's diet during pregnancy causes spina bifida, a birth defect that has largely been eliminated in the modern world thanks to a simple prenatal multi-vitamin.[572]

Similarly, a vitamin C deficiency was found to cause Scurvy, another disease that has practically been eradicated thanks to a basic vitamin.[573] Certain industrial chemicals,[574] food additives,[575] and household cleaners have been banned after it was discovered they caused birth defects when coming into contact with pregnant

---

[572] Mayo Clinic "Spina Bifida: Symptoms and Causes"

[573] T.K. Basu, D. Donaldson, in Encyclopedia of Food Sciences and Nutrition (Second Edition), 2003

[574] New York Times "A Study Finds Link Between Birth Defects And Solvents" by Gina Kolata (March 24th 1999)

[575] Fox News "Chemical in macaroni and cheese tied to birth defects, says study" (July 14th 2017)

mothers.[576]   What other birth defects and diseases could be prevented with a simple remedy that is being overlooked, or for whatever reason just isn't known, or if known, is suppressed?

The celebrity gossip website TMZ, which is run by homosexual Harvey Levin, once published a revealing story about Bruce Jenner's transformation into a "woman" which contradicted everything the gay community and the liberal media had been saying for years about "gay conversion therapy."   The article reported, "Several prominent doctors in the field tell us, the hormones often change sexual preference," and according to one study of 300 transsexuals, one third of them changed their sexual preference.[577]

The National Center for Biotechnology Information confirms these figures regarding sexual orientation changing due to hormone therapy.[578]

So since hormone therapy has been shown to change people's sexual orientation in over 30% of the cases, why isn't this area of science being explored to help homosexuals fix their sexual attraction disorder, thus

---

[576] Parents Magazine "Chemical Exposure During Pregnancy: What You Need to Know About Environmental Hazards in Pregnancy" by Richard Schwarz, MD

[577] TMZ "Bruce Jenner Sexual Preference Uncertain After Cross-Sex Hormone Therapy" (February 6th 2015)

[578] NCBI National Center for Biotechnology Information "Transgender Transitioning and Change of Self-Reported Sexual Orientation" by Matthias K. Auer, Johannes Fuss, Nina Hohne, Gunter K. Stalla, and Caroline Stevens via PLOA Online (October 9th 2014)

curing them?[579]   Same-sex attraction is obviously the result of a malfunction in the basic sex drive of humans, and it is a perversion in the same way a man in his twenties making out with an 85-year-old grandma is disgusting, because it is a violation of the fundamental sexual and social design of human beings.

---

[579] I'm not saying that they should be *forced* to have this done. Many homosexuals have openly expressed their hope for a cure, including Milo Yiannopoulos.

Incest

Since liberals have embraced gay relationships as "normal" and demand that gay "marriage" be accepted by all Americans because it involves "two consenting adults," the next logical step in their quest for "tolerance" leads down an even darker path. If, as liberals claim, consenting adults in homosexual relationships aren't abnormal, or disgusting, then this line of reasoning opens the door to accepting incest as perfectly "normal" as well.

In one of my Man on the Street segments for YouTube I interviewed people in San Diego about embracing incest as part of the LGBT community, and many of them said as long as the couples didn't have children, that sexual relationships between a father and his adult daughter, or a brother and a sister were no more abnormal than those in gay or lesbian relationships.[580]

Throughout human history incest has been looked at as not just taboo or gross, but also one of the most egregious violations of nature. Recently, however, we're seeing more and more incestuous couples "coming out of the closet" and have no shame about their relationships. Many of these couples consist of adult children and a parent whom they were separated from at birth and later

---

[580] YouTube "Incest Embraced by Liberals as 'Sexual Diversity' - "Nothing Wrong With It" Say SJWs" by Mark Dice (December 5th 2015)

reunited with.[581]   There appears to be a strange phenomena that happens in some of these reunion cases where the two feel a sexual attraction to each other, and instead of resisting the urge to act upon those desires, both the parent and child end up engaging in ongoing sexual relationships.

Scientists have called this Genetic Sexual Attraction, or GSA, and they report that the sexual attraction for each other is caused by the separation of a parent from their child and their reunion later in life.[582] This perversion of sexual attraction is a result of the disruption of the parent-child relationship they would have had if the parent had been around to raise the child.   And the adult child's desire to be loved by their biological parent is perverted into a sexual desire due to the separation.[583]

This is a disorder that develops from their social situation, not something that they are "born" with. The idea of having sex with one's mother or father is abhorrent for almost everyone, but something in the mind malfunctions in children separated from their parent and later manifests in GSA.

A similar situation may occur with people who are gay, which would contradict the widespread claim that people are "born" gay. Perhaps homosexuals don't have a birth defect, but may have their sexual attraction

------

581 The Guardian "Genetic sexual attraction" (May 16th 2003)

582 The Telegraph "Disgusted by incest? Genetic Sexual Attraction is real and on the rise" by Charlie Gill (September 9th 2016)

583 Ibid.

mechanism malfunction because of a disruption in their psycho-sexual development as Freud had suspected.[584]

These GSA couples aren't just being reported on by fetish websites or in sleazy porn magazines. They're making national news in major outlets, and many of the people are using their real names and showing their faces. A 51-year-old mother and her 19-year-old son "fell in love" after being reunited, and the son actually left his wife to be with his mother which he described as having "incredible and mind-blowing" sex with. He told his wife, "Every time I have had sex with you since I met her, I imagine its her I am kissing, otherwise I can't perform."[585]

Of course this kind of madness isn't just limited to heterosexual incestious couples. In Oklahoma a woman married her mother after the two were reunited and "hit it off" and "fell in love" with each other.[586] They were arrested since incest is against the law. It's important to point out that this is totally different than a parent molesting a small child who doesn't know any better.

These "children" are adults, and they're not your typical phonies on the *Jerry Springer Show* just making up a story and acting it out to get on TV. These are real

---

[584] Basic Freud: Psychoanltic Thought for the 21st Century by Michael Kahn, Ph.D page 77 - on the negative resolution of the Oedipus complex.

[585] Daily Mail "'Every time I had sex with my wife, I imagined it was my mother I was kissing otherwise I couldn't perform': In love British mother, 51, and son plan to have BABY after she broke up his marriage" by Jennifer Newton (April 8th 2016)

[586] Fox News "Oklahoma woman who married mother after two 'hit it off' pleads guilty to incest" (November 10th 2017)

people and real stories, and Genetic Sexual Attraction is getting more widely reported.

A father-daughter couple in North Carolina were recently arrested for incest after the daughter had the father's child.[587] While some outlets are framing these stories in the proper light, that this kind of behavior is abnormal and these people are sick; others are sensationalizing and seemingly glorifying it. *Cosmopolitan* magazine published a story with the headline, "Girl describes what it was like to have sex with her dad," and quote her as saying, "The sexual intensity was nothing like I'd ever felt before. It was like being loved by a parent you never had, and the partner you always wanted, at once."[588]

She went on to say, "We understood each other's bodies as if we'd been life-long lovers. I've had to teach most of my partners how to do things — and obviously he's a middle-aged man, he's had lots of sex, but there was more than that to it, some deep psychic connection. It felt like he knew me better than I knew myself. The sex was intense in a way that no other sex has been."[589]

Cosmopolitan did a similar story about a brother and a sister who were separated at birth and later reunited, and then became sexually involved with each other. "It was love at first sight, absolutely the craziest thing I have ever experienced," the woman says. "The sexual force was

---

[587] Fox News "North Carolina father-daughter couple arrested for incest after having love child" (February 4th 2018)

[588] Cosmopolitian "Girl describes what it was like to have sex with her dad" (February 19th 2015)

[589] Ibid.

like I was levitating off the earth. Your body instantly craves the other person."[590]

A 33-year-old woman in Florida was charged with incest after she gave birth to a baby fathered by her brother.[591] The two were living as a couple and had been in a sexual relationship for the last five years. These are just a few of the cases that make headlines and that we know about. There are countless more happening right now that only the perpetrators and perhaps their immediate family and friends are aware of.

It's likely only a matter of time before there is a public campaign attempting to normalize incest, and add one more letter to the ever-growing LGBT acronym in the name of being "inclusive" for GSA couples. All it would take is a famous celebrity who was put up for adoption when they were a baby and then entered into a sexual relationship with their father or mother once they were reunited to be rolled out as the poster child for "incest rights."

Actress Mackenzie Phillips, best known for her role in *American Graffiti* (1973), admitted that as an adult she had a ten-year-long sexual relationship with her biological father, but this admission came before the trend of

---

[590] Cosmopolitian "This is what it's like to fall in love with your brother" by Asher Fogle (October 30th 2015)

[591] New York Post "Woman in 'romantic' relationship with brother charged after giving birth: cops" by Jackie Salo (March 27th 2018)

incestuous couples coming out of the closet started making headlines. [592]

A society that gets offended when someone says "Adam and Eve, not Adam and Steve" will likely draw no distinction between two men in a sexual relationship, or a father and his daughter, or two adult siblings. If they're both consenting adults, "loving" who they want to "love," then to liberals that's no different than a regular heterosexual couple. There are actually blogs, Reddit threads, Tumblr accounts, and YouTube videos dedicated to promoting "incest rights" by people calling themselves "consanguineous couples," meaning blood relatives, who want incest laws repealed. [593]

One such blog concludes, "For those brought together through GSA who are enjoying their consanguineous relationships, nothing else compares. They should be free to share love, sex, residence, and marriage with each other, if that is what they want, and they should not be bullied or discriminated against." [594]

Did you ever think you'd see a world where incest is considered "normal"? Or where those on the Left would start pushing for "incest marriages" to be legally recognized, and for a repeal of the long-standing anti-incest laws on the books? It may not be an exaggeration

---

[592] ABC News "Mackenzie Phillips Confesses to 10-Year Consensual Sexual Relationship With Father" by Russell Goldman, Eileen Murphy and Lindsay Goldwert (September 23rd 2009)

[593] YouTube Account "Jane Doe" posted a seven part series titled "Consensual Incest"

[594] https://marriage-equality.blogspot.com/p/genetic-sexual-attraction.html

to say that there is no limit to the abominations that liberals are trying to promote as "normal."

Christians tried to warn people that gay "marriage" was just the beginning of the LGBT agenda, but now the Supreme Court has ruled, and so the Left continues marching along the path to perdition, advocating for perversions that extend beyond what most people could possibly imagine.

Author's Note: Please take a moment to rate and review this book on Amazon.com or wherever you purchased it from to let others know what you think. This also helps to offset the trolls who keep giving my books fake one-star reviews when they haven't even read them. Almost all of the one-star reviews on my books are from NON-verified purchases which is a clear indication they are fraudulent, hence me adding this note.

These fraudulent ratings and reviews could also be part of a larger campaign trying to stop my message from spreading by attempting to tarnish my research through fake and defamatory reviews, so I really need your help to combat this as soon as possible. Thank you!

Transgenderism

What once consisted of just a small handful of eccentric people brought on stage at the *Jerry Springer Show* for entertainment has exploded into an epidemic of "women" supposedly born in men's bodies and vice versa in some kind of strange birth defect. But that's just the tip of the transgender iceberg. Liberals now claim there are dozens of different genders, and that some people's gender is "fluid," meaning it changes from week to week (or even day to day), and some people say they have no gender at all.

For years liberals argued that gender is just a social construct, meaning the only difference between men and women is that baby boys and baby girls are treated different from birth, solely on their genitals alone, so we are each "brainwashed" into thinking and acting like a boy or a girl. Of course this is completely contradictory to the basic principals of biology which show there are distinct differences between the bodies *and brains* of males and females, not just in humans, but all mammals (and even insects).

Under the premise that a female brain can develop in a male body, then this new hypothesis of transgenderism embraces the idea that the person will feel like a woman trapped in the wrong body because their brain is hard wired to feel "female." And if the human brain is hardwired either male or female then one's gender cannot be fluid, it cannot change, and it cannot be neither. It is fixed. Not only is it fixed, but they are only *two genders,* not fifty-eight like the number of options of Facebook listed as genders in 2014.[595]

As I mentioned earlier it turns out fifty-eight weren't enough so instead of having a drop-down menu with the fifty-eight different gender identities to choose from, Facebook changed it to a fill-in-the blank so people can just put whatever they want as their gender, whether that's a reindeer or a jar of peanut butter.

It's hard to keep up with the metastasizing pathogen of liberalism today and nobody in their right mind would want to waste too many brain cells learning all the intricacies of their insanity, so if you missed it from a previous chapter, one new term they like to throw around is "cisgender," meaning someone whose gender matches their biology; or in other words a biological male with an x and y chromosome, an Adam's apple and a penis who identifies as a male. Or a "person" with breasts and a vagina who "identifies" as a woman. Quite simply, a cisgender person is a normal person.

If, in some cases, people are born in the wrong body with a brain of the opposite sex, then instead of claiming that these transgender people are "normal" people, science should find out what is causing this kind of debilitating birth defect and cure it, rather than treating them as some kind of trailblazers who are "helping" society uproot "ancient stereotypes" about sex and gender.

But the transgender epidemic raises many serious questions that most of the LGBT community don't really

---

[595] ABC News "Here's a List of 58 Gender Options for Facebook Users" by Russell Goldman (February 13th 2014)

want the scientific answers to. And their ideas about gender and what exactly a man or a woman is are rooted in delusions rather than science. But how can we deal with this problem in a way that those afflicted with transgenderism don't feel ostracized or hated, while those uncomfortable with the implications of transgenders in our society don't feel like their privacy or their safety is put in jeopardy?

What is Causing This?

What is causing this recent outbreak of transgenderism? Is it literally something in the water (or the food) that's disrupting peoples' bodies and brains like chemicals that have been found to be doing with frogs and fish?[596] Is it the radiation from cellphones, tablets and laptops disrupting the development of the fetus?

Or is it a simple vitamin or mineral deficiency during pregnancy like the cause of spina bifida? Could it be from children growing up with only one primary parent, and they're not properly imprinting what a boy or a girl is or how they should act, so their entire identity is distorted?

Many transgenders actually regret their decision after getting surgery, particularly men who have their penis removed hoping to become a "woman."[597] Some even

---

[596] Berkeley News "Pesticide atrazine can turn male frogs into females" by Robert Sanders (March 1st 2010)

[597] Newsweek "Transgender Surgery: Regret Rates Highest in Male-to-Female Reassignment Operations" by Lizette Borreli (October 3rd 2017)

have a second surgery in attempts to reverse their "transition." Britain's youngest sex change patient, who switched from being a boy to a "girl" at the age of fifteen, later got a second surgery to transition back to a man at the age of eighteen, and lived as a gay man for a few years. Then at the age of twenty-three, this person decided to get a third surgery and "transition" back into a "woman."[598]

The former top psychiatrist at Johns Hopkins Hospital, Dr. Paul R. McHugh, believes that transgenderism is a mental disorder similar to other body dysmorphia disorders like anorexia.[599] An anorexic person "feels" fat, despite being extremely (and even dangerously) thin, and doesn't feel comfortable in their own "fat" body, so they keep trying to lose weight. Similarly, Dr. McHugh and others argue that transgender people see their bodies as "defective" and don't feel comfortable in their own skin due to the same kind of mental illness.

Not only is this making *them* feel uncomfortable, but others around them as well since a Pandora's box of social complications has been opened because scientists so far haven't figured out how to prevent or cure transgenderism.

---

[598] The Mirror "Britain's youngest sex swap patient reveals why she's undergoing surgery to switch gender for the third time" by Grace Macaskill (August 5th 2017)

[599] CNS News "Johns Hopkins Psychiatrist: Transgender is 'Mental Disorder;' Sex Change 'Biologically Impossible'" by Michael W. Chapman (June 2nd 2015)

The Locker Room Question

After a woman in Michigan got uncomfortable from seeing a biological male using the women's locker room at a Planet Fitness gym she complained to the front desk, but to her surprise instead of calling the police or canceling the membership of that individual, the club revoked *her* membership instead![600]

The gym said the person with a penis using the women's locker room self-identified as a woman, so that was good enough for them. The woman whose membership was revoked for being uncomfortable with a biological male using the same locker room as her then sued Planet Fitness for invasion of privacy, sexual harassment and breach of contract, but the court ruled against her!

An editorial in *The Charlotte Observer* in 2016 said that girls need to start accepting seeing people who have "different genitalia" than them in changing rooms and showers and while, "the thought of male genitalia in girls' locker rooms — and vice versa — might be distressing to some...the battle for equality has always been in part about overcoming discomfort — with blacks sharing facilities, with gays sharing marriage — then realizing that it was not nearly so awful as some people imagined."[601] Yes, they literally compared forcing girls to

[600] The Daily Caller "The New normal: Women at Planet Fitness have to accept biological men in locker rooms" by Amanda Tidwell (June 8th 2017)

[601] Charlotte Observer "Taking the fear out of bathrooms" by The Observer Editorial Board (May 13th 2016)

shower with men to blacks sharing the same bathrooms as whites.

CNN's Chris Cuomo, the brother of New York Governor Andrew Cuomo (D) said if a father doesn't want his 12-year-old daughter to share locker rooms and showers with naked people who have a penis, that he's "intolerant."[602]

At Northern Arizona University activists put up a sign outside a bathroom encouraging students not to question whether someone is using the "right" bathroom because it would offend "gender variant people" or put them at risk of "verbal, sexual, and physical assault."[603] The sign also said that cisgender people have "pee privilege" because nobody gets uncomfortable with them using the bathroom.

As this push to allow biological males to use any women's bathroom, locker room, or shower they want by self-identifying as a "woman" began to gain momentum, normal people became concerned about sexual predators being able to enter the facilities where women would be easy prey. While you will never hear about it in the mainstream media, there have been dozens of recent cases where men dressed as women have been caught

---

[602] Washington Examiner "Cuomo absent from CNN after transgender comments" by Eddie Scarry (February 24th 2017)

[603] Washington Times "Arizona college asks students to consider 'pee privilege' over transgender issues" by Douglas Ernst (May 9th 2017)

videotaping girls in bathrooms, showers, and changing areas.[604]

There have also been many women physically attacked by these kinds of crossdressing perpetrators.[605] For example, a transgender prisoner who "identifies" as woman despite not having sex-change surgery, was incarcerated with the female prisoners for an unrelated crime and within just a few days had sexually assaulted four of the women inmates, so authorities moved him to a male prison.[606]

When this gender-bending phenomena was heating up in 2016, I did an experiment by asking random people on the beach to sign a petition which I said would mandate a few urinals be installed in all women's public restrooms for the transgender "women" who use the women's bathroom despite having a penis "so they feel more welcome" there and can pee in a urinal like they're used to. You can watch the video on my YouTube channel, which was shot in San Diego, California and a shocking number of people eagerly signed it.[607]

---

[604] Breitbart "Top Twenty-Five Stories Proving Target's Pro-Transgender Bathroom Policy Is Dangerous to Women and Children" by Warner Todd Hudson (April 23rd 2016)

[605] Toronto Sun "Predator who claimed to be transgender declared dangerous offender" by Sam Pazzano (February 26th 2014)

[606] Daily Mail "Daily Mail: Trangendered prisoner who was put in a female jail despite not having sex-change surgery 'sexually assaulted four women inmates'" by Rod Adehali (July 17th 2018)

[607] YouTube "Urinals in Women's Bathrooms" by Mark Dice (June 13th 2016)

Women's Spa Under Attack

A women's spa in Toronto caused an uproar after it was discovered they had a "no male genitals" rule in their full nudity facility. After one trans "woman" took to Twitter to complain (when don't they?) the spa released a statement signaling they would soon change their policy. "Because Body Blitz Spa is a single-sex facility with full nudity, we are not like other facilities. We recognize that this is an important discussion for single-sex facilities to have and we will seek to find a satisfactory resolution."[608]

York University Professor Sheila Cavanagh claimed the spa was violating gender discrimination laws and that, "There are many ways of being trans and there are many ways of being a woman. And certainly surgery or hormones, per se, do not make a woman.... I think it's gender identity that matters and what is between our legs is our own business."[609] So if I decided to be "gender fluid" for a day to try out "being" a woman, I would be allowed in a fully nude women's spa?

The way gender discrimination laws are being interpreted means that if I decided one day that that I was gender "questioning" and wanted to live as a woman to see how I liked it, then I could use the women's showers at the gym and there is nothing anyone can do to stop me. In fact, if the gym kicked me out, I could sue them for

---

[608] The Star "Trans community speaks out against Body Blitz women-only spa" by Briony Smith (June 16th 2017)

[609] The Globe and Mail "Toronto's Body Blitz Spa in hot water for turning away transgender women" via The Canadian Press by Cassandra Szklarski (June 14th 2017)

discrimination. I asked a police officer what would happen if the gym reported me for doing so and he said the police in California would do nothing, and couldn't stop me.

The Cotton Ceiling

Liberals have even come up with the term "cotton ceiling" (a spin-off from "glass ceiling" which they claim prevents women from advancing in their careers). The "cotton ceiling" though describes the 'obstacle' that transgender "women" face from straight men not wanting to have sex with trannies. "The cotton ceiling is real and it's time for all queer and trans people to fight back," reads one blog post about it on QueerFeminism.com.[610]

The term was coined by a transgender "woman" and is also said to describe trans "women" or "men" being excluded from female or male "spaces." They've also coined the acronym TERF, which stands for "Trans-Exclusionary Radical Feminist," meaning feminists who don't accept transgender "women" as women, and so the TERFs are labeled hateful bigots.[611]

On *Celebrity Big Brother* in the UK, one of the contestants was a transgender "woman" who asked American singer Ginuwine if he would date a transgender person and he replied "no." The "woman" then leaned over and said "Let's have a kiss" and tried to kiss him,

---

[610] QueerFeminism.com "The Cotton Ceiling Is Real and It's Time for All Queer and Trans People to Fight Back" (March 27th 2012)

[611] New Statesman "Are you now or have you ever been a TERF?" by Terry MacDonald (February 16th 2015)

causing him to back away. BET [Black Entertainment Television] asked if this was "transphobic behavior" with many viewers denouncing him on Twitter for being a bigot and transphobe![612]

Riley J. Dennis, a "woman" whose Adam's apple sticks out almost as far as "her" nose, thinks that the reason most men are sexually attracted to vaginas is because men are brainwashed to think that's what they're supposed to feel. "Maybe your preference for women with vaginas over women with penises is, to some degree influenced by our cis-sexist society," Dennis says in a YouTube video titled "Your dating 'preferences' are discriminatory," promoting this ludicrous idea.[613] You may have to read through what "she" said a few times before you can begin to wrap your mind around just how delusional these people are.

Men are now bigots if they aren't attracted to transgender "women" who have a penis, according to the latest arguments from the trans community. *Vice News* complained about the negative responses the video generated, saying, "This video struck a nerve in far-right circles, which led to a harassment campaign against Riley carried out by an angry cyber-mob of thousands of users systematically down-voting her videos and sending her hurtful content, comments, and venomous response

[612] BET "Ginuwine Refused To Kiss A Trans Woman On Live TV And Now The Internet Is At War" (January 8th 2018)

[613] https://twitter.com/RileyJayDennis/status/884991412202229760

videos."[614] The writer then complained about people having a "no trans dating preference."[615]

Vice went on to argue, "Sexuality and gender aren't simply something that comes from some biological imperative. They are phenomena that are developed through a messy brew of social, cultural, historical, and psychological factors. They can also prove to be lightly malleable if we try to dig into the foundations of how those oppressive structures influence the ways we see and understand the world."[616] You must not be opposed to hooking up with a tranny, or else you are a "cis-sexist" bigot now.

Aerobics icon Richard Simmons sued *The National Enquirer* after they reported he had been living his life as a tranny, claiming it was defamation. He was not living as a tranny, but lost the case because the judge claimed that being called transgender shouldn't be seen as an insult, even if it's a false claim and the person is not. Richard Simmons not only lost the defamation case, but had to pay *The National Enquirer* $130,000 for their legal fees.[617]

Since the culture has changed so much recently, and in the wake of Richard Simmons losing his lawsuit, it's likely that if someone is falsely smeared as a homosexual

---

[614] Vice News "What's Wrong With the 'No Trans' Dating Preference Debate" by Abigail Curlew (February 23rd 2018)

[615] https://twitter.com/vicecanada/status/967121462418063360

[616] Vice News "What's Wrong With the 'No Trans' Dating Preference Debate" by Abigail Curlew (February 23rd 2018)

[617] Page Six "Richard Simmons must pay $130k to National Enquirer, Radar Online" by Kathleen Joyce (March 13th 2018)

in the press, they may have no legal recourse since the courts will follow the precedent set by Richard Simmons' lawsuit and claim that being called gay isn't defamatory because "there's nothing wrong that that."

"Some Women Have Penises"

Transgender activists on social media like Riley J. Dennis and Zinnia Jones claim that "some women have penises" and "men can menstruate."[618] Jones says, "We need to resist this push to misgender trans women using very specifically chosen definitions and applications of 'biological' and 'male.'"[619] And that "If we accept the use of terms like 'male' or 'male genitals' for trans women, people now have an excuse to call us partially or fully male."[620] "She" went on to say that, "Referring to a trans woman's penis as 'male genitals' might seem harmless or even common-sense. It's not. It's the thin edge of the wedge."[621]

Just enter a search into Twitter for "some women have penises," and you'll find countless tweets from social justice warriors arguing that this is the case and engaging in online arguments with others trying to convince them

---

[618] The Blaze "Transgender 'feminist' lays down the law: 'Some women have penises'" by Dave Urbanski (March 23rd 2017)

[619] https://twitter.com/ZJemptv/status/885209576257327104?lang=en

[620] https://twitter.com/ZJemptv/status/885210401042038784

[621] https://twitter.com/ZJemptv/status/885209894483349506

of this. There are even people selling T-shirts online that say, "Some Women Have Penises. Get Over It."[622]

The infamous "Pussy Hat" came to prominence during the 2017 feminist Women's March which was the day after President Trump's inauguration where participants carried signs that read "Pussy Power" and "This Pussy Grabs Back" to console each other after Hillary Clinton's loss, but the "Pussy Hat" becoming the symbol of the Women's March was offensive to some because it was too "reproductive system-focused" and marginalized transgender "women" who don't have pussies. One transgender activist wrote an essay for the University of Oregon's student newspaper, *The Daily Emerald*, to complain that too many women were equating womanhood with having a vagina.[623]

Another social media maniac tweeted, "Today I'm talking about my vagina for #VaginaFriday, promoting women's health. Did you know, you don't have to have a vagina to be a woman?"[624] Reading through these people's Twitter feeds is like taking a tour of an old fashioned insane asylum, but it's not just a few random weirdos online making these kinds of claims. These ideas are being fully embraced by mainstream media, major universities, and the Big Tech giants.

---

[622] https://www.google.com/search?q=some+women+have+penises+t-shirt&ie=utf-8&oe=utf-8&client=firefox-b-1

[623] The Daily Emerald "Griggs: Intersectionality in reclaiming words" by Taylor Griggs (March 25th 2017)

[624] https://twitter.com/adorkablegrrl/status/880820632010854400

"Some Men Have Periods"

Google has installed tampon dispensers in men's bathrooms at their headquarters in Silicon Valley because they love being on the cutting edge of "diversity."[625] Brown University also installed tampon dispensers in men's bathrooms,[626] and there is a "movement" to have all colleges (and businesses and public bathrooms) do the same thing in what they call the "Free the Tampon" movement.[627]

"Nobody expects you to carry around your own toilet paper, and so in the same sense we don't think it should be required or expected of people to pay for or carry around their own tampons or pads," says one proponent.[628] They're literally calling it the fight for 'menstrual equality.'

A 24-year old transgender "man" named "Cass" Clemmer began free bleeding to "raise awareness" that "Periods are Not Just For Women" and that "It's harmful

---

[625] Breitbart "Rebels of Google: Tampons Kept in Men's Restrooms Because 'Some Men Menstruate'" by Lucas Nolan (August 17, 2017)

[626] Breitbart "Brown University Providing Tampons in Men's Bathrooms Because 'Both Sexes Menstruate'" by Ben Kew (September 8th 2016)

[627] Chronicle of Higher Education "Tampons in Men's Rooms? It's Just a Small Part of 'Menstrual Equality,' Campus Activists Say" by Alex Arriaga (May 16th 2017)

[628] Teen Vouge "Colleges to Offer Free Menstrual Products in Men's Bathrooms" by De Elizabeth (May 22nd 2017)

to equate periods with womanhood."[629] "Free bleeding" means she doesn't wear a tampon and has her period blood seep through her pants which creates a large bloodstain on her crotch. How it's not illegal for a woman to walk around and sit on chairs in restaurants or other public places and leave them smudged with period blood is a question that remains to be answered.

The Daily Beast, an online website run by the parent company of *Newsweek*, declared, "Yes, Men Can Have Periods and We Need to Talk About Them" in a bizarre article claiming, "Menstruation isn't just a 'women's issue.'"[630] The writer got triggered by a joke on Twitter about "if men had periods" and penned a lengthy essay about how some "men" do "have periods." "We do not need to hypothesize what the world would be like if men had periods. Some men do have periods, as do some non-binary people."[631]

A popular health website called Healthline.com, which is one of the top 250 most-visited websites in the United States according to Alexa (the Internet web traffic analytics firm)[632] has decided to stop using the word "vagina" when referring to women's genitals in their "safe sex guide" because they're concerned the term is

---

[629] People "Transgender Activist Freebleeds to Show Men Can Menstruate Too: It's 'Harmful to Equate Periods with Womanhood'" by Julie Mazziotta (July 25th 2017)

[630] The Daily Beast "Yes, Men Can Have Periods and We Need to Talk About Them" by Zoyander Street (September 21st 2016)

[631] Ibid.

[632] https://www.alexa.com/siteinfo/healthline.com

associated with women, and have opted to start calling them "front holes" to be more "gender-inclusive."[633]

They explained that historically sex education "discriminated" against trans and gender nonbinary people, and that, "These guides also often unnecessarily gender body parts as being 'male parts' and 'female parts' and refer to 'sex with women' or 'sex with men,' excluding those who identify as nonbinary. Many individuals don't see body parts as having a gender — people have a gender."[634]

The post, which it notes was "medically reviewed" by a doctor before being published, says, "the notion that a penis is exclusively a male body part and a vulva is exclusively a female body part is inaccurate. By using the word 'parts' to talk about genitals and using medical terms for anatomy without attaching a gender to it, we become much more able to effectively discuss safe sex in a way that's clear and inclusive."[635]

"For the purposes of this guide, we'll refer to the vagina as the 'front hole' instead of solely using the medical term 'vagina.' This is gender-inclusive language that's considerate of the fact that some trans people don't identify with the labels the medical community attaches to their genitals."[636]

---

[633] Yahoo News "People are angry over this safe sex guide, which calls the vagina a 'front hole'" by Elise Sole (August 21st 2018)

[634] Healthline.com "LGBTQIA Safe Sex Guide" by Mere Abrams (July 13th 2018)

[635] Ibid.

[636] Ibid.

It continues, "For example, some trans and nonbinary-identified people assigned female at birth may enjoy being the receptor of penetrative sex, but experience gender dysphoria when that part of their body is referred to using a word that society and professional communities often associate with femaleness. An alternative that's becoming increasingly popular in trans and queer communities is front hole."[637]

"Some Men Get Pregnant"

In 2014 the Midwives Alliance of North America updated their website to be more "inclusive" of transgender people by removing all references to mothers being women, and now calls them "pregnant people" or "birthing individuals" because in their mind, "men" can be pregnant too.[638]

Another midwife organization, Woman-Centered Midwifery, denounced the move, posting an open letter reading, "We know as midwives that biological sex occurs at the level of our DNA and the gametes we produce, and is immutable." While acknowledging, "gender is cultural and gender norms vary across the globe," they pointed out that, "Sex is natural, biological and objectively factual," and "Human beings, like the majority of other mammals, are sexually dimorphic. i.e. there are two distinct biological sexes."[639]

---

[637] Ibid.

[638] https://mana.org/healthcare-policy/use-of-inclusive-language

[639] https://womancenteredmidwifery.wordpress.com/take-action/

It went on to say, "by embracing the idea that any human other than those in a class called women carry offspring to term, give birth to them and nurse them, we are prioritizing gender identity over biological reality," and that, "We are allowing gender identity to be the primary way that we refer to one another, even for a biological process like birth."[640]

"The very few gender-identified males that have given birth or accessed an abortion have only done so because they are female-bodied people, and that scientific fact cannot be erased...We must fight the forces destroying the living material world and telling us that cultural distractions are more real than life itself. There is life-giving power in female biology. As midwives we protect the lives of the life-givers: women, mothers, females, and their offspring. We must not become blinded to the biological material reality that connects us."[641]

The British Medical Association has declared that the term "expectant mothers" is offensive to transgender people, and insists they be called "pregnant people" instead because some "men" can get pregnant too.[642] The British government then recommended an amendment to the International Covenant on Civil and Political Rights, a UN treaty, to reflect the "more inclusive" language

---

[640] Ibid.

[641] Ibid.

[642] The Telegraph "Don't call pregnant women 'expectant mothers' as it might offend transgender people, BMA says" by Laura Donnelly (January 29th 2018)

because "It's not women who get pregnant — it's 'people.'"[643]

When a Planned Parenthood clinic tweeted out that "Some men have a uterus," the post was celebrated by Leftists online and was "liked" over 63 thousand times.[644] One clothing company even sells "gender neutral" maternity wear, because "not all pregnant people are women."[645] It's probably only a matter of time before major retailers like Target and Walmart start carrying maternity clothes for "men."

In April 2017 the Dove soap company put out a commercial featuring "real moms" called "No Right Way," showing new moms with their babies and praising the 'diversity' in how they were raising them. "We are both his biological parents," says a man who now identifies as a woman as he is shown rocking his new born baby. "You get people that are like, 'What do you mean you're the mom?' We're like, 'Yep! We're both gonna be moms.'"[646]

Facebook suspended me for a week and locked me out of my page for posting a link to an article about the commercial because I added the comment, "Excuse me now while I go grab some Irish Spring [a competitor's

---

[643] The Sunday Times "It's not women who get pregnant — it's 'people'" by Andrew Gillian (October 22nd 2017)

[644] https://twitter.com/PPIndKentucky/status/969384341636861952

[645] Mashable "Gender-neutral maternity wear: Not all pregnant people want to wear pink" by Haley Wilbur (June 6th 2016)

[646] NewsBusters "Dove Ad Features Transgender Mom: 'No One Right Way'" by Sarah Stites (April 12th 2017)

soap] to clean up my puke." That was "hate speech" they said.[647]

"Some Men Can Breastfeed"

In our backwards world we're now seeing articles from *Time* magazine (not the *Onion*) that read, "My Brother's Pregnancy and the Making of the New American Family," which is an essay by a woman about her "brother" who was born female but now identifies as a man, and who got pregnant and gave birth to a poor unfortunate baby who was then breastfed by its bearded lady mother (photos of this were included in the article.)[648]

"Americans are just starting to open up to the idea that you may be born into a female body, but believe that you are really a man. But what if you are born into a female body, know you are a man and still want to participate in the traditionally exclusive rite of womanhood? What kind of man are you then?" the essay begins.[649]

The woman who wrote the "pregnant brother" article has a father who later divorced her mother at age 50 and then came out as gay, so you know there's something seriously wrong with their gene pool or family life.

The La Leche League USA, (a breastfeeding educational and support organization with more than

---

[647] Breitbart "Facebook Suspends YouTuber for Disliking 'Transgender Mother' Commercial" (April 14th 2017)

[648] Time "My Brother's Pregnancy and the Making of a New American Family" by Jessi Hempel (September 12th 2016)

[649] Ibid.

300,000 Facebook followers) wished "Happy Father's Day to all the chestfeeding dads out there," and said that they are "excited to support you."[650]

What is "chestfeeding," you ask? Their post went on to explain, "Chestfeeding is the term often used by transgender men and nonbinary people who nurse their babies. Although both men and women have breast tissue, the word 'breast' is most often associated with women. Trans men may be more comfortable referring to their 'chest' and 'chestfeeding' or 'nursing' their infants rather than 'breastfeeding.'"[651]

It continued, "When we think about breastfeeding, the image that comes to mind — the one pushed on us by society, medical professionals and the media alike — is that of a mother nursing her newborn baby. Brochures, websites and PSAs promote the picture of a woman lovingly looking at her child as the baby suckles at her breast. The language accompanying this imagery is inevitably gendered, specific to cisgender women who are nursing a baby that they themselves gave birth to."[652]

Jake Kathleen Marcus, a lawyer who is "the nation's foremost expert on breastfeeding law," suggests we "rethink" the term "Nursing Mother." "The term 'mother' is itself problematic," she insists, because, "Kids are

---

[650] https://www.facebook.com/LaLecheLeagueUSA/photos/a. 264537160241504.82770.253475138014373/1676238509071355/? type=3

[651] Ibid.

[652] The Huffington Post "The Troubling Erasure of Trans Parents Who Breastfeed" (November 30th 2015)

nursed by people who are not their mothers all the time."[653]

The Huffington Post is of course on board with changing the terminology because saying "nursing mothers" and "women who nurse" is offensive to transgender and "non-binary" parents. They're not happy about the slogan for La Leche League International either because it is "Happy Mothers Breastfed Babies."[654]

In fact, to call breastfeeding natural is offensive and "unethical," according to *The Journal of Pediatrics* now. "Coupling nature with motherhood...can inadvertently support biologically deterministic arguments about the roles of men and women in the family (for example, that women should be the primary caretaker," they claim.[655]

"Referencing the 'natural' in breastfeeding promotion...may inadvertently endorse a set of values about family life and gender roles, which would be ethically inappropriate."[656]

"Men Can Have Abortions"

The brain damage-inducing website "Everyday Feminism" is upset that medical clinics and society as a whole use 'gendered' language when referring to women

---

[653] Ibid.

[654] Ibid.

[655] Journal of Pediatrics "Unintended Consequences of Invoking the 'Natural' in Breastfeeding Promotion" by Jessica Marucci and Anne Barnhill (April 2016 Volume 137 Issue 4)

[656] Ibid.

getting abortions, because in their world — men can have abortions too, and so can gender non-binary people because, "not everybody who has a functioning uterus identifies as a woman."[657]

They published an article that is accompanied by a video of a woman from the "All Access Coalition" pro-abortion group who looks and sounds like a woman, but identifies as a non-binary person and was upset because when she went to get an abortion at the age of twenty, "The people at the clinic constantly read me as a woman and called me 'ma'am,' 'she,' [and] 'miss.'"[658]

She was literally upset that people at the abortion clinic were referring to her as a woman! Who the hell else is going to be getting an abortion?!! "Having an abortion is tough enough without having to navigate constant misgendering. It's like being slapped every two seconds," she said.[659]

In the description of the video posted on the All Access Coalition's YouTube channel, it reads, "Jack was 20 when they had an abortion. The forms, paperwork, and language left them feeling isolated. They share their story to remind everyone that we don't all identify with the gender we were assigned at birth. By changing our language and being mindful of others, we can make

---

[657] Everyday Feminism "Why we need gender neutral language for abortion access" by Jack Qu'emi (September 13th 2016)

[658] Ibid.

[659] Ibid.

abortion care more accessible to all. Support Jack by sharing their story."[660]

It should read "she" shared her story, but instead it's a complete grammatical mess because her "preferred pronouns" are "they," "them," and "their" so the description says "they shared their story," when it's referring to only one person — her!

Sports

If a man wants to wear makeup, a wig, and a dress in the privacy of their own home, as long as they're not hurting anyone, that's fine. But we shouldn't have to go along with their delusion or treat them like a normal person when they step outside into the public. And we shouldn't have to allow them to compete in sports as a woman either — whether in a private league, a high school sports team, or professionally. But unfortunately many people are doing this and it's getting out of control.

A transgender weight lifter in New Zealand won a series of competitions and despite looking like a man, having the muscle structure of a large man, and weighing over 200 pounds, "she" has been allowed to compete as a woman because that's how "she" identifies.[661] "She" even set several new international records for the "women's competition."

A transgender MMA fighter named Fallon Fox was born male, but identifies as a woman and fought other

---

[660] https://www.youtube.com/watch?v=sFmba7xtUlo

[661] Washington Times "Transgender weightlifter sets New Zealand records for second time" by Bradford Richardson (April 30th 2017)

women in mixed martial arts competitions, once fracturing the eye socket of "her" opponent and giving her a concussion during a 2014 fight. In the post-fight interview Fox's opponent said, "I've fought a lot of women and have never felt the strength that I felt in a fight as I did that night. I can't answer whether it's because [he] was born a man or not, because I'm not a doctor. I can only say, I've never felt so overpowered ever in my life, and I am an abnormally strong female in my own right."[662]

Light-heavyweight kickboxing champion Andrew Tate joked about identifying as a woman for a while in order to become the best female kick boxer in his weight class just to illustrate how absurd it is to allow biological males to fight in the women's division.   He was denounced as a transphobe for bringing up the issue.

A biological male won the women's division in the El Tour de Tucson cycling race in November of 2016.[663] A transgender high schooler in Alaska runs track on the girls team, despite being a biological male.[664] A six-foot-tall transgender "woman" plays on a women's semi-pro football team in Minnesota.   At first the league turned "her" down for obvious reasons, and due to safety concerns about letting men play against women in the

---

[662] WhoaTV "Exclusive: Fallon Fox's latest opponent opens up to #WHOATV" by Alan Murphy (September 17th 2014)

[663] World Net Daily "Female athletes crushed by 'women who were once men'" (March 26th 2017)

[664] Anchorage Daily News "At Alaska state track meet, a transgender athlete makes her mark" by Beth Bragg (May 31st 2016)

league. "She" then sued for discrimination to force the league to let "her" play.[665]

A six-foot, eight-inch tall male joined a women's basketball team at a Jr. college in Santa Clara, California in 2012 after a judge awarded "her" with a new birth certificate indicating he was a "female."[666] A 24-year-old male joined the UC Santa Cruz women's volleyball team in 2016, an NCAA Division III level team,[667] and there are many, many more instances which raise serious concerns about fair competition.

UFC announcer Joe Rogan said, "If you had a dick at one point in time, you also have all the bone structure that comes with having a dick. You have bigger hands, you have bigger shoulder joints. You're a fucking man. That's a man, OK? You can't have... that's... I don't care if you don't have a dick anymore..."[668] That was back in 2013 before the PC Police started trying to ruin the careers of anyone who resisted the radical LGBT agenda. It's surprising Rogan hasn't been fired for his comments.

Pandora's Box has been opened. Courts have already ruled on many of these cases and there doesn't appear to

---

[665] MPR News "Snubbed by one team, transgender football player feels at home at last" by Laura Yuen (March 10th 2017)

[666] CBS 13 Sacramento "6-Foot-8 Transgender Player Takes Court Against Delta College Women's Team" by Steve Large (December 18th 2012)

[667] UC Santa Cruz News Center "Student challenges assumptions about transgender athletes" by Nicole Freeling (September 8th 2016)

[668] Bleacher Report "UFC's Joe Rogan to Transgender MMA Fighter Fallon Fox: 'You're a F***ing Man'" by McKinley Noble (March 18th 2013)

be much of a chance of putting the toothpaste back in the tube. The best thing you can do is keep your own family functioning properly and do your best to insulate them from the backwards culture that liberals are creating.

Trans Privilege

Transgenders are a "protected class" of people, which means that they are legally provided special treatment by the government, not to mention from the social media giants who consider any disparaging remarks about them to be "hate speech." At most major award shows now, like the Grammys, Oscars, and MTV's Video Music Awards, transgender celebrities like "Caitlyn Jenner," "Lavern Cox," and "Gigi Gorgeous" are regular presenters or given front row seats to the events so the cameras can pan over to them at some point to capture their reactions to the show.[669]

Barack Obama commuted "Chelsea" (Bradly) Manning's prison sentence, setting "her" free after just a few years into serving "her" 35-year sentence for stealing classified documents and turning them over to Wikileaks. There was no reason to grant "her" clemency, since "she" put Americans' lives at risk by stealing the classified information, and the only reason Obama let "her" out of prison is because "she" is a famous transgender.

If there's any doubt that this was to throw a bone to the LGBT community, then you should know that Obama issued the clemency order on "International Day Against

---

[669] Time "Laverne Cox Told Everyone to Google This Transgender Student at the Grammys" by Maya Rhoda (February 13th 2017)

Homophobia, Transphobia & Biphobia," another made-up "holiday" for liberals to promote their agenda.

Caitlyn Jenner is perhaps the world's most celebrated transgender person, largely because "she" was part of the hideous Kardashian family, marrying Kim Kardashian's mom after her divorce from Robert Kardashian, one of O.J. Simpson's lawyers. Shortly after Bruce Jenner came out as trans, "she" was even given an ESPY award by ESPN for "excellence," an award that usually goes to an athlete who has overcome tremendous challenges.

But ESPN decided "Caitlyn" Jenner deserved the award over an Iraq veteran who lost an arm and a leg yet went on to become a competitive runner and crossfit athlete, and also passed over a college basketball player who played with a brain tumor.[670]

In 2015 "Caitlyn" was involved in a deadly car crash on Pacific Coast Highway in Malibu, California where Jenner's SUV rear-ended another vehicle, causing the victim's car to be pushed into oncoming traffic where it was then hit head-on, killing the driver instantly. Jenner was facing manslaughter charges, but the Los Angeles District Attorney decided not to file them, leading some people to believe that "she" got let off not just because "she" was from the Hollywood royal family, the Kardashians, but because it would have been a PR nightmare since "she" had recently become a huge

---

[670] National Review "Yes, ESPN Did Pick Caitlyn Jenner Ahead of Iraq War Vet and Amputee Noah Galloway for the ESPY Courage Award" by David French (June 3rd 2015)

transgender star, and they can do no wrong. The victim's family then sued Jenner for wrongful death.[671]

Liberals' love for "Caitlyn" soon turned to scorn after "she" mentioned "she" was a Republican and admired Republican Senator Ted Cruz because he's a Constitutionalist.[672] Apparently transgender people are only supposed to be Democrats.

Emojis Not "Inclusive" Enough

We're all unfortunately familiar with emojis. And while a few of them, like a smiley face or a laughing face with tears of joy may help convey what we mean in a text message, unfortunately the number of emojis just keep growing and growing and now include symbols of food, buildings, and just about anything one can imagine. Anything except a pregnant man, so the SJWs are upset about this "lack of diversity."

"If Unicode [the organization responsible for which emojis are added to smartphone keyboards] wants proper gender representation in emoji, it needs to be able to represent pregnant people who aren't female," said one

[671] Los Angeles Times "Caitlyn Jenner settles lawsuit with stepchildren of woman killed in PCH crash" by Christie D'Zurilla (January 28th 2016)

[672] National Review "'Tolerant' Liberals Start Insulting Bruce Jenner When He Says He's Conservative" by Katherine Timpf (April 27th 2015)

activist who got upset when they added a softball emoji, but no transgender or non-binary people.[673]

She complained, "Adding gender to Unicode was a massive mistake right from the start. The basic premise just didn't make sense to me [but] now that they have done it, they stubbornly refuse to actually do gender properly," she said.[674]

Up until 2015, emojis were all yellow, like PacMan, but the SJWs wanted different races represented, so then new options were added to the emoji keyboard which allowed users to choose the shade of skin tone for the emojis, ranging from pale to very dark.[675]

How come all the emojis are of people with two eyes? What about people who have only one eye due to a birth defect or an accident? Why aren't *they* represented? Why do they all look like they're people of an average weight? Where are the obese emojis? How come the emojis all have two arms and two legs? Why are amputee people not represented? Of course I'm being sarcastic, but I'll bet that soon social justice warriors will seriously try to argue these points and persuade the tech companies to include even more "diversity" emojis to satisfy them. And I have little doubt that the emojis will then be added.

---

[673] ABC.net.Au "The case for a 'pregnant male' emoji" by Tiger Webb (February 15th 2018)

[674] Ibid.

[675] CNN "Black emojis are coming" by Aaron Smith (November 4th 2014)

They Can't Take A Joke

Since most liberals are miserable because of their strange fixations and hallucinations of racism and sexism around every corner, they can't have any fun and also try to ruin the fun for the rest of us. One of the things that triggers them the most are jokes about "trannys." Just the word "tranny" sets them off, but they're also extremely sensitive about any jokes making fun of "trannys," or any of the gender-bending nonsense.

After Michelle Obama spoke at the Democrat National Convention in 2016, I sarcastically tweeted how nice and "inclusive" it was of the Democrats to include a transgender speaker, and people went so nuts I started trending on Twitter from all the hate. When cartoonist Ben Garrison depicted Michelle Obama as being a muscular, angry-looking person with a bulge in her crotch, people freaked so bad calling it "racist" and "transphobic" that it made headlines.[676]

While hosting the iHeartRadio Music Awards in 2015, Jamie Foxx upset idiots on the Internet for cracking some jokes about Bruce Jenner, who had recently announced his plans to "transition" into a woman. "We have some groundbreaking performances here, too, tonight," Foxx began. "We got Bruce Jenner, who will be here doing some musical performances. He's doing a his-and-her duet all by himself." Some of the audience groaned, to which he responded, "I'm just busting your balls…while I

---

[676] Dallas News "Here's why this Michelle Obama/Melania Trump cartoon is despicable" by Leona Allen (May 18 2016)

still can."[677]   Of course the tweets flooded in to Twitter accusing him of "transphobia" and denouncing iHeartRadio for allowing him to host the show.

During the taping of Spike TV's *Guy's Choice Awards* in 2015, 85-year-old Clint Eastwood cracked a joke about Caitlyn Jenner transitioning, but when the show aired a few days later, the network had cut the "inappropriate" joke out.[678]

When Dave Chappelle returned to the spotlight with two Netflix specials in January 2018, he upset some of his fans because he said he finds transgender people to be hilariously strange.[679]   Despite saying he has empathy for them, and supporting their goals of being accepted in society, he just pointed out how he's surprised most of them don't see the humor in their predicament.   His jokes were called "reckless" and "hateful."

Saturday Night Live has been under fire for their *It's Pat* skits from the early 1990s which featured a gender ambiguous person named Pat, and depicted him (or her) in various situations where people interacting with Pat struggled with trying to discover his/her gender so they wouldn't offend Pat by using the wrong pronouns. During a GLAAD [Gay & Lesbian Alliance Against Defamation] panel at the Television Critics Association in 2017, the creator of *Transparent* (a transgender drama

---

[677] Time "Jamie Foxx Blasted for 'Transphobic' Bruce Jenner Jokes" by Laura Stampler (March 30th 2015)

[678] Deadline "Clint Eastwood's Jenner Joke Cut From Spike's Guys Choice Awards" by Erkik Pedersen (June 8th 2015)

[679] The Guardian "Dave Chappelle's 'reckless' #MeToo and trans jokes have real after-effects" by Brian Logan (January 4th 2018)

produced by Amazon Studios) blasted *It's Pat* saying it was an "awful piece of anti-trans propaganda."[680]

Actress Julia Sweeney who played Pat responded, "None of the jokes were made at Pat's expense, but I can see how today that what we did is so next-door to laughing *at* the person for not having clear gender characteristics. So, I can see how it might seem like you're laughing at the person."[681] She also acknowledged that the skit probably wouldn't be allowed on network TV today because, "It seems so completely inappropriate at this point in time."[682]

How much longer until Jim Carrey's old *In Living Color* sketches of him being a "female body builder" are censored from the Internet for being "transphobic" as well? Or Martin Lawrence's skits of him playing the character, Sheneneh? Or Tyler Perry's movies for him playing female characters for comedic effect? The slippery slope of censorship will likely continue, and careers will be derailed or destroyed when someone dares to poke fun at the now-forbidden topic.

In 2016, ESPN analyst and former All-Star pitcher Curt Schilling was fired after he posted a "transphobic" meme on his personal Facebook page denouncing a recently proposed law aimed at allowing anyone to use

---

[680] SFGate "Jill Soloway Cites 'SNL' Sketch 'It's Pat' as 'Awful Piece of Anti-Trans Propaganda'" by Tony Magilo (August 4th 2017)

[681] The Wrap "Julia Sweeney Responds to Jill Soloway's 'It's Pat' Transgender Criticism" by Tim Kennealy (Septermber 6th 2017)

[682] Ibid.

any bathroom or locker room they wanted to if they self-identified as that gender.[683]

The meme showed a hideous looking transgender "woman" with the caption "Let him in to the restroom with your daughter or else you're a narrow-minded, judgmental, unloving racist bigot who needs to die." ESPN released a statement saying they are an "inclusive company" and that, "Curt Schilling has been advised that his conduct was unacceptable and his employment with ESPN has been terminated."[684]

YouTube often removes videos and issues community guideline strikes on channels that make fun of other gender-bending YouTubers.[685] You can't call them crazy, you can't criticize them, and you can't even laugh at them now without risking career-ending repercussions.

Transgender Trojan Horse

At first "transgender rights" were just about the "bathroom bill" and the Left wanting anyone to be able to use whatever bathroom they wanted, no matter what their biological sex is, but this was just a trojan horse so they could unleash their actual plan. It was never just about

---

[683] The New York Times "Curt Schilling, ESPN Analyst, Is Fired Over Offensive Social Media Post" by Richard Sandomir (April 20th 2016)

[684] Ibid.

[685] Cowger Nation "EXPOSED: Screenshot from Riley's private Facebook reveals he engages in censorship" by Hunter Avallone (April 1st 2017)

bathrooms, it's about locker rooms and showers at schools and gyms.

The "bathroom" angle was a straw man because bathrooms are generally private with stalls or allow just one person in the room at a time, but in school showers and locker rooms, naked transgender people walk around right next to everyone else, and if there is no objective standard for what actually makes someone "transgender" or "gender questioning" then what's to stop *anyone* from just deciding one day they want to use the women's showers at their local gym?   Nothing.   And that's horrifying.

Since transgenders tend to be mentally unstable, do we really want to allow men who think they're a woman, or who could just *say* that they think they're a woman — to be able to walk into women's locker rooms at will?

Just like legalizing gay "marriage" was the radical LGBT lobby getting their foot in the door so they could spread their agenda in schools and get ahold of children, the early push for "transgender bathroom rights" was just a smokescreen. Instead of being satisfied with gays being able to marry, the LGBT groups kept pushing even more radical agendas like having teachers read elementary school children books about gay characters, and now hold "Drag Queen Story Hour." They are even attacking the very nature of boys and girls as their assault on normalcy has accelerated to the point that just calling a boy, a "boy" or a girl a "girl" is offensive!

A website called TransKids.biz actually sells prosthetic penises for young "trans" girls (called silicon packers) along with underwear for boys that will help hide their penis (called "Tuck Buddies Underwear"). The

TransKids website was started by a "woman" who had previously launched a similar site for adults. "After years of helping adults find high-quality gender expression gear, she saw the need for a site and store that focused more on kids and their unique needs," reads the "About Us" page on TransKids.biz.

It goes on to say, "Searah [the founder] hopes that all parents coming here can trust that this is a safe and affirming place, where helping your kids live fully and embodied is our only goal."[686] The website shows photos of the horrifying child products you will wish you had never seen.

And if you dare call these people "mentally ill" then they scream that it's "hate speech" and want you banned from social media, and your career ruined. They are determined to mold society into their image and will try to destroy anyone who gets in their way. One can only begin to imagine what they have in store for the future if we allow them to keep cramming their agenda down our throats.

---

[686] https://transkids.biz/pages/about-us

Transracialism

Liberals painted themselves into a corner by denying basic biology when they began accepting people who "identify" as dozens of different genders and embracing this "choose your own gender" insanity, and this kind of backwards "logic" has now led to people "identifying" as someone of another *race*, despite what their actual heritage and DNA is.

Many liberal media outlets embraced Rachel Dolezal, the first woman to popularize "transracialism," as a black woman. She is the blonde-haired, blue-eyed white woman who uses skin bronzer and dyes her hair trying to pass herself off as black. She was thrust into the spotlight after a local TV news station asked her about her race after rumors began circulating that she was pretending to be black in order to work at the local NAACP [National Association for the Advancement of Colored People] in Spokane, Washington.

MSNBC host Melissa Harris-Perry (who herself is black) asked, "Is it possible that she might actually be black? Some of us are born cisgendered, some of us are born transgendered, but I wonder can it be that one would be cis-black and trans-black, that there is actually a different category of blackness that is about the achievement of blackness despite one's parentage. Is that possible?" Her guest, an associate professor at Stanford, responds, "It's absolutely possible, I mean, why not?"[687]

Trying to capitalize off the controversy, Dolezal soon wrote a memoir about why she thinks she's really black, and when CNN interviewed her about it, instead of pointing out that she's mentally ill, the host Michael Smerconich compared her "transracialism" to transgenderism and believes that she actually is black! Smerconich began the interview saying, "Let me share with my audience some of what I learned about you from the book. I learned that as a child at age four — put this up on the screen — when you were asked to sketch yourself, you sketched yourself as a black child. You fantasized that you were from Africa. When Aunt Becky wanted to get you a Raggedy Ann or Andy doll, you finish the story, what kind of doll did Aunt Becky get you?"[688]

Rachel Dolezal responds, "Well, she actually made me a black Raggedy Ann and Andy doll."

Smerconish sets her up for her next talking point, asking "How come?"

"Well, because she kind of recognized and seemed to understand my affinity for black is beautiful and black is inspirational," she responds.

The host continues, "You went to Howard University for your masters. You were raised with four adopted black siblings. You braided their hair. You married a

---

[687] MyNorthWest "Rachel Dolezal is everything that's wrong with political correctness" by Jason Rants (June 17th 2015)

[688] CNN "Smerconish" Interview with Rachel Dolezal (April 1st 2017)

black guy. I was thinking Caitlyn Jenner as I was reading the book. Is there an analogous situation here?"

"Well, I think a lot of people have drawn that parallel," she concludes.

Rachel Dolezal recently changed her name to Nkechi Amare Diallo, and unfortunately this woman is not just a lone nut and the nation's only "transracial person." There are others who suffer from this same delusion.

Trans 'Korean' Man

A blonde hair blue eyed man from Brazil decided to undergo plastic surgery to get "slanted eyes" to make himself look Korean after he spent a semester studying abroad there and fell in love with the country.[689] Of course he dyed his hair black and also wears brown contacts hoping to achieve the look. He also changed his name from Max to Xiahn. If you see his pictures, he looks like a bizarre anime character or an Asian doll, and says it took ten different surgeries to get him the results he desired.

White Man Identifies as Filipino

A Florida man fell in love with Filipino culture after watching a documentary on the Discovery channel and then decided to start identifying as a Filipino.[690] Unlike

---

[689] Fox News "White Florida man says he now identifies as Filipino" (November 13th 2017)

[690] New York Post "'Transracial' man was born white, identifies as Filipino" by Jackie Salo (November 13th 2017)

the man who wanted to be Korean, this "trans-Filipino" man didn't get any plastic surgery, he just started identifying as Filipino and changed his name from Alex to "Ja Do."

He also bought a small vehicle called a Tuc Tuc, which is popular in the Philippines, and uses it as his mode of transportation. "Ja Do" also dyed his hair pink and identifies as a woman, making him the world's first transgender, transracial individual. It's possible that he's just pranking the media to see if they would accept his ideas, but it's impossible to tell because people are that crazy, and people do accept him as a Filipino.

When psychologist Dr. Stacey Scheckner was interviewed about "Ja Do's" new racial identity, instead of recommending he actually see a psychologist, she said, "If someone feels that they feel at home with a certain religion, a certain race, a certain culture, I think that if that's who they really feel inside life is about finding out who you are. The more knowledge you have of yourself, the happier you can be."[691]

Wiggers

In the 1990s when rap music went mainstream, a lot of white suburban kids began to idolize rappers like Dr. Dre, Snoop Dogg, Ice Cube, and other gangster rappers who had become counterculture figures. These kids not only emulated their ridiculous clothes by wearing pants five sizes too big so they sagged so low their butts were

---

[691] USA Today "'Transracial' man born white feels like he is Filipino" by Garin Flowers (November 15th 2017)

hanging out, and turned their baseball caps sideways so they looked like goofballs. They also started talking like them too, sounding as if they grew up in an inner city ghetto, despite living in white suburban America for their entire lives. They were called wiggers, (white niggers), and there were so many of them the term is now listed in the dictionary, which defines them as, "White youth who adopt black youth culture by adopting its speech, wearing its clothes, and listening to its music"[692]

With the help of bullying, thankfully many of these kids straightened up and later began speaking proper English instead of ebonics, but some wiggers still exist. I'm not sure if these people are guilty of "cultural appropriation" or have embraced transracialism, but one thing is certain — these are the dumbest kids on the block whose very identities have been destroyed by the noise pollution they call music.

Indian Man Pretends to Be Black

And if all this isn't crazy enough, an Indian man (meaning his ancestors are from India, not a Native American) who kept getting turned down from medical schools he applied to decided to identify as black, figuring he could get accepted because of affirmative action. So when applying to new schools he checked the "African American" box for his race, shaved his head and trimmed his eyelashes, (apparently because Indians have long eyelashes or longer eyelashes than black people), and he

---

[692] Dictionary.com definition of "Wigger"

was soon accepted to Saint Louis University Medical School.[693]

Unlike other "transracial" people, he did this partially as a joke and as an experiment since it's widely known that many schools give preferential treatment to black people when considering their acceptance, allowing them in over other students who have better grades just because they are black. He later wrote a book about his experience called *Almost Black: The True Story of How I Got Into Medical School By Pretending to Be Black.*

An interesting side note is that he is the brother of actress Mindy Kaling, best known for her role on NBC's *The Office.* After her brother's book came out and his story started making headlines she publicly denounced him and his fakery, but he says when he was first considering the idea she actually encouraged him and thought it was a great and hilarious plan.

Embracing "Transracialism"

The Rhode Island School of Design now offers a course on transracialism, not as part of a psychiatry or psychology class to explore this newly emerging mental illness, but to embrace it as part of the broader trans movement. The course description reads, "Technological advances in surgery, hormonal therapy, psychiatry, [and] cultural warfare are catching up to the transgender presence: the gendered body is not necessarily that with

---

[693] New York Post "Why I faked being black for med school" by Vijay Chokal-Ingam (April 12th 2015)

which we were born, but one that can be crafted to match the real body of our psyche, our dreams."[694]

It went on to express disappointment that people's "racial self remains tethered to biology," and "Blackness, Whiteness, Asianness, Latinness, the whole rainbow of racial identification, is still construed as biologically inescapable and inevitable." It noted the mockery that "transracial" people like Dolezal have received, claiming that it is "contrary to the everyday experience that actually finds racial identification as a process that is always transracial...Declaring ourselves racially, we all cross restricted zones in becoming ourselves."[695] The description concludes, "In this course, we will use the discourse of transgenderism to build an alternate vocabulary of race."

So the Left have accepted transgender and transracialism as "normal" and so some of you may be wondering, "what's next?" Identifying as a different age? Or a different species? I'm sorry to tell you, but the crazy train hasn't stopped. It's still going full steam ahead.

---

[694] Campus Reform "Rhode Island college offers 'Transracial Bodies' course" by Anthony Gockowski (July 26th 2017)

[695] Ibid.

Trans-Species

Since the Left have embraced the idea that a man can be a "woman" if he "feels" like one with no medical evaluations or scientific benchmarks to support this belief, and that a white woman can be black, and a white man can be a Filipino woman because that's how they "identify" despite the clear opposition to basic biological facts; then what's to stop them from embracing the idea that some "people" have decided that they're not even human?

On the Internet you can find communities of people who do just about anything, no matter how obscure, strange, or disturbing. And the ability of crazy people to seek out and find others online who are afflicted with the same fetish or mental illness has emboldened them by making them feel that because there are others out there who feel the same way, their behavior or beliefs aren't something to be ashamed of, but instead something to be proud of because it's just "who they are."

Since many "open minded" and "non judgmental" liberals are accepting the idea that there are fifty-eight different genders and a white person can be black or Filipino if they "feel" like it, then the next step down the path of liberal logic is to embrace people who identify as animals. This group of "people" exist, and they have a name: Otherkind, as in "another kind of" or a "different kind of" creature, and they are people who do not identify as human, or identify as only partially human.

Some believe that they are genetically part animal (or elves, dragons, or aliens, as you will see) and others believe that because of reincarnation, they have an animal spirit but are stuck living in a human body for this life. Some even use the term "species dysphoria" to describe this disorder, a spinoff of body dysphoria that anorexic and transgender people suffer from.

Some of these "Otherkind" work at Google, as was revealed in a wrongful termination lawsuit filed against the company by James Damore who was fired for writing his infamous "anti-diversity" memo which called in to question Google's hiring practices and "diversity" goals.

One part of the lawsuit reads, "Google furnishes a large number of internal mailing lists catering to employees with alternative lifestyles, including furries, polygamy, transgenderism, and plurality, for the purpose of discussing sexual topics. The only lifestyle that seems to not be openly discussed on Google's internal forums is traditional heterosexual monogamy."[696] It then notes that, "For instance, an employee who sexually identifies as 'a yellow-scaled wingless dragonkin' and 'an expansive ornate building' presented a talk entitled 'Living as a Plural Being' at an internal company event."[697]

You would expect such deranged people to be embraced by tabloid TV shows and exploited by clickbait websites that feature stories about freaks and weirdos, but the fact that Google is catering to these "Otherkind"

---

[696] Breitbart "Damore Lawsuit Claims Google Let Employee Who Identifies as 'Yellow-Scaled Wingless Dragonkin' Give Presentation" by Lucas Nolan (January 10th 2018)

[697] Ibid.

identities proves there is virtually no limit to the level of mental illness they will enable in the name of diversity.

The Cat Girl

A 20-year-old woman in Norway apparently believes that she is a cat living in a human body. With the mass mental illness we're seeing affecting so many people around the world, it certainly is possible that she isn't joking, and really is this crazy. She wears cat ears and walks on all fours around her house, saying, "Sometime I hiss when meeting dogs in the street," because of her "instincts."[698]

The "cat girl" even claims that she can see better in the dark than during the day. She is seeing a psychologist who told her that she can "grow out of it" but she doubts it and thinks she'll be a "cat" for the rest of her life.

A man who went by the name of "Stalking Cat" transformed himself to look like one using 14 different surgeries after he says a "medicine man" told him that he was born with the spirit animal of a tigress.[699] He also attended furry conventions and once lived with a couple he met at one. He committed suicide at the age of 54.

There is even a company that sells tongue brushes which people stick in their mouth and then "lick" their cat with. I'm not sure if they're meant as a joke or not. The Amazon listing says, "Licking your cat is an oddly

---

[698] New York Post "This woman has the biggest dating red flag ever" by Lindsay Putnam (January 29th 2016)

[699] New York Daily News "'Cat Man' found dead in Nevada, rumors of suicide" (November 13th 2012)

meditative practice, soothing for both you and your cat." It also says the brush will help people "bond" with their cat, "by communicating in their language," and using it will help your "relationship" with your cat "deepen."[700]

The Elf Man

A 25-year-old man in Argentina who became obsessed with elves as a child spent tens of thousands of dollars on plastic surgery to transform himself into one by tattooing the whites of his eyes black, having his facial and body hair surgically removed, and got a nose job and liposuction on his jaw. He wears pointy prosthetic ears and is saving up his money for more surgery to make them permanently pointed. He also wants to undergo a "limb lengthening" operation to make himself six and a half feet tall and wants several of his ribs removed to make his waist thinner.

"I consider myself trans-species, in the same way transgender people feel," he says. "I need to become how I feel inside, I don't expect people to understand but I ask they respect it."[701]

He explains, "I was bullied as a child and as an escape I would submerge myself in fantasy movies like

---

[700] https://www.amazon.com/PDX-Pet-Design-Licki-Brush/dp/B07793L9ZZ?th=1

[701] Daily Mail "'I consider myself trans-species': Fantasy fan transforms himself into an ELF with £25,000 of plastic surgery including full body hair removal, skin bleaching and eye colouring" (May 3rd 2017)

Labyrinth and *The NeverEnding Story*, as well as other fantasy tales."[702]

On a personal note, I was picked on as a child too, for being extremely skinny because I was such a picky eater. People often called me an "Ethiopian" because of the mass starvation there and the popular Sally Struthers' TV commercials airing when I was a kid asking for donations to help feed the people. And do you know how I dealt with the bullying? I started eating right and working out, and by the time I was in my early twenties, I was 200 pounds of solid muscle and was dating the most beautiful girls you could imagine.

That's how you should overcome being bullied as a kid, or you can focus on building a successful career, leaving your bullies in the dust as you climb to the top of your profession. Meanwhile the "tough" guy who picked on you in school ends up working at a local factory making minimum wage and is only happy when he's watching his favorite football team on TV while he's getting drunk hoping to forget about how pathetic his life has become for a few hours before Monday morning rolls around again.

By being afraid to judge others for the abnormal ways they deal with life's difficulties we are only contributing to a perpetual cycle of maladjusted weirdos running around making things worse for everybody.

---

[702] Ibid.

Puppy Identity

Everyone has likely heard of the BDSM [Bondage and Sadomasochism] subculture of sexual deviants whose brains are fried from watching too much porn, so they turn to mixing sex with violence in attempts to get off. And this "community" has recently given birth to the "Puppys" which are mostly gay men (go figure) who like to dress up in elaborate full-body latex BDSM dog costumes.

There is an entire documentary on these psychos that aired on Channel 4 in England in 2016 and the London *Guardian* reported the "Secret Life of the Human Pups is a sympathetic look at the world of pup play, a movement that grew out of the BDSM community and has exploded in the last 15 years as the Internet made it easier to reach out to likeminded people. While the pup community is a broad church, human pups tend to be male, gay, have an interest in dressing in leather, wear dog-like hoods, enjoy tactile interactions like stomach rubbing or ear tickling, play with toys, eat out of bowls and are often in a relationship with their human 'handlers.'"[703]

"You're not worrying about money, or food, or work," one of the "puppies" said. "It's just the chance to enjoy each other's company on a very simple level." Another one of these freaks interviewed in the "Human Pups" documentary explains, "It's pre-rational, pre-conscious. It's an instinctive, emotional space. But within every puppy is a person. This is part of my identity, but it's only

---

[703] The Guardian "The men who live as dogs: 'We're just the same as any person on the high street'" by Nell Frizzell (May 25th 2016)

part. I'm also a vegetarian, play the piano; I have a parrot. I was planting tomatoes on my allotment this morning. I can go months without going into pup space."[704]

He continues, "There is an immense amount of pleasure from gambolling around in a club playing with squeaky toys because you're making people laugh, you're being a cute little puppy. The gay scene can be very serious, scary and offputting. But if you're going in with a little puppy hood, ears and a tongue, you look cute. You're allowed to bound around and be enthusiastic, mischievous and friendly."[705]

Another "puppy" says, "People automatically jump to the conclusion that this is gear we wear to have sex. I used to get asked awful questions like, if I liked having sex with dogs. But it's certainly not that, and it's not always sexual. Members of my pack, we spend a lot of time together at home just being dogs. There's nine of us and my partner is our handler. A big part of it is a feeling of family and belonging; we're there to look after each other."[706]

Genderless Alien

A 23-year-old Oregon man wants to have his genitals surgically removed as the final step in his quest to transform himself into a "genderless alien." He had

---

[704] Ibid.

[705] Ibid.

[706] Ibid.

already spent $60,000 on surgery, including a nose job, tattooing the whites of his eyes black and having his facial hair removed by laser treatments.

He wants his nipples and belly button removed too so his body is just one smooth surface, and says, "My goal in regards to my look is to become an exact, scientifically proportioned, sexless human being."[707]

"People talk about 'gender reassignment' but I'm looking to have 'gender unassignment.' I'm looking to change my genitals so there is nothing there. There will just be a hole to pee out of."[708]

Plastic surgeons are reluctant to perform the kind of operation he wants because there are muscles in the genital area that prevent the urethra from leaking urine, so they are recommending the typical male to female gender reassignment surgery instead, but he's not happy with that option. "I don't want to become a woman, I just want to have nothing," he says.

His sister was concerned about his final step, but now supports his decision. "I do worry that he'll change his mind about surgery later in life but the more we talk about it, the more it actually feels like this is actually truly what he needs and wants to be more authentically him."[709]

---

[707] The Sun "Man who wants his GENITALS removed to become a 'sexless alien' is warned it could be impossible... as he'll have no way to urinate" by Becky Pemberton (May 26th 2017)

[708] Ibid.

[709] Ibid.

Transgender Dragon Lady

A 55-year-old Arizona man decided to transform himself into a transgender "dragon lady" by having his ears and nose surgically removed, and then had the whites of his eyes tattooed green, his tongue forked, added prosthetic horns on his head using subdermal implants, and had "scales" tattooed all over his face, chest, and arms. He was born Richard Hernandez, but as part of "her" transformation, he changed his name to Eva Tiamat Baphomet Medusa and now identifies as a dragon.[710]

On it's website the creature explains, "I shed my human skin and my physical appearance and my life as a whole leaving my humanness behind."[711] "She" once worked as a banker, but it's unclear how "Tiamat" earns a living today. I assume it's only income is from getting paid to make appearances at freak shows and tattoo conventions. "She" is also HIV positive.[712] What a surprise.

As you know, these aren't the only cases of people undergoing extreme body modification. We've all seen the photos of the people with their entire faces tattooed and have subdermal implants protruding from their face, but the "Transgender Dragon Lady" takes the cake for the

---

[710] Mirror.co.uk "Transgender woman 'Dragon Lady' chops ears off to look like a reptile" by Kara O'Neill (September 9th 2016)

[711] Ibid.

[712] Daily Mail "Transsexual 'dragon lady' who was born a man reveals how an HIV diagnosis inspired her to morph into a reptile, complete with a forked tongue and HORNS - because she 'didn't want to die a human.'" By Unity Blott (February 27th 2018)

craziest of them all. It's also amazing that any licensed doctor would actually perform unnecessary surgeries like cutting off someone's ears and nose. Perhaps he had to go to Mexico, but who knows.

Feminism and Sexism

To liberals, sexism is just a one-way street where women are always the victims and men (the patriarchy) are always the perpetrators. And to fight back against this massive masculine conspiracy some women have united together in the name of feminism, which in the past did have a legitimate purpose, but as time went on has morphed into an angry mob of misfits who blame men for all of the world's problems.

Feminism is broken down into four different "waves." The first wave started in the early 1900s and involved the right to vote (women's suffrage), the second wave continued to dismantle legal inequalities in the 1960s, and then by the 1990s what's known as the third wave had lost its focus since there were no real goals that needed to be accomplished anymore in order to establish "equality" in America. But that didn't stop them from trying to do *something*.

The fourth wave of feminism, which is the current incarnation, started around 2012 when social media had become a huge part of our lives, connecting fat, ugly, crazy women from different parts of the country through the Internet so they could hang out together in delusional online echo chambers where they come up with new "causes" to "fight" for since they're too intellectually weak to have any real hobbies and too emotionally abrasive to have boyfriends.

Their social media campaigns kept getting more insane with no real purpose other than to shock people and get them some attention. In 2016 the "Shout Your Status" campaign was started on Twitter in which feminists began publicly admitting to having various sexually transmitted diseases as a way to 'reduce the stigma' of having one![713] They were embraced by other radical progressives who called the campaign "amazing" and encouraged more women to "come out" of the STD closet.[714]

Free Bleeding

One of the countless crazy modern feminist causes they're fighting for today is the right to not use tampons, or any kind of feminine hygiene product while they're on their period—a practice they call "free bleeding." As you can imagine the blood visibly seeps through their pants leaving a big red splotch on their crotch that is impossible not to notice. One yoga teacher posted photos on her Instagram of her "free bleeding" in white yoga pants while striking up various poses in order to raise awareness for the cause.[715]

---

[713] Breitbart "Feminists: It's a 'Privilege' to Have a Sexually Transmitted Disease" by Dr. Suzan Berry (April 15th 2016)

[714] Revelist "This is the amazing reason women are telling the world they have STIs" by Emily Shugerman (April 7th 2016)

[715] https://www.instagram.com/carleebyoga/

She's a mother of three who free bleeds and breastfeeds her 18-month-old all while doing yoga at the same time![716] In one photo she posted, she can be seen striking a yoga pose with one leg up in the air while her two small children hug her other leg, appearing to bleed, or almost bleed on their heads because her period blood was running down her leg right by the children's faces.[717] Why would anyone do this, you ask? "I take time each cycle to be grateful that I can bleed and I incorporate it into my yoga practice to honor all of the women who have it and those that can not," she explains.[718]

A woman ran the London Marathon during her period without a tampon and bled all over her crotch and had blood running down her legs to "raise awareness" of periods (as if we aren't already painfully aware of them), and to encourage women not to be embarrassed about them. "Despite cramping and pain, [many women] hide it away and pretend like it doesn't exist. I ran to say, it does exist, and we overcome it every day."[719]

Olympic gold medalist Aly Raisman was pressured by *People* magazine to "free bleed" and stop using tampons. "Aly Raisman has her fair share of period woes, but the Olympic gold-medalist says she won't take to free bleeding like other athletes," the magazine said,

---

[716] Metro UK "Meet the mum who freebleeds and breastfeeds while doing yoga" by Jessica Lindsay (February 20th 2018)

[717] Ibid.

[718] Ibid.

[719] People "Woman Runs London Marathon Without a Tampon, Bleeds Freely to Raise Awareness" by Char Adams (August 7th 2015)

271

disappointed in her. "Raisman, 22, recently teamed up with Playtex Sport to take away the stigma surrounding women and their periods. But the athlete says letting her period flow freely — not using a cup, tampon or pad while menstruating — just isn't her thing."[720]

Another free bleeding "activist" named "Barron" (who uses the gender neutral pronouns "they" and "their" because "it" doesn't identify as a woman) started free bleeding when "it" was a teen, in part because "it" was concerned that using tampons and pads would contribute to environmental waste.[721]

"It" also free bleeds in order to raise awareness of periods, because, "Society, in general, is really fearful of menstruation and people who menstruate. This is a bodily function that we're told is gross and that we have to conceal."[722] And for that reason, this woman (who denies she's a woman and identifies as gender non-binary) wants to bleed all over the place so everyone knows when that time of the month rolls around.

A woman who identifies as a "witch" gave herself a facial using her menstrual blood, "to show that periods are nothing to be ashamed of."[723] Free bleeding may have actually started out as a 4Chan prank after people from

---

[720] People "Aly Raisman Won't Free-Bleed Like Other Athletes: I Don't 'Have the Confidence'" by Char Adams (April 7th 2017)

[721] Canadian Broadcasting System "Free the period: Why some women choose to free-bleed" by Katrina Clarke (October 30th 2017)

[722] Ibid.

[723] The Sun "BLOODY HELL: Self-proclaimed 'blood witch' smears period blood on her face to break stigmas around menstruation" by Nicola Stow (January 9th 2018)

the infamous Internet forum posted fake photoshopped images of women "free bleeding" for various causes and spread them around online as a way to mock radical feminists, but it appears that nothing is too crazy for them to actually do, and they again erased the line between parody and reality.

The Vagina Challenge

In June 2017 women began posting videos online of themselves yelling the word "vagina" as part of "the Vagina Challenge," after the Vagisil feminine itch cream company announced they would donate $5 to Planned Parenthood for every video that was posted. Many women literally yelled "vagina" in public places like coffee shops and busy sidewalks.[724]

The "Vagina Challenge" seemed like a 4Chan prank trying to trick women into doing something so ridiculous since tons of people had been jumping on the latest "Internet challenges" lately, but it was a real campaign started by Vagisil, and women were actually doing it.[725]

If men started yelling "penis" in public as loud as they could and posting video of themselves doing so, they would likely be arrested for sexual harassment, but feminists thought making fools of themselves was fun and felt they were supporting a good cause by screaming at strangers about their vaginas.

---

[724] PJ Media "Feminists Shout 'VAGINA' in Public for Planned Parenthood. WTF." by Megan Fox (July 26th 2017)

[725] DigiDay "Vagisil shrugs off 'Vagina Challenge' backlash" by Ilyse Liffreing (August 1st 2017)

Grilling Out is Sexist

Grilling up some burgers and brats, or God forbid some steaks, is now under assault for "perpetuating sexism" and "toxic masculinity." A "man" who writes for the London *Guardian* griped that barbecuing is, "a biologically deterministic blizzard of bullshit that sees women as salad-spinners and men as the keepers of the grill, the tenders of the flame, lords and masters of the meat.   It's a sausage-fest out there, and it's getting ugly."[726]

He went on to say, "don't we share stuff such as childcare, cooking and cleaning?   This grilled-food gender split is ubiquitous, odd and unacknowledged."[727] It sounds like this loser is afraid he'll burn himself if he fires up the grill, or doesn't know how to cook a basic burger.

"How — and why — do men continue to claim this sacred fire-space as a male-owned sanctuary where women are not permitted?" he asks.   It's because for thousands of years men ventured out into the wild to hunt for protein, and then came back to the camp and cooked it while the women watched after the children so they wouldn't stumble into the fire, moron!   And normal people like to keep some of the traditions that our ancient ancestors developed because its part of the human experience, and by dividing up the necessary activities to

---

[726] The Guardian "Why do normal men turn sexist when they get in front of a barbecue?" by Mike Power (July 19th 2013)

[727] Ibid.

get through life, men and women can work in concert together to make it more enjoyable for everyone!

After a group of college kids put a funny and entertaining ad on Craigslist looking to hire a "BBQ Dad" for an afternoon of grilling out with them, feminists were upset because it was, "a harsh reminder of how gender roles become the star of the stage during a BBQ."[728] The ad said they were looking for an older fatherly figure to join them to, "Talk about dad things, like lawnmowers, building your own deck, Jimmy Buffett, etc. Funny anecdotes are highly encouraged. All while drinking beer."[729] But a group of college guys aren't allowed to enjoy the tradition of grilling out with each other anymore.

One feminist critic complained that the meat is the central focus of a barbecue, saying, "All the annoying, extra bits that make a barbecue work go unpraised, but the meat? That's the star of the show. Whoever cooks the meat gets praised and thanked for their brilliant job."[730]

A male feminist who writes for *Slate* is so conflicted about being a feminist and liking to grill, that he wrote a whole article describing his struggle. "I hate how much I love to grill," it starts. "It's not that I'm inclined to vegetarianism or that I otherwise object to the practice itself. But I'm uncomfortable with the pleasure I take in something so conventionally masculine. Looming over

---

[728] Metro "why do barbecues bring out our inner sexists?" by Rebecca Reid (June 6th 2017)

[729] Ibid.

[730] Ibid.

the coals, tongs in hand, I feel estranged from myself, recast in the role of suburban dad. At such moments, I get the sense that I've fallen into a societal trap, one that reaffirms gender roles I've spent years trying to undo. The whole business feels retrograde, a relic of some earlier, less inclusive era."[731]

Another triggered feminist complains, "there's one aspect of the barbecue that I just can't get my head around. Not the desire to use a substandard cooking facility for no better reason than that it's outside, but the way that having a barbecue sends groups of intelligent, emancipated people back to the 1950's."[732]

She goes on to complain that men, "stand around the big fire, drinking beer and discussing the best way to cook meat [but] the women sit around a table, drinking rosé and perhaps making a salad," and asks, "where else socially do we segregate ourselves so strongly?"[733]

Apparently it's not just grilling meat which is a problem. Just eating it is. A Ph.D. candidate at Pennsylvania State University argues that simply eating meat perpetuates "hegemonic masculinity." She argues that, "Doing vegetarianism in interactions drives social change, contributing to the de-linking of meat from gender hegemony and revealing the resisting and

---

[731] Slate "Grillax, Bro. I'm a feminist. I'm a dude. And I hate that I love to grill" by Jacob Brogan (July 22nd 2015)

[732] Metro "Why do barbecues bring out our inner sexists?" by Rebecca Reid (June 6th 2017)

[733] Ibid.

reworking of gender in food spaces."[734]   She also said that, "vegetarians defy attempts to hold them accountable to gendered social expectations," whatever the hell that means.

Air Conditioning is Sexist

Virtually nothing is safe from being sucked into the social justice warrior vortex where everything is racist, sexist, homophobic, transphobic, ablest, etc., etc.— not even air conditioning. As you know, most women wear skirts even in the winter time (which is completely asinine), but they want to show off their legs and as much skin as possible, so they wear skirts and sleeveless low cut tops to the office, whereas men wear a suit and tie (which is also asinine, but that's a subject for a whole other book).

And because women choose to wear such skimpy clothes, they often get cold, even in the office during the summer time since the air conditioning keeps room temperatures down in the low seventies or upper 60s, depending on who is in control of the thermostat.

But for feminists there's more to it than that. They see a sexist conspiracy behind it all. "Most AC units are designed for a man's body temperature — not a woman's" says one columnist who whined about the "sexist air-conditioning" problem in offices in an article titled "Air

---

[734] Gender, Place & Culture: A Journal of Feminist Geography by Anne DeLessio-Parson (Volume 27, 2017- Issue 12)

Conditioning In Your Office is Sexist: True Story."[735] She went on to explain, "In modern offices, most climate control systems are based on the resting metabolic rate of a 40-year-old man, which runs up to 30 per cent faster than a woman's."[736]

Since men have more muscle, their core body temperature is slightly higher on average than women (only .4 degrees higher), and one study cites the average hand temperature for women is 87.2 degrees, while men's are 90 degrees.[737]

This particular columnist went on to warn about the "dangers" of offices being too cold saying they cause "thicker blood," an "increase in blood pressure" and the "tightening of the airwaves." She concludes her sob story by saying, "If that's not an incentive for employers to finally sort out the AC problem once and for all, I don't know what is."[738] What the hell does she want employers to do? Segregate men and women, putting them into different offices so the women can have a separate HVAC unit and keep the temperature warmer?

Other outlets have covered this "controversy," including *The Washington Post* with their "investigation"

---

[735] The Telegraph "Air conditioning in your office is sexist. True story" by Radhika Sanghani (August 3rd 2015)

[736] Ibid.

[737] Ibid.

[738] Ibid.

titled, "Frigid Offices, Freezing Women, Oblivious Men."[739]

A *Time* magazine writer was upset that the issue wasn't being taken seriously enough by society and also concluded that air conditioning is sexist. "Certain facts, no matter how well-established, are always being contested by those who think that just because they themselves do not understand or experience them, that they are not, in fact, facts," she wrote, pointing to the same "evidence" of women's body temperature being lower than men's.[740]

The New York Times reported, "Chilly at Work? Office Formula Was Devised for Men," and mentioned a recent "study" that looked into the conspiracy by the *Nature Climate Change* journal which recommended it's time to end "gender-discrimination" in "thermal comfort."[741]

Since feminists think the world revolves around them, the solution to this "problem" isn't to just put on a sweater, or stop wearing skimpy clothes to the office, but that the standardized office temperature should be raised by a few degrees, which would obviously cause men wearing heavy sports coats and tight collars wrapped with ties around their necks to become uncomfortably warm

---

[739] Washington Post "Frigid offices, freezing women, oblivious men: An air-conditioning investigation" by Petula Dvorak (July 23rd 2015)

[740] Time "It's August, It's 2016, Let's Just Acknowledge the Office A/C Issue" by Kastallia Medrano (August 24th 2016)

[741] New York Times "Chilly at Work? Office Formula Was Devised for Men" by Pam Belluck (August 3rd 2015)

with no recourse because most dress codes require men to wear a suit and tie.[742]

"Abortions are Cool"

After a viral meme game on Twitter of people wishing for certain kinds of Disney Princesses called "We Need a Disney Princess Who…[fill in the blank], a Planned Parenthood branch tweeted (and then later deleted), "We need a Disney Princess who's had an abortion," sparking outrage and disgust among conservatives. But *Jezabel*, a radical feminist website created by Gawker Media and currency owned by Univision, endorsed the idea and posted an article titled, "Statistically, at Least 2 Disney Princesses Have Had Abortions,"[743] and cited a poll claiming 23.7 percent of women will have had an abortion by the age of 45.

Some researchers say that figure is inaccurate because it's based on certain subgroups of women (poor, and black) who have a much higher abortion rate compared to the general population, and then those numbers were extrapolated to represent *all* women, which is a flawed methodology, but that's a whole other story.

Jezabel then tallied up the number of Disney Princesses and concluded, "That means statistically around two and a half of these strong women have gotten

---

[742] The New York Post "The war against neckties is heating up" by Christopher Cameron (July 23rd 2018)

[743] Jezabel "Statistically, at Least 2 Disney Princesses Have Had Abortions" by Joanna Rothkopf (March 27th 2018)

abortions and aren't telling you about it because of a national culture of shame and misogyny!!!"[744]

It continued, "We also know that emotionally authentic portrayals of these experiences are still extremely rare — and that's part of a much bigger lack of honest depictions of certain people's lives and communities. Okay, this is all fine, but cartoons can have abortions and two of these ones—if not more!—almost certainly have."[745]

One Planned Parenthood branch president issued a statement about the controversy saying, "Planned Parenthood believes that pop culture—television shows, music, movies—has a critical role to play in educating the public and sparking meaningful conversations around sexual and reproductive health issues and policies, including abortion."[746]

In 2004, a feminist launched the "I Had an Abortion" campaign, encouraging women to "come out" and publicly admit that they had an abortion in order to "reduce the stigma" around it. Some women even wore "I Had an Abortion" t-shirts, including *Ms Magazine* founder Gloria Steinem.[747]

A few years later a woman decided to start the "Shout Your Abortion" challenge by posting on her Facebook

---

[744] Ibid.

[745] Ibid.

[746] Fox News "Backlash after Planned Parenthood branch tweets: 'We need a Disney princess who's had an abortion'" by Elizabeth Zwirz (March 27th 2018)

[747] http://abortionandlife.com/photos.html

page that she got an abortion at a Planned Parenthood facility the previous year and encouraged other women to brag online about their abortions too.[748] Actress Lena Dunham said she wishes she had an abortion so she could better identify with other women.[749]

The online dating website OkCupid partnered with Planned Parenthood to allow users to include support of abortion on their profiles and enable people to find others on the site who also support abortion. As you know, all dating sites (and apps) allow people to search for others with common interests like sports, cooking, and other hobbies; but OkCupid was the first to include supporting abortion as a common interest.

"OkCupid's partnership with Planned Parenthood is really exciting because it enables us to help people connect on the issues that matter to them," said their Chief Marketing Officer Melissa Hobley.[750] "In this current climate, this matters more than ever when it comes to finding 'your person.' We know that Planned Parenthood is driving conversations, support and education that millions care about. When we looked at the data, we saw that our community on OkCupid was talking about Planned Parenthood, so we decided to make

---

[748] The New York Times "#ShoutYourAbortion Gets Angry Shouts Back" by Tamar Lewin (October 1st 2015)

[749] Time "Lena Dunham Said She Wishes She Had an Abortion" by Samantha Cooney (December 20th 2016)

[750] OkCupid.com "Our New Profile Badge Helps You Filter for Planned Parenthood Supporters" (September 13th 2017)

it easy to find the folks who cared about the same thing."[751]

Since there are countless unplanned pregnancies due to reckless sexual behavior by many who use dating apps, I guess OKCupid wanted to ensure guys that if they got one of their dates pregnant she would be happy to kill the baby so it wouldn't interfere with their future online hookups.

Prostitution is "Freedom"

Prostitution is most often a result of desperate and drug addicted women or young girls who are coerced or forced into the business by gangs and organized crime syndicates. While there are some "high class" escort services, the majority of the sex trade is a dirty and dangerous business that almost everyone agrees is morally bankrupt. Everyone except for liberal feminists.

After the FBI shutdown BackPage.com, an infamous website used by sex traffickers, the organizers of the "Women's March" (which spawned the creation of the "pussy hats" and hosted Madonna when she said she wanted to blow up the White House), denounced the crackdown. The group's official Twitter account tweeted, "The shutting down of #Backpage is an absolute crisis for sex workers who rely on the site to safely get in touch with clients. Sex workers rights are women's rights."[752]

---

[751] Ibid.

[752] https://twitter.com/womensmarch/status/982689439574085634

They retweeted a post from another group which said, "The crackdown on BackPage is not about ending trafficking; it's motivated by the patriarchal notion that women should not be free to do what we want with our bodies."[753]

The tweet included a graphic that said, "People choose sex work for a wide range of reasons — flexible schedules, higher pay than many entry-level jobs, or just because they enjoy it. There are also many people who engage in sex work because it's the only option available to them while experiencing homelessness."[754]

Liberals' casual attitude towards prostitution is causing college students to turn to sugar daddies for help paying their tuition and student loans, and of course there are websites (and probably apps) to facilitate that. One of which is Sugar Baby University which claims they have several hundred students signed up from most major universities.[755]

A *Washington Examiner* reporter noted, "College is so expensive that students are willing to prostitute themselves to pay for it. While SeekingArrangement.com is not "technically" an escort service, students are, at the very least, objectifying themselves for supplemental income. The vast number of college students signing up demonstrates how the sugar baby trend is quickly emerging as a socially acceptable and typical way of paying for college. Some students are willing to do

---

[753] https://twitter.com/SafeSpacesDC/status/982429621198249985

[754] https://twitter.com/SafeSpacesDC/status/982429621198249985

[755] https://www.seekingarrangement.com/sugar-baby-university/usa

anything to eliminate student loans, leaving less of a stigma for sugar daddy relationships."[756]

USA Today reported on one girl who admitted registering at SeekingArrangement.com, saying, "For the next four years, she met with 30 different men between the ages of 42 and 75. She says the average sugar daddy she met on the site would pay around $1,000 for a one-time meeting, or would set up monthly allowances to help cover her expenses." She says she made nearly $300,000 while earning her masters degree in writing.[757]

"I treated it like any other dating site. If you think of it like a normal dating site, it's just like OkCupid, but for money. So then you think, what's the point of doing it for free if you can do it for money?"[758]

A Liberal Democrat politician in England named Dennis Parsons has suggested that career counselors in high schools be able to encourage girls to get into prostitution, saying, "Why shouldn't they?"[759] He's disappointed that there is a stigma attached to sex workers and he's upset that recommending such a "career" to students is a violation of school policy. "The fact that we are asking 'should we seek to prevent people entering sex work?' is part of the problem," he said. You wouldn't ask

---

[756] Washington Examiner "Students joining 'sugar baby' program to pay school tuition" by Brendan Pringle (January 25th 2018)

[757] USA Today "To pay for college, more students are becoming sugar babies" by Ginger Hervey (July 21, 2016)

[758] Ibid.

[759] Daily Mail "Liberal Democrat politician says schools should be able to suggest PROSTITUTION as a career to pupils" by Abe Hawken (September 17th 2016)

the question 'should we prevent people from becoming accountants?' You'd just take it for granted."[760]

Wonder Woman is Sexist

When the film *Wonder Woman* (2017) came out, many feminists celebrated a female super hero starring in her own big blockbuster film, but some were upset that she shaved her armpits. "It's really hard to believe that Wonder Woman, who has been on an island filled with strong women her entire life, is worried about waxing and then bleaching her pits," whined one feminist reviewer.[761]

"It also comes down to freedom," she went on. "To have or not have armpit hair is a woman's choice and it's one that she's often judged for. With Wonder Woman standing in as an example of female strength, it would have been exciting to see her with a little hair under her arms. To prove that women — even those who are superheroes — don't have to cater to beauty standards that are meant to make them more attractive to men. Women can instead celebrate their bodies in whatever way they see fit, hairy pits and all."[762]

It isn't only Wonder Woman's lack of armpit hair that upsets feminists. A protein bar company called ThinkThin Products had a Wonder Woman tie-in campaign which also angered them because it was "body

---

[760] Ibid.

[761] Refinery 29 "Is Wonder Woman Allowed To Have Armpit Hair?" by Shannon Carlin (March 15th 2017)

[762] Ibid.

shaming" fat women by promoting the idea that they could be fit and healthy like Wonder Woman since that's offensive to those who are overweight.[763]

The Millennial generation and Generation Z are offended by countless movies and television shows enjoyed by the older generations. James Bond films are sexist. *Friends* is sexist. *Crocodile Dundee* is sexist, racist, and homophobic.[764] *Indiana Jones and Temple of Doom* is sexist because the audience isn't told much about his love interest and, "almost all that we know about her is that she loves perfume, diamonds, and shrieking."[765]

Even the Christmas classic *It's a Wonderful Life* is sexist to them too.[766] So is *Revenge of the Nerds*, *Return of the Jedi*, *Blade Runner*, *The Breakfast Club*, *Weird Science*, and many, many, more.[767]

Female Favoritism

In early 2018 it was revealed that Oxford University in England increased the amount of time allowed for

[763] Washington Times "'Wonder Woman' protein-bar promotion has critics spinning: Report" by Ken Shepherd (May 15th 2017)

[764] The Guardian "Crocodile Dundee was sexist, racist, and homophobic. Let's not bring that back" by Luke Buckmaster (January 22nd 2018)

[765] Bustle.com "15 Movies You Didn't Realize Were Sexist" by Loretta Donelan (January 22nd 2017)

[766] CNN "Is 'It's a Wonderful Life' sexist?" by Carol Costello (December 20th 2017)

[767] SheKnows.com "'80s Movies Were Full of Sexism That Would Never Fly Today" by Shanee Edwards (January 17th 2018)

exams in math and computer science by fifteen minutes hoping it would help boost women's scores since twice as many men were getting degrees in those two subjects. The school felt that, "female candidates might be more likely to be adversely affected by time pressure," so in the name of "equality" they granted everyone more time.[768]

This discrepancy is just more evidence that men and women have different brains and different abilities, and each sex is generally better suited for certain tasks than the other,[769] but facts or hypocrisy never gets in the way of the Liberal Agenda.

A University of Akron professor planned to give all the female students enrolled in his Systems Analysis & Design class higher grades because on average women were "not doing well" in the class, and some were going to have to repeat the course or drop out of the program if he didn't.[770] When others learned of his plan (which he emailed to all his students) a senior administrator stepped in and stopped him.

"While the professor's stated intention of encouraging female students to go into the information sciences field

---

[768] The Telegraph "Oxford University extends exam times for women's benefit" by Tony Diver (February 1st 2018)

[769] The Guardian "Male and female brains wired differently, scans reveal. Maps of neural circuitry show women's brains are suited to social skills and memory, men's perception and co-ordination" by Ian Sample (December 2nd 2013)

[770] Washington Examiner "Professor tries to give female students better grades just for being women" by Emily Jashinsky (May 16th 2018)

may be laudable, his approach as described in his email was clearly unacceptable," he said.[771]

In 2017 feminists celebrated the first woman who was attempting to get into the Navy SEAL program, but she soon dropped out because she couldn't handle the tryouts.[772] Twenty years earlier the film *G.I. Jane* came out staring Demi Moore who was depicted as the first woman to become a Navy SEAL, proving that the idea was just a Hollywood fantasy, because twenty years later not a single woman had been able to complete the training.

The U.S. Marines recently canceled their Combat Endurance Test for infantry soldiers because many women aren't strong enough to pass it.[773] In fact, only one female Marine in history has successfully completed the course, so instead of appearing "sexist" and not having any female Marines in the infantry units (the brave ground-based combat force), they scrapped the test altogether!

In 2015 the Colorado Springs police department in Denver suspended the mandatory fitness test after a dozen female officers sued, claiming the tests were "discriminatory" because many of them were just too weak to pass them. The test consisted of two running

---

[771] New York Post "University nixes tech professor's grade fix for female students" by Greg Re (May 18th 2018)

[772] San Diego Union Tribune "1st woman drops out of Navy SEAL training pipeline" by Jeanette Steele (August 11th 2017)

[773] Marine Corps Times "Passing Combat Endurance Test is no longer required for infantry officers" by Shawn Snow (February 7th 2018)

exercises, and officers had to also do 52 pushups in two minutes, as well as 45 sit-ups within two minutes.[774]

Many local residents were shocked because they want police officers to be able to chase down and/or subdue a suspect, and obviously a certain amount of strength is needed in order to do that. But in the name of feminism, the department stopped the test because the women who couldn't pass it were assigned to desk duty instead of being allowed out in the field, so they sued.

A writer for the *Washington Post* thinks that women have it so bad in society that we should actually stop putting them in jail "for anything" when they commit crimes.[775] She says, "It sounds like a radical idea" but claims, "The argument is actually quite straightforward: There are far fewer women in prison than men to start with — women make up just 7 percent of the prison population. This means that these women are disproportionately affected by a system designed for men."[776] She went on to argue that "there is evidence that prison harms women more than men," and concluded we should just stop sending them there.

The Patriarchy is Behind it All

To feminists, its not just men who are the root of all evil in the world, but more specifically it's the social

---

[774] CBS 4 Denver "Springs Officers Will No Longer Take Fitness Tests After Discrimination Lawsuit" (November 10th 2015)

[775] Washington Post "We should stop putting women in jail for anything" by Patricia O'Brien (November 6th 2017)

[776] Ibid.

structure itself, which of course, they say, was carefully constructed by men.   One popular feminist website explains, "Patriarchy perpetuates oppressive and limiting gender roles, the gender binary, trans phobia and cissexism, sexual assault, the political and economic subordination of women, and so much more. And it is of the utmost importance that we prioritize dismantling the patriarchy in our intimate lives, as well as in a larger systemic sphere."[777]

Let me translate this liberal nonsense for you.   In other words, the Patriarchy is the social structure of society which developed in a way where men tend to be in positions of power and authority, and women tend to be in roles involving nurturing and caring. Kind of like how female animals stay in the den with their newborn young while the males go out and get food to bring back for the family. Males and females of all species have different roles in terms of gathering food and taking care of their young, but feminists aren't happy with these differences. As you know, they're never happy about anything.

After a viral video showing a man giving a live interview on the BBC about North Korea's nuclear threats was hilariously interrupted when his two small children, a toddler followed by a baby in a wheeler, burst into his home office and stole the show, everyone thought it was the funniest thing they'd seen all week and it became an instant meme.   Well, everyone except for one woman,

---

[777] EverydayFeminism.com "What Is Patriarchy (And How Does It Hurt Us All)?" by Marina Watanabe (November 24th 2014)

who decried that it was the "patriarch in a nutshell," and declared it was "not funny."[778]

"Basically, the message this video delivers to me is: being a man is playing life on the easy setting," she said. "It also exposes one reason why there are more men delivering their opinions all over our televisions most days — because women are doing the behind the scenes work needed to make that feasible. True equality will not have been achieved until we see a father desperately clawing at a baby wheeler while a woman talks about the rising threat of nuclear war."[779]

A recent CNN report says, "Guns alone don't kill people, patriarchy kills people," and went on to claim "Patriarchy is a social system that defines men as being inherently violent, dominant and controlling while rewarding them with power for being that way. It is no secret, especially these days, that we live in a patriarchal society. Why are we continually surprised when a man takes up arms and commits mass murder?"[780]

Actually, statistically boys who grow up in fatherless homes tend to take up arms and commit mass murder. In fact 26 of the 27 deadliest mass shootings were committed by men (or teenage boys) who grew up without a father.[781] That's why in Chicago's south side

---

[778] New Statesman "The BBC pundit's children video is not funny. It's patriarch in a nutshell" by Moley Tant (March 10th 2017)

[779] Ibid.

[780] CNN "Guns alone don't kill people, patriarchy kills people" by Richard Edmon Vargas (May 1st 2018)

[781] Real Clear Politics "Of 27 Deadliest Mass Shooters, 26 of Them Were Fatherless" by Mark Meckler (February 27th 2018)

(the black community) every weekend during the summer there are dozens of shootings, and Chicago is the murder capitol of America. It's not "the patriarchy" which is spawning those who commit gun violence, it's the collapse of the patriarchy.

The Biological Reasons

In his historic analysis of human mating behavior, evolutionary biologist David Buss explained in his book *The Evolution of Desire* that, "Feminist theory sometimes portrays men as being united with all other men in their common purpose of oppressing women. But the evolution of human mating suggests that this scenario cannot be true, because men and women compete primarily against members of their own sex. Men strive to control resources mainly at the expense of other men. Men deprive other men of their resources, exclude other men from positions of status and power, and derogate other men in order to make them less desirable to women."[782]

He continues, "A startling consequence of sexual strategies, for example, is that men's dominant control of resources worldwide can be traced, in part, to women's preference in choosing a mate. These preferences, operating repeatedly over thousands of generations, have led women to favor men who possess status and resources and to disfavor men who lack these assets. Ancestral men

---

[782] Buss, David -*The Evolution of Desire* page 214

who failed to acquire such resources failed to attract women as mates."[783]

What this means is that the primary reason men strive to achieve positions of power and status in society is because women are hardwired to be attracted to those kinds of things. Buss explains, "Women's preferences for a successful, ambitious, and resourceful mate and men's competitive mating strategies evolved together. These strategies include risk taking, status striving, derogation of competitors, coalition formation, and an array of individual efforts aimed at besting other men on the dimensions that women desire. The intertwining of these co-evolved mechanisms in men and women created the conditions for men to dominate in the domain of resources."[784]

So the women who complain about men "ruling" the world and dominating positions of power in society don't understand that men only strive towards those goals in order to impress women! It's in our DNA. Buss says, "The forces that originally caused the resource inequality between the sexes, namely women's preference and men's competitive strategies, are the same forces that contribute to maintaining resource inequality today."[785]

The same feminists who complain about this "social inequality" and about the "wage gap" (which is a long-

---

[783] Buss, David -*The Evolution of Desire* page 212

[784] Buss, David -*The Evolution of Desire* page 213

[785] Ibid.

debunked myth)[786] also ignore the fact that men often work dangerous and dirty jobs that expose them to enormous safety risks and health hazards. Not to mention men doing backbreaking manual labor that isn't just physically exhausting, but over time wears out parts of their bodies. Jobs like roofing, pouring concrete, brick laying, tree trimming, road construction, etc.

Feminists also overlook other facts like men accounting for 92% of workplace deaths because of these dangerous jobs,[787] men making up the majority of homeless people,[788] they are 76% of homicide victims,[789] not to mention 97% of combat deaths are men.[790] Feminists claim to want "equality" in the workplace and whine about there not being enough women in certain industries, while ignoring that fact that men are happy to work dirty and dangerous jobs so that women won't have to.

---

[786] Time "6 Feminist Myths That Will Not Die" by Christina Hoff Sommers (June 17th 2016)

[787] Bureau of Labor Statistics "Fatal Work Injuries and Hours Worked by Gender of Worker, 2002"

[788] The Telegraph "Homelessness is a gendered issue, and it mostly impacts men" by Glen Poole (August 6th 2015)

[789] FBI Expanded Homicide Data https://www.fbi.gov/about-us/cjis/ucr/crime-in-the-u.s/2010/crime-in-the-u.s.-2010/offenses-known-to-law-enforcement/expanded/expandhomicidemain

[790] AVoiceForMen.com "The Facts About Men and Boys"

Feminism's End Game

Feminists want to uproot and destroy every single social tradition that has been practiced by men and women since the beginning of time. The idea of grandma cooking dinner while grandpa fixes the car in the garage is seen as "old fashioned," and "oppressive."

A woman sewing a button back on her husband's shirt after he comes home from work at the office or factory and sits on the couch watching TV to relax for a bit isn't seen as the two sexes working in harmony with each other, but instead is just more "oppression" from the Patriarchy. How dare a woman be "expected" to know how to sew just like her mom and grandma, and all the women in her family tree going back to the beginning of civilization.

Even the tradition of men asking women to marry them is under attack, as the Leftists are trying to "reverse the roles" and are encouraging women to do the proposing.[791] Some feminist men are actually taking their wives last names![792] As you would expect, a recent study shows that men who do this are less masculine than normal men.[793] It would be fair to ask if they are even men at all.

---

[791] New York Post "Women proposing to their boyfriends are the latest #MeToo cultural shift" by Sara Dorn (February 10th 2018)

[792] New York Post "Why I took my wife's last name" by WHIMN (December 19th 2017)

[793] StudyFinds.org "Men Viewed As More Feminine, Lacking Pants If Wives Keep Last Name, Study Finds" by Daniel Steingold (November 27th 2017)

Because of modern feminism, stay-at-home moms are now frowned upon, and women are pressured to get back to work right after giving birth and let some daycare center or state-run school raise their kids. *Forbes* magazine declared, "The rate of millennial women choosing to become stay-at-home moms is on the rise. Bad work-life balance and lack of flexibility may be to blame."[794] They make it sound like being a stay-at-home mom is a bad thing, and that outside factors are forcing women into such a horrible situation.

Feminists get upset when a man has to explain something to a woman that she doesn't know anything about, or when a man corrects them when they're spouting nonsense because this makes feminists feel inferior since they want to dominate men in all things. They call it "mansplaining," short for "a man explaining," and it's seen as condescending and more evidence of the sinister Patriarchy in action.

Telling a woman something about cars, tools, or science is now deemed a micro-aggression. Apparently we're just supposed to let them live in bliss with their ignorance. Since many women specialize in things like applying makeup, doing their hair, and fashion, while men tend to be more knowledgeable in practical areas of life, like knowing how to fix cars or stop a leaking faucet, feminists get triggered when faced with the obvious fact that their area of "expertise" has left them largely inexperienced in other important fields.

One of their slogans is "The Future is Female," showing that they don't want "equality," they want

---

[794] https://twitter.com/Forbes/status/962087465669611520

dominance. Today's feminists are mostly women who struggle to fit in with society and instead of taming their wild ideas or accepting the laws of Nature, they try to fight them. It's like an apple tree being upset that it produces apples, and instead wants to grow oranges.

Sorry, but that's not what you were designed to do, and no amount of bitching about it is going to change that. Just learn to be happy with how God created you, or your life will forever be in disharmony and out of balance.

Most feminists are fat, ugly, and bitter about life and since most of them were raised by a single mother they didn't experience what a normal life with a mother and father working together to raise a family should be. Their entire view of the world has been skewed and they have been emotionally scarred without even knowing it. And because of their constant complaining and distorted view of the world, many are unable to find stable relationships with men which only fuels their frustration.

Those who do land a husband instead of just getting knocked up and being a single mom themselves, often have their marriage end in a divorce, or the poor husband puts up with them out of fear that she'll take half his income for the rest of his life through hyper-inflated child support payments and alimony. Many men married to feminists often resort to alcoholism trying to cope with the hell on earth they've been trapped in, hoping to drink away their problems by numbing themselves to the reality of who they're married to and what their life has become.

Like an old and outdated VHS recorder, feminism has outlived its usefulness. At one time it had noble and valid goals, but now feminists find themselves an army without a war, and instead of disbanding and finding other productive things to do with their time and energy, they engage in imagining new enemies, picking pointless fights, and perpetuating perversions which only prevent themselves from facing what their real problems actually are.

Breakdown of the Family

The root cause of most of the craziness we are witnessing in society today is the breakdown of the family. Ever since the divorce laws were changed in the 1960s we've seen a dramatic increase in the number of broken homes in America. With so many children being raised by single parents, the harsh truth that few people want to admit is these kids don't have the proper supervision, guidance, or role models to help them grow up to be well-adjusted adults.

Evolutionary biologist David Buss explains that children raised without the presence of a father, "suffer from the absence of his teachings and political alliances," which have irreparable effects on their lives.[795]

No matter how "good" of a mom a single mother is, no matter how much she loves her kids, and no matter how hard she tries, the fact is that not having a father in the home dramatically impacts the development of the children. The same is true if the child is raised by only a father without a mother in the home, which is rare because mothers get primary custody of the children in the vast majority of cases.

---

[795] Buss, David - *The Evolution of Desire* page 50

What's worse than parents who get a divorce while their children are growing up is the situation of women having children when they're not even married at all. Often these children are fathered by men who they're just casually dating and with whom they don't have the necessary commonalities required to maintain a stable and happy longterm relationship.

There are countless problems caused by not having a father in the home, like missing out on learning the father's technical skills and seeing the day-to-day interactions of how a man and a woman relate with each other. But there are even more devastating effects. Most mass shooters grew up without a father in their home.[796] ISIS often recruits members for their terrorist organization from homes with no father.[797]

It's impossible to argue that the lack of supervision, guidance, and discipline a father living in the home provides children doesn't dramatically impact the psychological wellness of the children and without it they are put at risk for a wide variety of potential dangers.

But Democrats love single mothers for multiple reasons. First of all, it's because they often rely upon the government for assistance in raising their kids, and are thus inclined to become lifelong members of the Democrat Party and keep voting Democrat which grows the Nanny State larger every year. As Tucker Carlson

---

[796] RealClear Politics "Of 27 Deadliest Mass Shooters, 26 of Them Were Fatherless" by Mark Meckler (March 27th 2018)

[797] Washington Times "Link between mass shooters, absent fathers ignored by anti-gun activists" by Bradford Richardson (March 27th 2018)

once said when Democrats were protesting the separation of parents and children who were detained after sneaking across the U.S.-Mexico border, "You think any of these people care about family separation? If they did, they'd be upset about the collapse of the American family, which is measurable and real. They're not. They welcome that collapse, because strong families are an impediment to their political power."[798]

Our culture is in a downward spiral because of the collapse of the nuclear family. Even friendships seem to be a thing of the past for many of the younger generations who now "talk" with their friends on Instagram or Snapchat since face to face interactions (and even talking on the phone) seem old fashioned.

Most young men today wouldn't even know how to approach a beautiful girl in person, chat her up, and ask for a date. Instead they sit on their phones and "swipe" through Tinder profiles as if they're scrolling through a magazine or a menu.[799]

Dating is seen as strange to them. "Going out" has been replaced by "Netflix and Chill" which is their only idea of a good time, and Millennials are having less sex than previous generations because they are afraid of real intimacy due to their stunted social skills from spending too much time living in their virtual worlds.[800] Many of those who are having sex see one-night stands or "friends

---

[798] https://twitter.com/TuckerCarlson/status/1008873030066626561

[799] Vanity Fair "Tinder and the Dawn of the 'Dating Apocalypse' by Nancy Jo Sales (August 6th 2015)

[800] Rolling Stone "Inside the Awkward World of Millennial Dating" by Elisabeth Sherman (November 15th 2016)

with benefits" as the norm and sleep around with multiple different people within their group of friends without entering into long-term or serious relationships.

There are core principles that happy couples have practiced for thousands of years, but unfortunately today many people shun the long-held traditions thinking they can reinvent the wheel and come up with odd new ideas about what relationships should be, which only lead to disaster.

So many people are starving for human affection in our online and isolating world that a new industry has been growing: Professional Cuddling. People actually pay money to cuddle with complete strangers. One business in Portland was booked for two months after it first opened. It's called "Cuddle Up to Me" and they have an office with six different "cuddling rooms" where customers pay up to $80 an hour.[801]

This isn't a front for prostitution. It is literally a place where people go to cuddle with someone they've never met before and pay for it because they are so lonely and desperate for human touch.

Many psychologists also believe that too much porn and video games are causing a "masculinity crisis" for the younger generations since they have an endless supply at the tips of their fingers.[802] Many boys now turn to porn instead of pursuing relationships with girls because

---

[801] CNBC "This 34-year-old gets paid to cuddle people" by Jane Wells (April 2nd 2018)

[802] The Independent "Porn and videogame addiction are leading to 'masculinity crisis' says Stanford prison experiment psychologist" by Doug Bolton (May 9th 2015)

they're so afraid of getting rejected since they don't have the adequate social skills to confidently communicate with someone they're attracted to. Porn addiction is a real problem, and it literally rewires the reward centers of our brains and over time actually causes erectile dysfunction when in the presence of an actual naked female from what's called "porn-induced erectile dysfunction."[803]

Unprotected sex is a danger too many people continue to ignore which is also part of the problem. The term should be "safer sex" not "safe," because condoms often break or aren't used properly, and birth control pills can fail or are forgotten, and even the combination of the two can, and does fail. Most people have sex with someone they've known just a few hours, and with whom they don't have enough in common with to enjoy an hour-long lunch, but they jump into bed with each other putting their entire future family tree at risk of becoming dysfunctional.

Having a child with a woman who your interests, values, and goals aren't compatible with, and who you won't partner up with to raise the child is automatically putting the kid at a tremendous disadvantage in life by forcing him or her to grow up in a single parent home.

Of course there's the financial burden of being a parent, and the incredible amount of time they have to invest in raising the child. So don't ruin your life, and don't ruin your child's life by having one with a person you're not in love with and know you won't marry. Does this mean no sex until marriage? That can be pretty

---

[803] Time "Porn and the Threat to Virility" by Belinda Luscomb (March 30th 2016)

tough, but at the least it should mean no sex until commitment, and even then, be extremely careful and always use condoms, birth control, pull out, and throw in some spermicide too!

While relationships and marriage can be difficult, liberals often exacerbate these difficulties because they keep doing the fundamentals wrong. Many now are openly calling for an end to marriage altogether. Feminist Merav Michaeli is hoping for a "paradigm shift" regarding marriage, and wants society to "cancel marriage."

In 2012 she gave a Tedx talk saying that marriage is out-dated and "unevolved." She clarified, "Not only religious marriage...also civil marriage. I want all secular states to totally eliminate all registration and regulation of marriage. I want to cancel the very concept of marriage."[804]

Feminist poet and novelist Robin Morgan agrees, saying, "We can't destroy the inequities between men and women until we destroy marriage."[805] A lesbian activist and author named Masha Gessen once admitted that the real goal of getting gay "marriage" legalized was to eventually eliminate marriage and monogamous relationships altogether. "Gay marriage is a lie," she said, while on a panel at the Sydney Writers Festival in 2012. "Fighting for gay marriage generally involves lying about what we're going to do with marriage when we get there," she admitted. "It's a no-brainer that the institution of

---

[804] Tedx Talks "Cancel Marriage: Merva Michaeli at TEDxJaffa (November 10th 2012)

[805] ThoughtCo "Robin Morgan Quotes"

marriage should not exist," she concluded, which caused the audience to break out in applause.[806]

Open Marriages

There are an increasing number of news stories about couples in "open marriages" who are technically married, but date and have sex with other people. Swingers have been a small subculture that we've all heard about, but the practice is getting more accepted and the liberal media continues to publish glowing reviews about couples who do it.

On Father's Day in 2017, the *New York Times* published a video titled "Married, Dating Other People and Happy," featuring five different people who talked about how "great" their open marriages are. The *Times* chose Father's Day of all days to release the video because they wanted to attack the nuclear family on this special day by promoting this liberal poison.[807]

CNN published an article titled "Rethinking Monogamy Today" in the spring of 2017 and suggested, "consensual non-monogamy can be a healthy option for some couples and, executed thoughtfully, can inject relationships with some much-needed novelty and

---

[806] Yahoo News "Lesbian Activist's Surprisingly Candid Speech: Gay Marriage Fight Is a 'Lie' to Destroy Marriage" by Mike Opelka (April 29th 2013)

[807] New York Times "Married, Dating Other People and Happy" by Lesly David, Alexandra Garcia and Taige Jensen (June 16th 2017)

excitement."[808]   The story went on to tout the "benefits" of open marriages and quoted some whack job sex therapist who concluded, "couples say that consensual non-monogamy can improve their communication, because it requires a lot of talking, sharing and negotiating, (and) that can strengthen communication in other areas of the relationship, not just your sex life."[809]

It went on, "For some couples, non-exclusivity might take the form of attending 'play parties' together and swapping partners, watching other couples have sex, dating other people or even entering into polyamorous relationships with multiple partners.   It's also worth remembering that non-monogamy still carries a stigma in many circles, so think about how you and your partner will address that concern."

Slate.com, a fairly popular online outlet, featured an editorial written by a man who lives with his wife and her girlfriend in a "triad," and suggested that "balancing work, life, and leisure has never gone better."[810]   He says most people are concerned about such relationships because of jealousy issues and the other obvious complications, but insists, "We're finding that having more people around means less, not more complexity— more hands for the chores, more options for socializing

[808] CNN "Rethinking Monogamy Today" by Iran Kerner (April 12th 2017)

[809] Ibid.

[810] Slate.com "Easier With Three" by Evan Urquhart (May 3rd 2018)

and fun, an extra income to help with the bills, and more time for any one of us to spend going our own way."[811]

The Huffington Post publishes the same anti-family filth. "Do Open Marriages Work? How Dating Other People Brings Me Closer To My Husband," is one article, written by a mother of four.[812] She wrote how "sleeping with new people is a measuring stick of how connected you are to your spouse."

Other publications are now reporting that cheating on your spouse can actually be good for your marriage.[813] *Cosmopolitan* magazine enjoys publishing articles about the "benefits" of cheating too. One woman explained, "Cheating did not lead me to the love of my life, but it did lead me to look at my life and find happiness in myself."[814] Another explains, "If I never cheated on him, I don't think our relationship would have survived. It opened my eyes to how much I loved him."[815]

There's a reason why, in Biblical times, humans used to stone people to death for adultery. Because it violates the basic principles that hold together the fabric of society, and breaks the bonds necessary to hold families

---

[811] Ibid.

[812] Huffington Post "Do Open Marriages Work? How Dating Other People Brings Me Closer To My Husband" by Gracie X (August 28th 2015)

[813] Daily Mail "Relationship guru insists cheating in a marriage doesn't need to mean divorce - and claims it can even make a couple STRONGER" by Molly Rose Pike (October 29th 2017)

[814] Cosmopolitan "14 Confessions From Women Who Cheated and Don't Regret It" by Ali Drucker (January 26th 2017)

[815] Ibid.

together and can bring bastard children into the world who will grow up without the benefit of two committed parents, thus placing the children at a tremendous disadvantage from the very moment they are born.

But liberals have embraced sin and celebrate their debauchery, and perhaps don't even have a conscience to alert them just how disastrous their life's choices are.

Cuckolding

In January of 2018 CNN published a story advocating cuckolding as a way to "help" couple's relationships. For those who aren't familiar with "cuckolding" it's a term that refers to a man whose partner has been unfaithful, but has morphed into a kink fantasy that some couples carry out where a man watches another man have sex with his wife. CNN cited a "study" conducted by an infamous anti-Christian gay extremist named Dan Savage which claims that, "acting on cuckolding fantasies can be a largely positive experience for many couples, and hardly a sign of weakness."[816]

To be clear, this isn't about swinging, or an open relationship, or threesomes; it's about men watching their wives have sex with another man, and CNN's article portrayed the practice in glowing terms, and said that, "Acting on adulterous fantasies may strengthen a relationship, as counterintuitive as it may sound."[817] We should expect such a story from BuzzFeed or the

---

[816] CNN "Cuckolding can be positive for some couples, study says" by Ian Kerner (January 25th 2018)

[817] Ibid.

Huffington Post, but in recent years CNN has abandoned any affiliation with an actual news agency and is purely a propaganda platform of the Democrat Party and far-left political ideologies.

Sex Parties

Just a few generations ago it was taboo for a woman to have sex before marriage, but today *not* having multiple sex partners before marriage is seen as strange. And in the not so distant future, we will likely see the taboo of sex clubs, swinging, and orgies broken as well, and such activities may actually be considered "normal" by the general public.

We're already seeing the beginnings of this cultural shift with sex clubs popping up in major cities. While swingers have been a small subculture for decades, these modern day sex parties are quite different, and seem to have been inspired by the film *Eyes Wide Shut.*

It's not enough for liberals to have open "marriages" and "date" other people. Many are now so desensitized that they feel the need to attend masked sex parties and have orgies with complete strangers whose faces they haven't even seen in order to get off.

An "elite" sex club in New York called Snctm (pronounced sanctum) charges between $1500 and $1875 to attend each party which are held in five-star luxury hotels.[818] A *New York Post* reporter attended an event to

---

[818] New York Post "'A night of erotic freedom' at NYC's most exclusive sex party" by Heather Hauswirth and Jane Ridley (April 5th 2017)

write about the activities and said there were about 100 people there who participated in orgies and live sex shows, all while wearing masks to conceal their identities. The reporter said she observed one woman have sex with six different people by the end of the night.[819]

Another club called Killing Kittens has opened "franchises" in London, Los Angeles, and New York, where couples pay $250 to attend and engage in masked orgies with complete strangers.[820] A sex club in New York City for "millennials only" called NSFW charges members a $96 initiation fee and an additional $30 to $150 per party. Applicants must submit detailed answers to personal questions about themselves along with photos and links to their social media accounts.[821]

The NSFW club claims to have 700 members and a waiting list of hundreds more. The owner, who goes by the name of "Daniel Saynt" (pronounced *saint*), is a 35-year-old who grew up in the Jehovah Witness cult and had his first sexual experience when he was 13-years-old with another boy.[822]

Things are getting so strange that a group of nudists in Huntington Beach, California claimed the city is "discriminating" against them because of their lifestyle after it refused to rent them the city pool for their parties

---

[819] Ibid.

[820] New York Post "Kate Middleton's pal hosts the swankiest sex party in NYC" by Dana Schuster (March 10th 2015)

[821] New York Post "Inside NYC's host millennials-only sex club." Melkorka Licea (April 28th 2018)

[822] Ibid.

because they were creeping out the lifeguards who had to be on duty during their events.[823]

The sexual depravity in our society today is worse than you could possibly imagine and it's disturbing to just hear about it. Some of these communities strive to set "world records" for their perversion, such as holding the "world's biggest orgy" where an estimated 1000 people gathered in Las Vegas in the summer of 2018 to all have sex with each other.[824] The previous "record" was set in Japan in 2007 when a reported 500 people (250 couples) gathered to have sex together.

The porn industry has been known to organize "world record" events like these, such as when a porn star named "Candy Apples" had sex with over 700 different men in one afternoon trying to "achieve" a world record for gangbanging.[825] A few years later a woman named "Lisa Sparks" had sex with 919 different men, one right after the other, in order to break the previous record.[826]

[823] LA Times "Nudists claim discrimination after being banned from pool in Huntington Beach" by Anthony Clark Carpio (January 21st 2016)

[824] Mirror "Hundreds of sex enthusiasts to descend on Las Vegas for 'world's biggest ORGY' in X-rated world record attempt" by Sofie Evans (May 10th 2018)

[825] Adult Industry News "Gangbang 2000 Halted by Police Presence" by Steve Nelson (October 9th 1999)

[826] Culture Kiosque "Eroticon 2006: Sex and the Conservative City" by Colin Graham (January 30th 2006)

Sex Bots

Instead of getting a girlfriend, or a wife, some lost souls are turning to sex dolls instead, and it's becoming a big business. Blowup dolls used to be just a joke and something that guys would buy to bring along on a bachelor party to embarrass the groom. Very few people actually had "sex" with them, although *some* weirdos undoubtedly did.

But until recently, anyone who would admit that they actually owned and used a blowup doll would have been shunned and ridiculed by their friends (if they even had any friends at all) and encouraged to see a psychiatrist.

But the acceptance of such devices is rapidly growing and the sex doll business is now a multi-million dollar a year industry.[827] The president and founder of 1 AM Doll USA, told reporters, "I've had a couple of customers who have said, 'I go to the bar and take a girl home at 3am and she's a little fatter than I'd like her to be or she's not as cute'… So they turn to the doll because the doll can be put in the position they want."[828] He also thinks the dolls would be good for children, saying, "I do think that for education, it's got to be better than letting our kids find some pornography."[829]

---

[827] Daily Mail "March of the sexbots: They talk, they make jokes, have 'customisable' breasts - the sex robot is no longer a weird fantasy but a troubling reality" by Caroline Graham (October 29th 2017)

[828] Breitbart "Sex Doll Manufacturer: Sex Robots Would Be Better for Kids than Pornography" by Charlie Nash (March 5th 2018)

[829] Ibid.

People who prefer to be with sex bots over real women are sometimes called "digisexuals," and as you can imagine, they are extremely disturbed individuals, but what's even more unsettling is this kind of behavior is rapidly becoming more widespread. There are even "brothels" opening in Europe that rent out sex dolls by the hour which are then cleaned by staff in between customers.[830] When one opened up in Paris, some locals called for it to be shut down, concerned it "fuels rape fantasies."[831] The owner said all of the dolls, which are rented out at $100 for a thirty-minute session, were booked up for weeks as soon as they opened.[832]

There are actually a variety of companies building "artificially intelligent" sex bots that talk and answer questions, and are made more "lifelike" every day. These aren't your $20 blowup dolls from the local sex shop. These are extremely expensive devices with prices ranging from $5000 to $10,000.[833] Some in the industry are saying that by the year 2040, people having

---

[830] The Sun "Dublin brothel rents out 32E SEX DOLL for £80 an hour...and 'Passion Dolly' gets scores of visitors every week" by Megan Hill (July 9th 2017)

[831] Daily Mail "First sex doll brothel in Paris faces calls to close because it 'fuels rape fantasies'" by Khaleda Rahman (March 20th 2018)

[832] New York Post "Italy's first sex doll brothel 'booked out for weeks'" by Yaron Steinbuch (Steptember 3rd 2018)

[833] Engadget "Realdoll invests in AI for future sexbots that move, and talk dirty" by Andrew Tarantola (June 12th 2015)

"relationships" with sex bots will be the norm.[834]

Anton LaVey, the creepy man who founded the Church of Satan in 1969 and wrote *The Satanic Bible,* had dreamed of creating robots that people could have as sex slaves. "A humanoid always looks perfect, never has bad breath or any obnoxious habits that are suffered in human companions purely for reasons of sex or habit," he said.[835]

"How many people enter into emotionally unsatisfying or intellectually barren relationships just for sexual reasons?" asks LaVey. "With an artificial human companion, the sexual aspect would be completely satisfied, and a prospective mate would have to come up with something more enticing than just sex."[836]

One Internet porn giant even admitted that the rise of sex bots is a result of social media isolating so many people, saying, "It seems impossible in today's connected world, but loneliness is on the rise especially among the young. Social media seems to be anything but social, at least in the traditional sense of the word"[837] He went on to say that people watching porn are still "alone in an empty room" and thinks that sex bots will provide them with some company.

---

[834] Elle "Sex With Robots Will Be 'Socially Normal' By 2040, Says Technology" by Katie O'Malley (December 20th 2016)

[835] The Authorized Biography of Anton LaVey by Blanche Barton page 187

[836] Ibid.

[837] Daily Star "Sex robot boom driven by social media fuelled LONELINESS, reveals internet porn boss" by Henry Holloway (September 8th 2018)

"Slut-Shaming"

They can call Christians prudes and say that people who want to stay virgins until they're married are losers, but if you call a skank who regularly engages in risky sexual activity with complete strangers, then you are a sexist, judgmental bigot for "slut-shaming" them. Some forms of bullying can actually have a positive impact on society.

It can discourage people from behaving in a way that's detrimental to themselves and their communities, and bullying can help stigmatize the behavior enough for people to rethink their actions and cause them to stop going down the unsavory path they are on. But if you call a slut a slut, that's now "hate speech" and highly inappropriate because sluts are cool in Liberal Land.

Amber Rose, a "celebrity" best known for being Kanye West's big-butted ex-girlfriend with a shaved head, holds an annual "Slut Walk" now which is a festival for feminists to all meet up and celebrate being fat, ugly, STD-infected sluts. It includes guest speakers, booths, and even musical performances.

Being a slut is fun for feminists, including a blogger named Ella Dawson who is so proud of being a slut that she wrote an article for *Women's Health* magazine titled "Why I Love Telling People I Have Herpes."[838] There she explained, "Six months after my first outbreak, I started dropping the 'herpes bomb' into conversations casually. My logic was that every time I told someone, 'I

---

[838] Women's Health "Why I Love Telling People I Have Herpes" by Ella Dawson (April 14th 2015)

have herpes,' the words would get easier to say. I started looking for opportunities to share this fact about myself, seizing the chances presented by time spent waiting in line to pee at frat parties and by lively class discussions about health care."[839]

She's bisexual (surprise), and wrote a blog post titled, "I, Ella Dawson, Am a Slut with Herpes," where she explained she's non-monogamous and has a lot of needs as a "twenty-first century career woman and slut."[840]

One of the girls in MTV's *Teen Mom* documentary series showing the difficulties of getting knocked up at such a young age, sued MTV for $5 million dollars after she was cut from the show when she decided to do porn. After appearing in the show for several seasons, Farrah Abraham decided to get into the porn industry to make some easy money, but when the next season of *Teen Mom* was scheduled to be shot, MTV didn't want her, for obvious reasons, and so she sued, claiming they were 'slut shaming' her and discriminating against her because she sells sex tapes now![841]

AIDS

In California, LGBT extremists lobbied the government to reduce the penalty for *knowingly* exposing their sexual partners to HIV from a felony down to a

---

[839] Ibid.

[840] https://elladawson.com/2016/09/24/i-ella-dawson-am-a-slut-with-herpes/

[841] Variety "Farrah Abraham Claims MTV 'Sex-Shamed' Her for Doing Porn" by Gene Maddaus (February 21st 2018)

misdemeanor, and they succeeded. Governor Jerry Brown signed the bill into law, and it became effective January 1st 2018.[842] One activist said the old criminal laws "disproportionately harmed people of color and transgender women," and praised the "landmark" decision to reduce the penalty.[843]

The bill was proposed by State Senator Scott Wiener, who is, surprise — gay. Shortly before the law was passed an editor at *The Sacramento Bee* complained, "In California and more than 30 other states, dozens of laws remain on the books to punish people who willfully expose others to the virus. To this day, people still get charged with felonies over HIV and go to prison for five, 10 or even 20 years. In some states, those convicted must register as a sex offender for life."[844]

While any normal person would understand why willfully exposing others to HIV is a serious crime, this person went on to complain that those who supported criminal penalties for knowingly spreading AIDS were, "fear-based holdovers from the days of the 'gay plague.'"[845]

For decades, blood banks have refused to accept blood donations from gay men because of the extraordinarily

---

[842] The Los Angeles Times "Knowingly exposing others to HIV will no longer be a felony in California" by Patrick McGreevy (October 6th 2017)

[843] NBC News "New California Law Reduces Penalty for Knowingly Exposing Someone to HIV" by Julia Moreau (October 13th 2017)

[844] Sacramento Bee "The AIDS crisis is over. Why are people still going to jail over HIV?" by Erika D. Smith (April 24th 2017)

[845] Ibid.

high risk of the blood being tainted with HIV, and liberals have been crying that such a practice is "discrimination."[846] In Toronto a group of chefs opened a restaurant called June's that is run entirely by people infected with HIV, and they all wear aprons that read "Kiss the HIV+ cook."[847] They hope to expand their operation to San Francisco and New York.

A segment of the gay community actually engages in what is called "Bug Chasing" where they purposely have unprotected sex with someone they know is HIV positive for the "excitement" of the risk of getting infected themselves. Some psychologists think the act is a result of gay men's "resistance to dominant heterosexual norms" and by embracing the darkest aspects of the gay community, they are rejecting the heteronormative society they have come to despise.[848]

Rolling Stone did a story on the phenomenon in 2006 titled "Bug Chasers: The Men Who Long To Be HIV+" and found that the men who do it find the practice to be "the ultimate taboo, [and] the most extreme sex act left."[849] The issue has been addressed in various television series such as Showtime's *Queer as Folk* in which a character wants to get "the gift."

---

[846] The Atlantic "The Bigotry of Gay-Blood-Donation Bans" by Vann R. Newkirtk II (June 13th 2016)

[847] NBC News "Canadian Restaurant Run by HIV-Positive Staff Aims to Smash Stigma" by Reuters (November 9th 2017)

[848] British Journal of Social Psychology "'Resistance' and health promotion by Crossley Michelle (2004)

[849] Rolling Stone "Bug Chasers" by Gregory A. Freeman (November 16, 2006)

Grindr, the dating app for gays, actually includes a section in people's profile about their HIV status the same way normal online dating profiles list whether a user is a smoker or not, or what kind of music they prefer. If a dating app has to include a listing whether users are HIV positive or not, you know that the community of people using that app is infested with diseases because of their degenerate lifestyles and speaks volumes about the devastating effects their behavior is causing.

The End of Morality

If you ever wonder "can they get any more insane," the answer is always, yes. Like a once-friendly dog that gets rabies, there is no longer any resemblance to its former self after the infection takes hold. And as the final stages of liberalism kick in, there is no longer any hint of a human left, and what was once a person has turned into essentially a zombie.

Like most forms of cancer, if liberalism is detected and treated early, there is hope for recovery, but if left unchecked for too long of time, it metastasizes and spreads to the point where there is no hope to stop it.

The "identify however you want" ideology has ballooned from men wanting to be women and vice versa, to dozens of different genders and people who say they have no gender. There are even people who think they are of a different race. And since the Left has painted themselves into a corner by embracing every new level of craziness as "normal," there are now people who are identifying as "trans-age."

A Canadian man in his late 40s decided to leave his wife of 23 years and their three children to live as a six-year-old girl. "She" even found an "adoptive" family who took "her" in. "I can't deny I was married. I can't deny I have children. But I've moved forward now and I've gone back to being a child."[850]

This is not an isolated incident. A 38-year-old man in Chicago was arrested for sexually assaulting three different young girls aged 6 to 8, and told prosecutors he considers himself to be "trans-age" and is a 9-year-old boy stuck in a man's body.[851]

If you dare, you can search YouTube for ABDL, or Adult Baby Diaper Lovers, who are grown adults that like to live as small children, and even wear diapers. There you will see some of these people vlogging about their lifestyle. MTV aired an episode of *Real Life* titled "I'm An Adult Baby" which is on YouTube, and some of the top thumbed up comments defend them, saying things like, "It's just about a feeling of security. I get it. I don't think I could date someone with this fetish, but maybe if I really clicked with them, I could look past it. I don't judge. They all seem really nice. It's okay to be different."[852]

---

[850] The Independent "Transgender father Stefonknee Wolscht leaves family in Toronto to start new life as six-year-old girl" by Kate Ng (December 12th 2015)

[851] Chicago Tribune "Accused of assaulting 3 young girls, man says he's boy trapped in adult's body" by Deanese Williams-Harris (January 25th 2018)

[852] MTV's YouTube Channel "True Life | 'I'm An Adult Baby' Official Clip (Act 1) | MTV" (October 27th 2016)

If people reject their own age and don't "feel" like they're the chronological age according to the date on their birth certificate, then following the liberal logic of ignoring biology and common sense as they do with gender and race, then liberals may start to treat these people as children. Sure, some people have developmental disabilities that limit their cognitive functions to that of a child, but this is far different. This is mental illness.

The Huffington Post decided to feature a brick and mortar store dedicated to selling products for Adult Baby Diaper Lovers. The "Sex Heroes" series was dedicated to "explore[ing] the lives and experiences of individuals who are challenging, and thereby changing, mainstream culture's understanding of sex and sexuality."[853]

The article proclaimed, "Saying that people who identify as ABDL are misunderstood and maligned would be a colossal understatement. Even worse, not only do they face ridicule for having desires or inclinations that exist outside of what is considered by mainstream culture to be 'normal,' there are few places beyond the Internet to express their identity, find community or buy goods related to their interests."[854]

So what's next, will calling these people mentally ill psychos be equated with calling someone the n-word, or treated as the same kind of bigotry as someone who thinks gay people are an abomination?

---

[853] Huffington Post "Inside The Misunderstood World Of Adult Baby Diaper Lovers" by Noah Michelson (March 21st 2017)

[854] Ibid.

In George Orwell's *Nineteen Eighty-Four*, the main antagonist, O'Brien, reveals to Winston Smith that, "never again will you be capable of ordinary human feeling. Everything will be dead inside you. Never again will you be capable of love, or friendship, or joy of living, or laughter, or curiosity, or courage, or integrity. You will be hollow. We shall squeeze you empty, and then we shall fill you with ourselves."[855] This is what Leftists want.

They are miserable as a result of poor life choices combined with coming from dysfunctional families, which were most often the result of poor life choices, and their downward spiral is causing them to want everyone else to be miserable too. They are incapable of love and understanding, and have no logic or reasoning abilities. And the longer we let them openly exercise their mental illness and infest our schools, the media, courts and Congress, the more difficult it's going to be to stop them from completely destroying the human race.

---

[855] *Nineteen Eighty-Four* by George Orwell pages 228-229

Conclusion

The plague of liberalism is so much worse than what's been detailed in this book. I had to remove large sections and entire chapters to condense this material to around 300 pages in order to keep the printing cost down since I self-publish my books and don't have a mainstream publisher backing me to pay for large print runs. Many people have heard about some of the issues found in this book, but few know that they're just the tip of an iceberg of insanity that's spreading in our society. And what's worse is that courts have been ruling in favor of much of this and are legally forcing the rest of us to cater to it.

The social media companies are in lockstep with them, enforcing Orwellian terms of service designed to censor criticism from conservatives who disagree with this madness. And it's all in the name of "progress" and "creating a positive community" and "safe space" they say. Ronald Reagan once remarked that if fascism ever comes to America it will come in the name of liberalism, and it surely is.

They want us defunded and deplatformed, meaning our social media and YouTube accounts deleted. Major corporations like Uber and AirBNB are banning people from using their apps because of their political beliefs.[856] Services like PayPal, Venmo, and Patreon are shutting

---

[856] NBC News "Laura Loomer Banned from Uber & Lyft After Anti-Muslim Tweetstorm" by Chelsea Bailey (November 2nd 2017)

down accounts from some people because of what they've said on podcasts or in YouTube videos.[857] Restaurants have been refusing service to people for simply supporting President Trump.[858]

Conservatives understand that our rights come from God, not the government, and certainly not from corporations. The government's job is to *protect* our *inherent* rights, not to give them to us, or decide who gets them, when, and for what reason. We are born with them, but liberals are doing everything they can to take them away. We are up against a well-funded and dedicated group of conspirators who will stop at nothing to get what they want.

To fight back against them you must vote in the midterm elections, and in your local elections — not just every four years during the presidential election. Your local Republican Party should have a voter guide with their recommendations for who to vote for regarding various positions in your city from the mayor to school board members and the county treasurer.

As Plato famously said, "One of the penalties for refusing to participate in politics is that you end up being governed by your inferiors." You have to look at voting like paying your taxes. It takes a little bit of time and effort, and certainly isn't what you'd prefer to be doing, but if you don't do it, you're going to get screwed.

---

[857] Breitbart "Stripe, PayPal, Patreon: The Right Is Being Banned from Online Fundraising" by Allum Bokhari (July 24th 2018)

[858] USA Today "Restaurants kicking out Trump supporters: Unlike race or religion, it's legal" by Charisse Jones (June 27th 2018)

If you can afford it, put your kids in a private school, and learn the dangers that lurk for them on social media. And be sure to provide them with plenty of entertaining and educational alternatives to what the pop culture is programing kids to think is cool.

We are under assault and we have to fight back with lawsuits, with tweets, Facebook posts and YouTube videos to counter their propaganda on every platform with a flood of new conservative content every day. We need armies of anonymous trolls to engage in meme wars, producing clever and viral images which capture the essence of our message.

We need silent soldiers too, who are just as important, to quietly fight the liberal agenda simply by not adopting their ridiculous ideas, and instead live their lives in accordance with the truth as examples for their children and grandchildren.

Liberals want to turn our entire society upside down and dismantle the institutions which helped make our country so great to begin with. And they're trying to stab the very heart of humanity, hoping to cause the social fabric to completely unravel. They're targeting families, friendships, intimate relationships, and children; claiming humans have been doing it all wrong for thousands of years and that its time for a total revolution to overthrow the old order.

In the 1960s, drug-fueled teens and young adults experimented with "free love" and hippie communes as part of their rejection of modern society, but after a few years their lives became hopeless disasters. Their pipe dreams of a utopian society soon collided with the harsh realities of life their childish minds had ignored or hadn't yet contemplated.

The hippies later realized that as problematic as it could be, the traditional family which had been the way human beings lived for tens of thousands of years was the best way to live. And Capitalism, despite its flaws, was the best economic model for people to prosper. The fantasies of the '60s soon faded away and the flower children eventually grew up.

Let's hope we'll have a similar revival of traditionalism and that the progressive politics and toxic social experiments of modern liberalism will soon come to an end. Let's hope we can quickly put this dark chapter in the history books and move forward to a more rational, and reasonable society. While that is the goal, it is possible we may have passed the point of no return. There are so many vultures out there and they have sunk their claws so deep into the psyche of our species they may have permanently damaged a large segment of society. And they are enjoying it.

Like Jesus said, "For wide is the gate and broad is the road that leads to destruction, and many enter through it. But small is the gate and narrow the road that leads to life, and only a few find it."[859] So while we may not be able to "find a cure" for the liberal plague affecting the masses, you can find comfort in the fact that you can largely insulate yourself and your loved ones from the cultural craziness by continuing to practice the timeless traditions that have been proven effective around the world and across time.

---

[859] Matthew 7:13-14

No matter what the majority of people are doing or what the "news" claims is going on, or what the celebrities say we should think, or what the social media trends show is "right" or "wrong," we know the truth, and the truth will set us free.

Author's Note: Please take a moment to rate and review this book on Amazon.com or wherever you purchased it from to let others know what you think. This also helps to offset the trolls who keep giving my books fake one-star reviews when they haven't even read them. Almost all of the one-star reviews on my books are from NON-verified purchases which is a clear indication they are fraudulent, hence me adding this note.

These fraudulent ratings and reviews could also be part of a larger campaign trying to stop my message from spreading by attempting to tarnish my research through fake and defamatory reviews, so I really need your help to combat this as soon as possible. Thank you!

Made in the USA
Las Vegas, NV
16 March 2021